The Dynamics of
Psychological
Development

The Dynamics of
Psychological
Development

Alexander Thomas, **M.D.**

Professor of Psychiatry,
New York University Medical Center

and

Stella Chess, **M.D.**

Professor of Child Psychiatry,
New York University Medical Center

BRUNNER / MAZEL, *Publishers* • New York

Library of Congress Cataloging in Publication Data

Thomas, Alexander, 1914-
  The dynamics of psychological development.

  Bibliography: p.
  Includes index.
  1. Child psychology.   2. Personality.   I. Chess, Stella, joint author.
  II. Title.
  BF721.T4557   155   79-25425
  ISBN 0-87630-232-0

Published by
BRUNNER/MAZEL, INC.
19 Union Square
New York, New York 10003

To the memory of our two
dear friends and colleagues:

HERBERT G. BIRCH, M.D., Ph.D.
1918-1973

SAMUEL SILLEN, Ph.D.
1910-1973

Contents

vii

Foreword

This splendid monograph on developmental theory speaks clearly and forcefully for itself; it needs no exegesis masquerading as a Foreword. There may, however, be some value in placing it in the context of recent psychiatric history, particularly for readers who have recently entered the field of child development.

The work of Stella Chess and Alex Thomas first appeared in print early in my own career. I was then a student of Professor

Leo Kanner and had at his invitation joined in writing the reviews of progress in child psychiatry and mental deficiency which had been for many years a feature of the January issues of the American Journal of Psychiatry. We wrote, in our 1959 review article:

> Chess and Thomas (paper presented at the 1958 APA meeting) have reintroduced the issue of nonmotivational factors in behavior, a level of determination obscured by contemporary preoccupation with psychodynamic elements. In an effort to assess the extent to which characteristic response patterns may be intrinsically determined, they have launched a much needed longitudinal study of the nature, constancy and modifiability of the responses of infants to new stimuli at successive stages of development. The findings of this investigation will be awaited with considerable interest. . . . We see emerging from this year's progress in child psychiatry* the outlines of a comprehensive body of data on the longitudinal development of normal and disturbed children, data against which we can more meaningfully assess the significance of the behavior disorders that confront us in the clinic.

Three years later, after Dr. Kanner had asked me to take on the task of preparing the review alone, I noted in the 1962 article:

> The longitudinal studies of Chess, Thomas, Birch and collaborators provide evidence for the existence of primary reaction patterns detectable as early as the third month of life. Concurrent information on environmental events (weaning, toileting, etc. that are conventionally described as "traumatic" revealed far less evidence of behavior disturbed in response to these events than standard theory predicts. Development is viewed as a transactional process, with individuality of child, parents and life experience determining the resultant personality (Eisenberg, 1962).

---

* Our review included reference to the work of Lee Robins, Lester Sontag and Jerome Kagan, and Rema LaPouse and Mary Monk.

I could not resist prodding Stella and Alex to set their full findings forth and added (again) :

> Publication of details of methods, findings and data analysis in a promised monograph will be eagerly awaited by all workers in this field.

The monograph *was* forthcoming (Thomas, Chess, Birch, Hertzig and Korn, 1963) and proved well worth waiting for; its promise was more than fulfilled.

Why had Leo Kanner and I regarded this work, even in preliminary outline, as so important to the field of child psychiatry? Two decades earlier, Borden Veeder, a leader of American pediatrics speaking at the White House Conference on Child Health and Protection in 1930, had stated:

> I have a very definite feeling that the psychiatrist and psychologist have contributed somewhat to the pediatric attitude of suspicion or skepticism. The psychiatrist above all other people with whom I come into close contact has a penchant for obfuscating his thought with the most perplexing, and I feel unnecessarily complicated, verbiage (Kanner, 1957).

Not a year later, another distinguished pediatrician, Joseph Brenneman, wrote a paper with the ominous title: *The Menace of Psychiatry* (1931). He decried the armchair speculations, the absence of empirical data, and the confusing psychological theories of the dogmatic "schools." He warned his readership against the "bewildering nomenclature" and "confusion of theory and authority."

In response, James Plant of the Essex County Juvenile Court Clinic wrote a rejoinder under the title: *The Promise of Psychiatry* (1932). His concluding paragraph addressed pediatricians in these words:

> Whether you like it or not, the families which are your clientele are finding themselves face to face with new and profound

social problems. These matters affect the conduct and the health of the patients and serve to make every family part of our clientele, because every family is having to adjust itself to these changes. You cannot escape these problems and their implications to the child's health by deprecating them, nor can you solve or understand them by setting up a beautiful little experimental station where they do not exist. . . . The promise of psychiatry is the promise that if the pediatrician will address himself to these problems, he will face a vista of rare challenge. . . . Personally, I am sorry if he is only afraid of that challenge.

Such was point and counterpoint in the 1930s. For all the honor due to child psychiatry for having pioneered a broader view of patient-family-community interaction than had been comprehended by adult psychiatry, our horizons were constricted by our focus on the clinical study of the individual patients and families who passed through our clinic doors. It was only when population studies began that we recognized that clinic intake has unintended as well as deliberate bias built into it. Once appropriate controls for social class were introduced, it became difficult to verify the widespread assumption that such variables as age and method of weaning, toilet training practices, sex education, or the parental attitudes measured by standard inventories distinguish clinic patients from other children. Such factors do indeed vary significantly by social class but they fail to predict patienthood (Oleinick, Bahn, Eisenberg and Lilienfeld, 1966) .

Many of the formulations which seem to have explanatory value when applied in retrospect to patient populations which were skewed in unknown fashion by gatekeeping procedures disappeared into insignificance when appropriate sampling and control techniques were introduced.

Such errors stemmed, in part, from the isolation of the child guidance clinic from the practice of pediatrics and, in part, from its isolation from academic child development. No physiologist would describe a normal heart in terms derived solely from the study of the failing one; had he done so, Starling would have con-

cluded that ventricular output decreases rather than increases with
ventricular dilatation as it does within normal limits. Yet we had
generalized from our clinical work with troubled families to
theories of normal development. Freud's experience before the
turn of the century should have warned us of the unreliability of
our patients' reconstructions of their past; what he first thought to
be historical events he later discovered to be fantasy. Yet he and
we persevered in our preoccupation with those fantasies in lieu of
the more laborious task of accumulating detailed *prospective* accounts of the vicissitudes of development. It was only systematic
longitudinal studies which began to supply the information necessary for a meaningful account of the interactions between temperamental characteristics, parental behaviors and social experiences in generating observed behavior.

During the past half century, American medicine has been characterized by its pragmatism (what matters is what works). Yet,
during the same time period, American psychiatry has been a
curious exception to this guiding principle. Psychoanalytic theory,
transplanted to American shores, took stronger root here than it
ever had in Europe or the United Kingdom. Despite the failure
of research to establish the superiority of psychoanalytic psychotherapy over any other psychotherapeutic method, adherence to
its tenets remained the norm. Despite the failure of direct observation of infant and child development to affirm the theoretical
constructs of analysis, constructs which had been derived from
retrospective adult histories, faith in the doctrine remained un-
impaired.

This divergence between psychiatry and the rest of medicine is
in part explicable by differences in technology. Until the recent
past in adult psychiatry (and to the present in child psychiatry),
psychological methods were almost the only methods available for
treatment; furthermore, though psychiatric disorders may be
chronic and recurrent, most do respond to psychological interven-
tions. The problem responsible for our failure to adhere to scientific principles is not that psychiatrists sometimes fail in their

efforts to influence patients, but that they so often succeed, or, at least, appear to.

Independent of the theory on which the treatment rests, most studies of psychotherapy report improvement in two-thirds or more of the patients under care. I make the point, not to argue that we rest content with an outcome that we do not understand and that well may be unrelated to the medical training of the psychiatrist, but to stress that what is a bonus for the sufferer is an occupational hazard for the doctor. Just because we do so well, simply by "being" with a patient, whatever else goes on during the consultation, we are subject to the error of ascribing the observed effectiveness to irrelevant epiphenomena in the psychotherapeutic process. Doing well, in this sense, invites the hubris of crediting ourselves with greater understanding than we have.

Patients, in an all too human and unending effort to reduce the chaos that threatens to overwhelm them, attempt to impose meaning on puzzling and enigmatic events. At times, they generate hypotheses that we, from the perspective which distance and disinterest allow, can help them dismiss. But the problem only begins there. If they are persuaded to abandon spurious ideas, they remain in urgent need of new meanings to relate old events and are more than ready to accept our efforts to provide them. Worse, from the standpoint of testing the validity of tentative hypotheses (and all the better, for the reduction of anxiety), the new explanations are promptly incorporated into their belief systems. By acting upon them as if they were true, they make them, in a certain sense, true (that is, true for them). Thus, an idea put forth by the psychiatrist as a preliminary formulation, once it is assimilated by the patient, is so influential in altering the patient's behavior that it is only the unusual skeptic who will not mistake the social consequences of the psychodynamic interpretation for proof of its validity (Eisenberg, 1975).

Whatever complexities beset philosophers when they attempt to tease out the essential elements of the theory of causality and to explicate the logic of statistical inference, they do not have patients waiting upon them whose care must be based upon decisions which reek of imputed causal connections. The treating physician works in a context in which both he or she and the patient are bound together in a matrix of etiological hypotheses, frequently contradictory, often unsubstantiated, and most of the time with evidence inadequate for deciding on the relative merits of the alternatives. Worst of all, a significant component of the physician's therapeutic potency is his or her ability to make the patient feel the doctor "understands."

The most powerful test of truth in the scientific method is the susceptibility of predictions based on theory to disconfirmation by empirical evidence. Thus, international attention was focused on the study of the 1918 solar eclipse because the phenomena to be observed would provide a critical test for the theory of relativity. There was no reason to fear that the prediction would generate its own confirmation. Although the theory guided the observations that needed to be made, it could not affect the phenomena to be recorded. Behavioral theorists face an altogether different problem in this respect. As the sociologist W. I. Thomas pointed out almost 40 years ago: "If men define situations as real, they are real in their consequences." This proposition provides major problems in the evaluation of general theory in social science; it is compounded as a source of knotty difficulties for formulating and testing theory and practice in psychiatry.

These considerations made it all the more an occasion for celebration when I read the first reports of the study of infant temperament by Stella Chess, Alexander Thomas, Herbert Birch and their collaborators. At a time when many regarded the infant as a tabula rasa, they had the conceptual imagination to consider that the infant might be a principal actor in the drama of his own development; they had the methodologic sophistication to demonstrate that inter-individual differences could be reliably observed and followed over time. When I met Stella, Alex and Herb, I was enormously impressed by their vision and their dedication. Here were colleagues who were not only committed to the advance of knowledge but to its direct application in order to improve the lives of children.

As they followed the children in their original sample, they were able to relate temperamental differences, on the one hand, and styles of child rearing, on the other, to the evolution of healthy or unhealthy coping patterns in the growing child, an interactionist perspective that made sense, for the first time, of differences in outcome that could not be understood by looking at the child or the family alone. They added to the initial middle class white sample studies of working class Puerto Rican children and a large population of infants impaired by congenital rubella. Now one could see the impact of culture, on the one hand, and the impact of central nervous system damage, on the other, on the developmental process. What emerged was a remarkable demonstration of the plasticity of the human organism and the multiple paths by which either adaptive or maladaptive outcomes can be attained.

All of us in the field have been awaiting this volume in which the authors present a broad and enlarged scheme for the understanding of human development, based not only on their own work but on a scholarly assessment of the scientific literature. It is by no means a final statement, neither a final statement from them (I look forward to new and revised editions in the future), nor a final statement of developmental theory, which by its very nature is always tentative and subject to revision by new data and new concepts. The reader of this volume is in for a treat, an intellectual banquet. It is warranted to expand the horizons of every thoughtful reader and to enhance clinical understanding in the everyday practice of child psychiatry.

I consider myself privileged to have the opportunity to introduce it to the reading public.

LEON EISENBERG, M.D.
Maude and Lillian Presley Professor of Psychiatry
Harvard Medical School

REFERENCES

Brenneman, J. 1931. The menace of psychiatry. *American Journal of Diseases of Children*, 42:376-402.

Eisenberg, L. 1962. Review of psychiatric progress 1961: Child psychiatry; mental deficiency. *American Journal of Psychiatry*, 118:600-604.

Eisenberg, L. 1975. The ethics of intervention: Acting amidst ambiguity. *Journal of Child Psychology and Psychiatry*, 16:93-104.

Kanner, L. 1957. *Child Psychiatry*. Second Edition. Springfield: C. C. Thomas, p. 26.

Kanner, L. and Eisenberg, L. 1959. Review of psychiatric progress 1958: Child psychiatry: mental deficiency. *American Journal of Psychiatry*, 115:508-611.

Oleinick, M., Bahn, A., Eisenberg, L. and Lilienfeld, A. M. 1966. Early socialization experiences and intrafamilial environment. *Archives of General Psychiatry*, 15:344-353.

Plant, J. 1932. The promise of psychiatry. *American Journal of Diseases of Children*, 44:1308-1320.

Thomas, A., Chess, S., Birch, H. G., Hertzig, M. E. and Korn, S. 1963. *Behavioral Individuality in Early Childhood*. New York: New York University Press.

Preface

In this volume we venture beyond the specific research and clinical studies that have provided the basis for our previous publications. We now attempt a fresh overview of human developmental theory, indeed a most formidable challenge.

Three main streams have fed and continue to feed theory-building in human psychology: 1) the biological sciences of genetics, biochemistry, neurophysiology, and animal behavior; 2) child development research, including the contribution of social psychology; and 3) clinical and research psychiatry. In the main, these three streams have nourished a number of separate systems of conceptualization, rather than having achieved a confluence into one main current. The isolation of the fields of child development and clinical psychiatry from each other has been especially conspicuous and regrettable. Each has drawn in a rather ad hoc fashion from the biological sciences, but not from each other. We are constantly reminded of this gap in our conversations with psychiatrists and developmental psychologists in leading research and teaching positions. Each group recognizes the vital importance of the knowledge and ideas of the other field for their own conceptualizations of the dynamics of human psychological development. Each is troubled by their difficulties in absorbing and synthesizing the research findings of the other group with their own data and experience. Yet, with a few exceptions on both sides, the gap between psychiatrists and developmental psychologists has not been bridged.

It is this need for an integration of the data and concepts from the biological sciences, developmental psychology, and psychiatry which has motivated us to attempt this fresh overview of developmental theory. In this effort we have drawn upon our clinical and research psychiatric experience and our familiarity with developmental issues and data through our own longitudinal studies and our editorship of the *Annual Progress in Child Psychiatry and Child Development* series. Our knowledge of the basic biological sciences is more modest, but we have always considered it essential as clinicians, teachers and researchers to keep abreast of major developments and concepts in these fields.

All research and clinical practice rests upon some system of theoretical formulations, whether explicit or implicit, whether clearly or ambiguously stated. From the beginning of our own research activities, some 25 years ago, we have tried to make explicit to ourselves and to others the ideas which shaped our goals and methods of data collection and analysis. Our primary concepts at that time were derived from our psychiatric and psychoanalytic training, clinical experience, observations of the behavior and development of our own children and those of our friends, and a critical review of the existing literature. As formulated at that time, our theoretical constructs included the concepts that the child was an active agent from the moment of birth in the organism-environment interactional process, that temperamental individuality was a functionally significant influence in development at all age-periods, and that a dynamic interactionist model was required.

Though we were by no means the first to propose these ideas, they did run counter to the dominant one-sided environmentalist views and drive-reduction and stimulus-response models of the 1950s. A number of thoughtful students of behavior did find our formulations congenial with their own thinking, including the child psychiatrists Leon Eisenberg, John Rose and Michael Rutter, the pediatricians Berry Brazelton and William Carey, and the developmental psychologists Arthur Jersild and Jerome Kagan. Their interest and encouragement were of great value to us in those early days when we began to challenge so many entrenched theoretical positions. It has been, naturally, especially gratifying over the past decade to see these concepts that had been advocated by us and a small minority of other workers enter the mainstream of developmental theory.

Our longitudinal studies could not have been possible without the complete and continuous cooperation of the parents who have responded unstintingly and cheerfully over the years to our demands on their time and energies. Their children, also, have participated freely and easily as they have reached adolescence and early adult life and as we have made independent requests for their participation. Our co-workers have been numerous, and all have been consistently and thoughtfully devoted to their responsibilities and tasks. We do wish to express our special appreciation to Miriam Rosenberg, the administrative coordinador of our research unit, whose intelligence, imagination, and hard work have been invaluable assets over these many years, and gave us the time and energy to produce this manuscript.

A number of professional colleagues read an earlier draft of this volume and provided many valuable suggestions and criticisms which we have incorporated in the final text. Our thanks are extended to Martha Cameron for her skillful and intelligent editorial work, and to our publishers, Bernard Mazel and Susan Barrows, for their complete commitment to the production of a volume at the highest possible professional level.

Our longitudinal studies were initially aided financially by several private sources. Since 1960 we have received major support from the National Institute of Mental Health (MH-3614, 5-0359-4-11, 26414, and 3133), together with additional support from the National Institute of Child Health and Human Development, the Office of Education, the Children's Bureau of the Department of Health, Education and Welfare, and the Maternal and Child Health Research Office of Health, Education and Welfare (MC-R-360409), the New York City Health Research Council and the Foundation for Child Development. Most recently, additional financial support has come from the Children's Fund of the Okun Foundation. The views expressed in this volume are, of course, entirely the authors' and should in no way be construed as reflecting the opinions of any of the agencies that have given our studies financial support.

We have dedicated this volume to the memory of our dear friends and colleagues, Dr. Herbert Birch and Dr. Samuel Sillen. Dr. Birch was an outstanding figure in the international research community, who was at the height of his enormously productive and creative career at the time of his sudden death. He joined our longitudinal study group several years after its inception and remained committed to it thereafter. His contribution was at all times imaginative and stimulating. In his typical style, he sharpened our developmental and interactionist approaches, and formulated one important generalization after another from masses of detailed behavioral data presented to him. Dr. Sillen was our close editorial associate and co-author for many years on a number of projects. His own previous professional background in the field of literature proved uniquely useful when combined with his extraordinary ability to master the central questions in psychology and psychiatry. Looking at these issues analytically from the outside, so to speak, he was always able not only to broaden and deepen our formulations, but frequently to add significant insights of his own.

For the two of us, each succeeding year since Herb and Sam died increases our sense of loss of two irreplaceable friends and colleagues.

ALEXANDER THOMAS, M.D.
STELLA CHESS, M.D.

The Dynamics of
Psychological
Development

Chapter I

The Need for
New Theory

I believe fervently in our species and have no patience
with the current fashion of running down the human
being as a useful part of nature. On the contrary, we
are a spectacular, splendid manifestation of life. We have
language and can build metaphors as skillfully and precisely as ribosomes make proteins. We have affection.
We have genes for usefulness, and usefulness is about
as close to a "common goal" for all nature as I can guess

3

at. And finally, and perhaps best of all, we have music. Any species capable of producing, at this earliest, juvenile stage of its development—almost instantly after emerging on the earth by any evolutionary standard—the music of Johann Sebastian Bach, cannot be all bad.

Lewis Thomas, *The
Medusa and the Snail*

The beginnings of the scientific study of human psychological development and its pathological deviations were fashioned nearly a century ago by the creative seminal work of Sigmund Freud and Ivan Pavlov. They came to the study of human behavior from two different backgrounds—Freud as the neurologist and clinician, and Pavlov as a research physiologist. Their methods and conclusions were different, but both contributed basic creative insights into the dynamics of human psychological development. Both emphasized the process of the interaction of the biological and the environmental in the formation of behavior patterns. Both traced the effects of life experience in transforming simple patterns to more complex ones. Both provided methods for the study of human psychological functioning which proved to be enormously productive in their hands and for succeeding generations of investigators. In a deep sense, we are all "Freudians" and "Pavlovians."

In more recent times, the monumental work of Jean Piaget has provided detailed observations and formulations of the processes of cognitive development, an area ignored in the main by both Freud and Pavlov. Piaget, however, has not applied his genius to the elaboration of a general theory of human psychology and psychopathology.

As of today, the theories and practices of psychoanalysis and behaviorism, as derived respectively from Freud and Pavlov, continue to dominate the fields of developmental psychology and psychological medicine. Other theories have come and gone, many modifications in theory and practice have been introduced into psychoanalysis and behaviorism, but the central theoretical and

practical thrusts of both continue to reflect the fundamental formulations of their founders. Attempts have been made to integrate the concepts of psychoanalysis and behaviorism (Marks and
Gelder, 1966) and to find bridges to Piaget's work on cognition
(Wolff, 1960), but with only limited success.

But dominance does not necessarily mean contentment. Increasingly, in recent years, dissatisfaction with the adequacy of
the basic conceptual frameworks of both psychoanalysis and behaviorism has been expressed not only by outside critics, but by
authorities in each of these fields (Marmor, 1966; Schafer, 1976;
Rycroft, 1976; Bandura, 1974). It has become almost a cliché to
point out that Freud and Pavlov, no matter how great their genius
and insights, could not transcend in their theoretical formulations the primitive state of the basic neurosciences as well as the
psychology, psychiatry, and sociology of their time. Even understanding of the full implications of Darwin's revolutionary concept of natural selection was still far in the distance.

Essentially, both Freud and Pavlov relied on animal models
for their conceptualization of human psychology. For Freud, it
was the unfolding of a hypothetical predetermined sequence of
instinctual drives (1949); for Pavlov it was individual variations
in conditioned reflex structures. Pavlov did propose the existence
of a special additional system of conditioned reflexes in humans
called the second signaling system which made language and
thought possible. But, in his excursions into human psychology
and psychiatry, Pavlov's hypotheses rested on reflex systems and
presumed complex instincts (1928, 1941).

As these animal models proved inadequate in dealing with the
intrapsychic activity so characteristic of human beings, psychoanalysis and behaviorism took different approaches. Freud adopted
a traditional strategem of other sciences and filled in gaps of
actual knowledge with hypothetical reified constructs. Chemists
of an earlier era invented "phlogiston" to deal with their igno-
rance of the mechanism of combustion; physicists invented "the
ether" to try to explain the mysteries of the transmission of ra-
diant energy; biologists invented "spontaneous generation" to

account for the sudden unexpected appearances of living organisms. In a similar vein, Freud formulated concepts such as "libido," "cathexis," the "id," "primary narcissism," "infantile omnipotence," and "polymorphous perverse." These hypothetical reified entities served to fill out instinct theory as applied to the human infant, but did not receive support from any independent scientific testing.

Behaviorism, for its part, dealt with the challenge posed by human intrapsychic activity by fiat. The internal processes of the mind were declared "a black box," unknowable scientifically, and in any case unimportant. "Exponents of radical behaviorism have always disavowed any construct of self for fear that it would usher in psychic agents and divert attention from physical to experiential reality. . . . Internal events are treated simply as an intermediate link in a causal chain . . . one can explain behavior in terms of external factors without recourse to any internal determinants. Through a conceptual bypass, cognitive determinants are thus excised from the analysis of causal processes" (Bandura, 1978, p. 348).

Traditional behaviorism, thus, by its self-imposed limitations cannot deal with many of the most significant human psychological attributes—thought, complex emotions, temperament, motivation, self-concept, imagination, fantasy, defense mechanisms. With this approach, behaviorism "omits the psyche from psychology" (Simpson, 1963, p. 86). It is truly "Hamlet without Hamlet." Those behaviorists, like Bandura, who have incorporated intrapsychic factors into their conceptual models, now divorce themselves from "radical behaviorism," and use instead designations such as "social learning theory" (Bandura, 1978).

It is sometimes argued that in recent years many psychoanalysts have diverged significantly in theory and practice from traditional Freudian theory, and that criticisms of classical psychoanalytic concepts are therefore outdated. However, most modifications of Freudian theory that have been acceptable to the psychoanalytic movement "have not only been minor but are elaborations of theoretical positions he [Freud] had already explicitly introduced" (Stoller, 1973, p. 241). Where more radical revisions have been proposed, whether by Adler, Jung and others in the early years of the psychoanalytic movement or by Horney, Sullivan, Rado and others in more recent years, they have achieved no consensus among psychoanalysts as a group. Rather, the charge is always brought, and perhaps rightfully so, that such deviations are so drastic as to constitute a fundamental break with psychoanalysis. Given this state of affairs, we see no alternative in this volume to the consideration of psychoanalysis in terms of Freud's own formulations.

Freud and Pavlov could not transcend the animal models of their time. It is now finally possible to do so, to understand human development in terms of "the *human* nature of human nature" (Eisenberg, 1972, p. 123). The past 25 years have witnessed an explosion of knowledge and new ideas concerned with human psychological development—from neurochemistry and neurophysiology to clinical psychology and psychiatry to epidemiology and sociology. Child development research has uncovered a richness and complexity in the infant's behavioral repertoire previously unimagined. A number of long-term longitudinal behavioral studies have made important contributions to our understanding of individual patterns of psychological development. Contemporary biology has provided new conceptual approaches to the analysis of heredity-environment relationships and applied the evolutionary principle of natural selection to human behavior.

Our own research contribution has come from a series of longitudinal studies. In our major project, the New York Longitudinal Study, initiated in 1956, we have followed the behavioral development of 136 subjects from middle-class native-born families from early infancy into early adult life. To obtain a population of contrasting socioeconomic background, a group of 95 children of Puerto Rican working-class parents were followed from early infancy to the middle childhood years. We have also studied two longitudinal samples of deviant children. One group comprises 52 children with mildly retarded intellectual levels but without gross evidence of motor dysfunction or body stigmata, who were followed from age five to 11 years. The other population consists of 243 children with congenital rubella resulting from the rubella epidemic of 1964. This group was first studied at two to four years of age, and has been followed since, with a current evaluation in progress in early adolescence. This congenital rubella population has been of special interest because of the large numbers of physical, neurological and intellectual handicaps, including many with multiple handicaps. In all four longitudinal studies, similar protocols for data collection and analysis of behavioral characteristics have been utilized, to make various cross-group comparisons possible. Additional information pertinent to the special attributes of each sample has also been gathered (Thomas and Chess, 1977).

As the findings and formulations of the various longitudinal and early childhood studies have crystallized in recent years, a growing consensus around a number of basic concepts of the dynamics of human psychological development has become evident. This volume will attempt to integrate this new information and theory with the previously existing body of knowledge. The implications for personality theory will be explored, and various psychological phenomena and syndromes will be examined in the light of the theoretical formulations advanced.

Such a broad overview and integration of developmental data and concepts can be approached from a number of different vantage points. Our own preference is first to spell out a number of general formulations, then apply them to a number of specific areas of importance for theory and practice, and end with an overview of the main concepts presented in the various chapters. The general formulations start with an examination of the special and even unique adaptive function of the human brain, and its extraordinary potential for plasticity and alternative developmental pathways. These capacities of the brain, as they begin to manifest themselves in the neonate, make it possible for truly human development to start at birth. The overall characteristics of behavioral functioning which are basic to development we have categorized as *the goals of behavior, the structure of behavior,* and *the process of development.* The specific areas which follow are of necessity treated separately though they interact and intermesh intimately at all times in an individual's psychological functioning. The final overview will present a summation which we feel can provide a basis for a human rather than an animal model of developmental theory.

Chapter II

The Adaptive Function
of the Mind

Pessimism about man serves to maintain the status quo.
It is a luxury for the affluent, a sop to the guilt for the
politically inactive, a comfort to those who continue to
enjoy the amenities of privilege. Pessimism is too costly
for the disenfranchised, they give way to it at the price
of their salvation.

LEON EISENBERG, *The Human
Nature of Human Nature*

10

All surviving species possess genetically transmitted character-istics which enable the individual members to adapt successfully to their environment. This is the basic Darwinian principle of evolution by natural selection. Each species will show specific patterns and mechanisms of adaptation which are its characteris-tic modes of functioning and survival. This is especially true for us as human beings, with our exceptional capacities to invent and use tools, to communicate by language, to learn and to reason abstractly. These abilities are present to a greater or lesser de-gree in certain other species, but their extraordinary develop-ment in human beings has produced our unique ability to con-trol and exploit our environment (and the ominous present potential for destroying ourselves and all life on this planet). It is the human brain which has made these special adaptive char-acteristics possible—a brain with the largest mass of body weight of any species and with enormously developed cerebral hemi-spheres. As Sagan puts it: "The enormous amount of brain area committed to the fingers—particularly the thumb—and to the mouth and the organs of speech corresponds precisely to what in human physiology, through human behavior, has set us apart from most of the other animals. Our learning and our culture would never have developed without speech; our technology and our monuments would never have evolved without hands. In a way, the map of the human cortex is an accurate portrait of our humanity" (1977, pp. 33-34).

The human mind cannot be separated from the functioning of the brain. It is the mind which makes us human beings; it is the brain which makes the mind possible. The British psychiatrist Henry Maudsley stated this basic proposition succinctly over a century ago: "It must be distinctly laid down, that mental action is as surely dependent on the nervous structure as the function of the liver confessedly is on the hepatic structure: that is the fundamental principle upon which the fabric of a mental science must rest" (1867, p. 41).

The human brain is special in the animal world, and human behavior, language, and thought are unique. It would seem evident, therefore, that a theory of psychological development should give central consideration to the specifically human attributes of brain and behavior. But psychoanalytic formulations of "libidinal" development and the vicissitudes of instinctual drives still abound, and behaviorism remains committed to the conditioned reflex model. And this animal-centered bias has been reinforced by the recently developed discipline of ethology, the biological study of animal behavior. This latter field has developed speculative hypotheses such as "fixed action pattern," "innate releasing mechanism," and "action specific energy," very much in line with instinct theory, and has applied these formulations to human behavior (Eibl-Eibesfeldt, 1975).

Animal studies, of course, have made and will continue to make most essential contributions to our knowledge of the mechanisms of human behavioral development. Genetic studies, with plants as well as animals, have elucidated the fundamental principles of the interaction of heredity and environment in the production of the organism's individuality of structure and function. Pavlov's studies of conditioned reflexes in the dog opened the way to the identification of similar processes in human beings and to the recognition of their profoundly significant role in learning. Advances in our knowledge of the neurochemistry of the brain and its influence on normal and deviant psychological processes would be impossible without animal studies.

But the conditioned reflex in the human is not the same as in the dog. A water phobia may start in a three-year-old boy as a simple conditioned reflex after a frightening experience at the beach. But very quickly the anxiety symptoms create reactions in the parents, sibs and other children and adults, which modify the original conditioned reflex and give it symbolic meaning. A sequential interactional process is set in motion. When the boy is 10 years old, the same phobia has developed new aspects, new meanings and new influences on his functioning and social relations. And again, at 20 years, or 40 years, the same phobic symptom may still be present, but its significance for the individual and his family and friends will be different at these ages, since its meanings at these ages are different from the meaning it had at three or 10 years of age. Furthermore, a dozen three-year-olds might start with the same phobia, arising out of a similar traumatic experience in each instance; the phobic symptom might persist in each case into adult life and yet have vastly different meaning and importance in the lives of each of the 12 individuals. In one person the phobia may profoundly alter the life course, in another it may be only a trivial idiosyncracy; in one case it may remain an isolated symptom, in another it may become part of a complex psychopathological structure. In all instances it is the same conditioned reflex, yet it is the unique social nature of human psychological development which determines the outcome.

As to instinct theory, the insights of modern biology and sociology have made it clear that any such model is wholly inadequate as a foundation for human psychological theory. The issue is well stated by the sociobiologist Barash:

> Tight specification of the route from genotype to phenotype would be expected among organisms having simple nervous systems, little capacity for complex movements, and that experience relatively simple and unchanging environments. By contrast, the ability to modify behavior as a consequence of previous experience, learning in a broad sense, requires possession of a relatively complex nervous system. The need to interact with a variety of environments and the physical capacity to do so in complex ways also select for flexibility, that is, susceptibility to modification by experience. . . . Because of the prolonged dependency of wolf pups combined with the cohesive social organization of each pack, a young wolf has great opportunity to modify its behavior via its experience. In contrast, after hatching from its egg, a young spider is likely to float away on the first good breeze and will have to function independently. Spiders must therefore possess fully developed behavioral blueprints; reliance on instincts is more adaptive for them than it is for wolves, although wolves certainly possess some instincts as well.

Similarly, humans rely even less on instincts (1977, pp. 42-43, italics added).

The qualitative difference between animal and human models can be illustrated in the discussions of aggression and war, the complex sociopolitical phenomena which have played such a terribly destructive role in human history. Freud, in his well-known exchange of letters with Einstein on the issue of world peace, wrote that he saw "no likelihood of our being able to suppress humanity's aggressive tendencies," because they were innate and instinctual (Freud, 1950, p. 283). Lorenz, the dominant figure in ethology, in his volume, *On Aggression*, deals with human aggression by analogy with animal behavior, makes many references to "instinctual urges" and "aggressive drives," and asserts that human social behavior "is still subject to all the laws prevailing in all phylogenetically adopted instinctive behavior" (1966, p. 237). Tinbergen, another leading ethologist, endorses Lorenz's views on war and innate aggression and advocates as a prime necessity "the biological study of animal behavior for clarifying problems of human behavior of such magnitude as that of our aggression" (1968, p. 1418).

For dramatic contrast, there is the view of Jacob Bronowski, the mathematician-philosopher-humanist, the creative Renaissance man of our times. In his extraordinary document, *The Ascent of Man*, which is already a cultural treasure, Bronowski puts it simply:

> It is tempting to close one's eyes to history, and instead to speculate about the roots of war in some possible animal instinct; as if, like the tiger, we still had to kill to live, or, like the robin redbreast, to defend a nesting territory. But war, organized war, is not a human instinct. It is a highly planned and cooperative form of theft. And that form of theft began ten thousand years ago when the harvesters of wheat accumulated a surplus, and the nomads rose out of the desert to rob them of what they themselves could not provide. The evidence for that we saw in the walled city of Jericho

and its prehistoric tower. That is the beginning of war (1973, pp. 85-86).

A leading American psychiatrist, Judd Marmor, formulates this human psychosocial view of war with clarity. After challenging the theory of "a fundamental instinct toward destructive aggression in man," he goes on to say:

> It is meaningless to talk of modern war as though it were merely the sum total of countless human aggressions. Modern war is a complicated social institution—the resultant of the intermeshing of many intricate factors: social, economic, political and psychological. It involves large and complex social organizations which we call nations. It requires armies, weapons, supplies, scientific research, advanced technology, recruitment and propaganda. Like any other social institution, it is capable of evolution and change. . . . Other widespread social institutions of man's past, like slavery, dueling, ritual human sacrifice and cannibalism, which in their times and milieus seemed equally rooted in human nature and destiny, have been, in the course of history, almost entirely eliminated. It is also a fact that various societies have existed without recourse to war for many generations (1974, pp. 374-375).

If we reject animal models, what then is a human model for the biological basis of human psychological development? A human biological model must emphasize those genetically determined structural and functional characteristics of the brain which make learning, language, the use of tools, and abstract thought possible. These characteristics will have emerged through the evolutionary process of natural selection. "Natural selection can select for specific ways of being sensitive to experience, or for phenotypic structures that make experience possible, just as readily as it can for any other characteristics" (Lehrman, 1970, p. 73). The geneticist Dobzhansky spells out this fundamental concept: "What is biologically inherited are not body parts, or even

traits, but the ways in which the body reacts to the environment.
. . . We do not inherit culture biologically. We inherit genes
which make us capable of acquiring culture by training, learning, imitation of our parents, playmates, teachers, newspapers,
books, advertisements, propaganda, plus our own choices, decisions and the products of reflection and speculation. Our genes
enable us to learn and to deliberate. What we learn comes not
from the genes but from the associations, direct and indirect,
with other men" (1966, p. 14).

The human brain has the capacity to process, store, and re-
trieve literally trillions of bits of information. This makes for an
enormous capacity to learn, to communicate, and to reason. Plasticity and individuation in developmental courses become possible. Further, as Dobzhansky emphasizes in the above quote,
what we learn is in a social matrix, "from the associations, direct
and indirect, with other men." This social learning starts at birth.
As we shall see in succeeding chapters, our knowledge of the
genetic endowment of the newborn infant which makes this learning possible has greatly expanded in recent years.

The specific biochemical and neurophysiological mechanisms
involved in brain functioning are currently the subject of intensive research (Barchas et al., 1978; Gazzaniga, 1977; Guillemin, 1978). The findings are exciting and begin to spell out precisely how information is processed and stored, how different
mental functions are localized in the two cerebral hemispheres,
what the physiological correlates of sleep are, how language develops, etc. As the data and new ideas come in, however, they
reaffirm the basic principle stated by Dobzhansky above that
"what is biologically inherited are not body parts, not even traits,
but the ways in which the body reacts to the environment."

We do not inherit traits, and we certainly do not inherit fully
organized patterns of behavior, as organisms with simple nervous
systems do. We do inherit genetically the biological capacity to
form, elaborate, and extinguish conditioned reflexes. This form
of learning—contiguity learning—we share with other animal
species, even those with simple nervous systems. But this type of

learning does not provide the biological basis for all human learning, language, and thought—behaviorist theory notwithstanding.

In the past year a new discipline, sociobiology, has asserted that various aspects of human social behavior are genetically rather than culturally transmitted. The basic concept is that natural selection has operated to favor the genetic transmission of randomly produced genetic variations in social behavior which have superior adaptive value. The data are derived primarily from animal studies and applied ingeniously to human behavior. Even complex social phenomena such as altruism are subjected to this type of evolutionary analysis (Hamilton, 1964; Trivers, 1971). The leading figure in sociobiology, Wilson, whose text (1975) is authoritative in the field, does say that "few of the alternatives or directions that human culture has to take are under genetic control" (p. 12), but then asserts that altruism, incest taboos, and various phobias are genetically determined. Sociobiology has come under severe attack from social scientists for introducing a new and more sophisticated concept of the biological determinism of human culture (Sahlens, 1976).

Sociobiology does make it possible to explain the capacity of the newborn infant for social behavior, a capacity which precedes actual social experience. Such social functioning is certainly an adaptive asset for the neonate in cementing a bond for his nurturing caretaker and in communicating his needs. That this behavior arose randomly by genetic variation and was favored by natural selection appears a plausible hypothesis. The issue is different, however, once experience and learning take place and increasingly elaborate social functioning evolves. To ascribe such complex behaviors to genetic inheritance would appear dubious. That the behaviors can be explained by evolutionary theory does not in any way constitute proof of the hypothesis. To reason by analogy with the behavior of other animal communities is hazardous and highly unreliable. A quarter of a century ago, before the advent of contemporary sociobiology,

Herbert Birch spelled out the dangers of such arguments by anology.

> Man has something that is essentially new and which makes him human, *culture*. The tendency of the older generation to transmit its individually acquired and socially inherited experience to the younger generation is the essence of culture. It exists only in the most fragmentary form in primate societies, where each generation, in the main, must individually and painfully acquire the same stock of knowledge that was accumulated by its parents. . . . Culture affects not only the general structure and dynamics of a society but also the nature of interindividual relationships. Thus while social status and social role in the lower primates are determined by individual skill and biological structure, in human societies status and role are determined by genealogy, property or other institutional forms. Because of these differences it is inadvisable to seek for direct analogues of human social life in primate society (1954, pp. 473-474).

The special genetic endowment of the human species has made possible this second system of inheritance which is extragenetic, namely culture. As Campbell puts it, "social evolution is seen as a separate process from biological evolution, although made possible by it, as in the innate capacity for language, memory and perhaps group-affiliative tendencies. A number of modern evolutionary biologists have stressed the importance of social custom cumulation and the biological survival value of biological developments making sociocultural evolution possible" (1975, p. 1105). Cultural evolution, unlike biological evolution, is Lamarckian, in that social life experience is transmitted immediately and cumulatively to succeeding generations through social institutions. Biological change is slow and gradual. Cultural change is rapid, sometimes gradual and sometimes dramatic in its sudden shifts.

It is fruitless to pose the question of whether biology or culture is more important in individual psychology, just as the argument over heredity versus environment is fruitless. Psychological development occurs in a biosocial matrix through a continuous dynamic interaction of the biological and social. Mental functioning, whether adaptive or pathological, is always simultaneously biological and cultural. Operating as a dialectical unity of opposites, one cannot be separated mechanically from the other. "Human evolution is now the resultant of the interaction between biological and sociocultural forces, and it involves a constant feedback between them. In this respect also man differs qualitatively from the rest of the animal creation" (Dubos, 1965, p. 13).

Chapter III

Plasticity of Human
Development

The previous chapter has considered the special attributes of the human brain which make possible enormous capacities to learn, to communicate, and to reason. These represent the overall level of competence which characterizes our performance as a species. In addition, within the framework of its functional capacities the human brain has another attribute of the greatest developmental significance, namely flexibility and plasticity.

Normal children show a wide range of variability in their psychophysiological, perceptual, and cognitive attributes. Individual differences in temperament are striking and functionally significant. The time of emergence of motor capacities and skills and the effective use of language varies widely from one normal child to another. Children from different social classes and cultural backgrounds can show conspicuous differences in norms of behavior, speech, and values. Physical differences in height, weight, skin color, and facial configuration are obvious; less evident is the wide range of differences in the gross and microscopic anatomy of different organs, the composition of body fluids, and the specifics of physiological and chemical mechanisms. Even nutritional needs vary significantly. Roger Williams, who has studied this issue for decades, emphasizes this issue: "Nutritional needs are as unique as fingerprints; what makes a good diet for one person can be seriously deficient for another" (1978, p. 46).

This individual variability has vital evolutionary advantages for humankind. "The sociologically as well as the biologically most advantageous trait is a developmental plasticity of behavior. In any culture, a person meets in his lifetime a variety of challenges and a variety of opportunities. To be able to respond successfully to various challenges is better than to be specialized for just one. To be able to acquire competence in any one of several functions or professions is more useful than to be fit for a single one" (Dobzhansky, 1966, p. 14).

There are many different pathways to optimal learning and effective social functioning. In human development there are many roads to Rome, and many Romes. Unfortunately, this basic truth is all too often negated by rigidity of hierarchical formulations, in which differences in any category are ranged in a spectrum from the best to better to average to inferior to worst. Whether it be skin color, nationality, religion, social class, style of life, or material possessions, humanity has been cursed for thousands of years by the judgmental quantification of characteristics which intrinsically have no such hierarchical distribution.

The developmental plasticity of behavior must derive from the biological characteristics of the brain, as expressed in interaction with the variety of opportunities and expectations which the social environment provides. This potential of the brain is dramatically evident in the developmental course of children with severe physical handicaps. Also evident in these children is the futility and destructiveness of the hierarchical judgment that there is only one norm, with deviations from such a norm being of necessity unsatisfactory and inferior.

We have had a special opportunity to follow the developmental course of a group of children with a wide range of severe physical handicaps. These are the children in our congenital rubella longitudinal study, who have been followed from two to four years of age into early adolescence. The most frequent handicap has been hearing loss (in 65 cases as a single defect and in 112 combined with other defects). Visual loss has been next in frequency, followed closely by neuromuscular disturbances and cardiac abnormalities. Multiple defects are common.

THE DEAF CHILD

Deaf children can see the world but cannot hear it. There is no delay in motor skill acquisition. These children crawl or walk at the expected ages in pursuit of objects or people that catch their attention. They grab just as do the hearing children—and can equally get burned or cut or run over. The rules must be given visually, by touch, or by punishment; the deaf child cannot be warned of danger from afar unless he is already looking at the warner. Cause and effect cannot be explained, at least not in oral language. They cannot ask questions; they could not hear the answers. Rules for deaf children tend to be more restrictive and have fewer exceptions than is the case for hearing youngsters: This is a necessary substitution for explanation. Changes cannot be explained: Deaf children cannot anticipate events unless they have already experienced an equivalent happening that can be made a concrete referential point.

Yet, the deaf children as a group in our rubella sample showed a significant improvement in intellectual test performance level between the preschool and middle childhood years (Chess, 1978). Approximately 50 percent of those classified as retarded in the preschool period moved to either a lesser degree of retardation or into the normal range. A similar upward trend was strikingly evident in those scoring in the average, dull normal or borderline range at three to four years of age.

How do we explain the rising adaptation of these deaf children? The answer appears to lie in the development of communication skills which make language, thought, and conceptualization possible. The deaf child is deprived of the possibility of learning to communicate in early childhood through the spoken word as the hearing child does, and this is reflected in retarded cognitive and adaptive functioning. But she then develops her system of communication through visual cues such as gestures, sign language, and lip reading—what is called "Total Communication." Once she makes up in this way for her earlier inability to communicate and consequent retardation in learning, the deaf child can move ahead rapidly in cognitive and adaptive functioning.

By contrast, until very recently the vast majority of the schools for the deaf used only oral training, that is lipreading and voicing of words. This approach rested on the assumption that there was only one road to the development of language and abstract thinking—that taken by the normal hearing child. Sign language was labeled as inferior and incapable of stimulating cognitive development. Parents were instructed in the most authoritative terms to eliminate all gestures of any kind in communicating with their deaf youngsters, in order to insure the success of "oral" training. But the evidence accumulated indicated that this approach made it most difficult, if not impossible, for deaf children to master the use of language. Schlesinger and Meadows (1972) have shown that deaf children of deaf parents, who communicated with sign language and natural gestures from infancy onward, showed greater academic and language competence than did congenitally deaf children with hearing parents who did not have skill in sign language. In our own rubella sample of congenitally deaf children, oral speech training did not significantly enhance speaking ability. The use of sentences at the eight-to-nine-year age level varied inversely with the severity of hearing loss. Fewer than 15 percent of those with profound hearing disability used any kind of sentences—long, short, or telegraphic. Of those children who had only oral training in school, and had no single words in early childhood, only 7 percent were able to use sentences by middle childhood. On the other hand, the use of Total Communication led quickly to accelerated academic and social functioning (Chess et al., 1980).

Sign language is a true language with all that this means for learning and abstract thinking, thanks to the plastic potential of the brain. In a recent review of research studies on the acquisition of language, Moskowitz puts the issue well:

> Children who are deaf before they can speak generally grow up with the handicap of having little or no language. The handicap is unnecessary: Deaf children of deaf parents who communicate by means of the American Sign Language do not grow up without language. They live in an environment where they can make full use of their language-learning abilities, and they are reasonably fluent in sign language by age three, right on the development schedule. Deaf children who grow up communicating by means of sign language have a much easier time learning English as a second language than children in oral-speech programs learning English as a first language (1978, p. 108).

By the use of Total Communication, the deaf child's visual and motor abilities can be harnessed to compensate for his auditory deficit in learning language. It is the capacity of the brain for plasticity of development that makes possible this utilization of these alternative pathways to language mastery by the deaf child. She can argue, push limits, understand why and when safety rules are necessary, learn social necessities, express emotions clearly, explore ideas, and master abstraction and symbolization.

THE BLIND CHILD

Congenitally blind children show delays in achieving a number of motor developmental landmarks in infancy. They do not raise up their heads to visualize the world around them as other infants do—they can hear quite as well prone or supine. Their sitting, standing, and walking occur later than in their seeing peers—visually beckoning objects cannot stimulate the blind child to move into a better position to see or to come closer to grasp. But as they mature, these children catch up in neuromuscular skills and cognitive capacity, often in different sequences from sighted babies (Norris et al., 1957; Adelson and Fraiberg, 1974; Jan et al., 1977). Thus, for example, in a careful, detailed study of the development of 10 babies blind from birth on, Fraiberg (1977) reports that these infants showed the ability to search for a hidden object when they were eight to 11 months of age. This is the same age when sighted babies show this particular ability. The sighted babies, however, come to master this search for a hidden object with only a sound cue after first having learned at an earlier age to locate and grasp a visually apparent object. This earlier task the blind infants do not master.

Infants first learn to grasp objects with wide raking motions. As integration of visual and kinesthetic sensation develops, children with normal vision go on to develop precise pincer hand movements for grasping. The blind child remains with her raking motions—the same kind of sweeping movement any one of us would use in trying to locate an object in a pitch-black room.

The blind child does not respond to the caretaker's face and voice by smiling (Jan et al., 1977, pp. 189-90). The sighted baby who fails to respond to these stimuli with a smile may very well be showing the beginning of a disorder of affective and social development, such as autism. All too often the same interpretation is given to the blind baby's failure to smile, with a judgment that pathology of affective functioning exists. Those who work with blind children are quite familiar with how many psychiatrists and psychologists overdiagnose autism in such children. This misjudgment is bolstered by a lack of understanding of the adaptive significance of typical habitual behaviors of blind children. These include pressing the eyeballs, weaving the head from side to side, holding the face down, gazing at a light source with hand waving in front of the eyes, smelling foods before eating them, and smelling objects and people. These behaviors are so frequently found in blind individuals that they are categorized as "blindisms" (Jan et al., 1977, pp. 239-255). Similar habitual behaviors are also found in autistic children, where they are called "autistic rituals." But the functional significance of these behaviors is very different in the two groups. The blind child uses these behaviors to increase sensory stimulation and to substitute the use of an intact sense, such as smell, for the visual defect. Once such a child is otherwise stimulated, such as by someone talking to him, he easily stops the eyeball-pressing or head- or hand-waving. He can also be taught that smelling food or people is socially undesirable. The autistic child's behavioral rituals, by contrast, appear to reflect pathological self-preoccupation, and cannot be altered or extinguished in the same manner as in the blind child.

Just as a deaf child is capable of normal language development, so a blind child is capable of normal affective and social development. Such a child cannot see, but he can hear, smell, taste, feel, and be aware of kinesthetic stimuli. He can grasp, learn to cuddle and kiss, to play games identifying parts of the body, and then go on to more and more complex play and social activities that do not require vision.

Fraiberg describes the special developmental sequences and patterns of blind children and emphasizes their adaptive value. However, she fails to see that her own data confirm the key concept that the plasticity of the brain makes it possible to have more than one normal adaptive sequence of development. Committed to the theoretical position that there is only one normal biological program for behavioral adaptation, she comments that "what we have seen in this typical profile of a blind baby at five months of age is a biological program that has been derailed and for which adaptive solutions have not yet been found. . . . In the biological program it is 'intended' that vision and prehension evolve in synchrony" (1977, p. 154).

Once one assumes that there is only one biological program that is "intended," the different developmental sequence of the blind infant does represent a "derailment." If one views the data without such an a priori assumption, the behavioral patterns of the blind child which enable him to develop affectively and cognitively and cope with his environment become a dramatic tribute to the plasticity of the human brain—a plasticity which makes possible a host of alternative adaptive developmental pathways, depending on the characteristics of the child and the nature of the environment.

THE CHILD WITH MOTOR HANDICAPS

The infant with a motor handicap suffers from diminished sensorimotor experience. Depending upon the nature of the disability—absence or partial failure of growth of limbs, paresis, amyotonia, spasticity, athetosis—a corresponding limitation on the exploration of the world will be present. The handicapped infant may not be able to touch or hold objects with ease, move them from hand to hand, take them from or give them to nurturing adults.

In Piaget's theory of cognitive development (1954, 1963), the first stage is that of sensorimotor intelligence in infancy. In this period, the infant learns to coordinate sensory data and motor experiences, leading to an awareness of the external world as a permanent place, with objects having properties that are independent of one's own perceptions. Piaget designates the development of the basic psychological units as *schemata*. A primary scheme is that of prehension, which evolves out of the progressive modification of the neonate's grasping reflex by the infant's contact with different shapes, textures, temperatures, and weights as he grasps and handles one object after another.

For the infant with a severe motor handicap, her difficulties in grasping, holding and handling objects will make impossible the usual sequence of the formation of primary schemata. This sequence Piaget considers the essential first stage in the progressive development of cognition, as indeed it is for the nonhandicapped child. Yet, it is clear that the person born with a handicap which seriously limits her sensorimotor experience finds alternative pathways to normal cognitive development. The host of such individuals who attain a superior intellectual level which they use productively and creatively are again a vivid testimonial to the inherent capacity of the human brain for plasticity of development.

IMPLICATIONS

The deaf child, the blind child, the motorically handicapped child—each can find a developmental pathway consonant with his capacities and limitations, thanks to the plasticity of the brain. By the same token, the environmentally handicapped child is not inevitably doomed to an inferior and abnormal psychological developmental course. Whether the handicap comes from social ideology, poverty, a pathological family environment, or special stressful life experiences, the plastic potential of the brain offers the promise for positive and corrective change. This central human potential for plasticity and learning bears directly on a number of issues in developmental theory—the significance of early life experiences, continuity-discontinuity over time, and sequential patterning of developmental stages. These issues will be considered in subsequent chapters.

The promise which the plastic potential of the brain offers to the physically or environmentally handicapped child is not, however, a guarantee. The professional and political authorities who formulate educational, remedial, and therapeutic programs for these youngsters can translate this promise into a reality. To do so requires the abandonment of hierarchical judgments of a single normal sequence of development and a single standard for measuring social and intellectual growth. Otherwise, the assumption that the handicapped child's development must duplicate that of the nonhandicapped child, or else it is inferior, inevitably leads to self-fulfilling prophecies of actual inferior outcome.

The plastic potential of the normal brain is a crucial human asset. Damage to the brain which limits or destroys its capacity for plasticity will affect the individual's ability to respond with flexibility to environmental change. The consequences of such loss of flexibility can be far-reaching in their psychological consequences. These will be considered in the later section of this volume in which the dynamics of psychopathology will be considered.

Chapter IV

The Neonate
as a Human Being

In previous centuries, concepts of the neonate were dominated by two opposite views. In one, the newborn infant was considered a *homunculus,* an adult in miniature who already possessed all the physical and psychological attributes that would characterize him as an adult. In the other view, the neonate was a *tabula rasa,* as John Locke put it, a clean slate on which the environment would inscribe its influence until the adult personality was etched to completion.

The *homunculus* concept led to such labels as "constitutional inferior" and "constitutional psychopath," in which all kinds of complex patterns of deviant behavior were thought to be already present in the newborn infant. In a more idealized romantic view, there was Rousseau's vision of the child as a "noble savage," endowed with an "innate moral sense," with "intuitive knowledge of what is right and wrong," but thwarted by restrictions imposed on him by society" (Mussen, Conger, and Kagan, 1979, p. 11). (Freud also considered the infant a savage, dominated by "id impulses," but hardly "noble.")

By the beginning of this century, this mechanical constitutionalist view began to be discredited. Freud and Pavlov demonstrated how much of behavior that had been labeled as preformed and predetermined actually arose out of the child's life experiences. Psychodynamic-psychoanalytic and behaviorist studies expanded and deepened our knowledge of the profound significance of the child's environment in shaping his physical and psychological development. With the excessive swing of the pendulum that so often occurs, however, the rejection of the one-sided constitutionalist model led to an increasing trend to environmental determinism. In this country especially, from the 1920s to the 1950s, an environmentalist view which gave scant consideration to the importance of the infant's organismic characteristics was firmly in the ascendency. Thus, in the mid-1950s, as we ourselves began to explore the possible significance of the infant's own intrinsic behavioral style on later development, our psychiatric colleagues with few exceptions assumed we were returning to some outdated and discredited constitutionalist view.

Rather paradoxically, this environmentalist concept of the neonate as a *tabula rasa* was combined with adultomorphic interpretations of the young infant's behavior. The newborn was endowed with the egocentricity and omnipotence which would be pertinent labels for an adult with similar behavior, ignoring "the fact that the development of cerebral functioning of the young infant cannot ever approximate the level where such ideation is possible" (Chess and Thomas, 1959, p. 326). Thus, a widely cited text in psychiatry asserts that "the neonate possesses an omnipotence that he will never again possess. He but raises his voice and his needs are served. It is an omnipotence of helplessness, but he is fed, cleaned, cuddled, and kept comfortable" (Lidz, 1968, p. 114). In a similar vein, leading authorities in child development and child psychiatry assert that "the infant begins life as a completely self-centered and dependent individual, driven by his id forces" (Senn and Solnit, 1968, p. 3). Margaret Mahler, an authoritative theoretician in child psychoanalysis, puts it even more strongly: "I have applied to the first weeks of life the term *normal autism*, for in it, the infant seems to be in a state of primitive hallucinatory disorientation, in which need satisfaction belongs to his own omnipotent *autistic* orbit" (1968, pp. 7-8).

Jerome Kagan and his co-workers describe this adultomorphic issue well. "A potentially serious error in the study of infants is the use of comparative categories whose meaning is derived from a contrasting description for adulthoood. . . . Descriptive categories like *undifferentiated, oral, egocentric, narcissistic,* or even *sensorimotoric* connote qualities whose meaning is dependent upon a comparison of infant with adult. Babies seem to spend a lot of time feeding and mouthing objects, therefore it is tempting to conclude that oral satisfactions have a special place during the opening years of life. But if European adults at the turn of the century had devoted a large portion of their day to feeding, Freud probably would not have chosen that classification" (Kagan, Kearsley, and Zelazo, 1978, pp. 13-15).

As Kagan points out, changes in the cultural ego ideal lead to shifts in the traits ascribed to infants and children. "When a reasonable conformity to benevolent authority was the ideal, young children were described as willful. . . . When control of sexual impulse was the European ideal at the turn of the century, Freud described the young child as an uncharted libidinous surface. Now, "the Western adult is more preoccupied with finding some person or activity that will at least contain, but perhaps subdue, an anxiety that breeds on the absence of meaning in activity and of trust in human encounter. Correspondingly, modern theorists project onto the infant and young child, not shame, but anxiety over loss of a loving and caretaking adult" (Kagan, Kearsley, and Zelazo, 1978, pp. 12-13).

How many times over the years have we ourselves shuddered when psychiatric colleagues described an adult's behavior as "infantile" because it was unreasonable, with a demand for an immediate justification of self-centered impulses. Our protest that an infant doesn't really behave that way usually had as little effect as our challenges to explanations of disordered, disorganized adult behavior as "regression to an infantile state." Even in the current scene, a highly knowledgeable and thoughtful clinical and research psychiatrist, in constructing a hierarchy of adaptive ego mechanisms, says that in "the most primitive end of the continuum I have included the so-called psychotic defenses of delusional projection, psychotic denial and distortion. *Often, these mechanisms can be identified in normal individuals before the age of five*" (Vaillant, 1977, p. 81; italics added).

These adultomorphic and one-sided environmentalist views were difficult to challenge in the past as long as empirical research on the behavioral dynamics of the neonate and young infant was conspicuous by its absence. Speculative hypotheses always flourish in the absence of knowledge. As one leading researcher describes it (Schaffer, 1977, p. 27), "it was thought that in the early weeks of life a baby's senses were not yet capable of taking in any information from the outside world, so that to all intents and purposes he was blind and deaf. Unable to move much either, he seemed a picture of psychological incompetence, of confusion and disorganization. Only the regularity of his experience, provided principally by his parent, was thought to bring order to the baby's mind. Until that was achieved, all he could do was feed and sleep."

Research studies of the last 20 years have dramatically changed this view of the neonate's functioning. Careful, detailed, naturalistic observations and inductive content data analysis, combined with the use of new experimental techniques, have by now provided convincing evidence of the neonate's capacities. Another leading researcher summarizes the conclusions to be drawn from the recent explosion of knowledge: "A newborn thus begins life as an extremely competent learning organism, an extremely competent perceiving organism" (Bower, 1977, p. 35).

It is not possible or necessary here to document in detail the dramatic and surprising research data from the neonatal studies of the past 20 years. These have been summarized in a number of recent publications (Bower, 1977; Dunn, 1977; Kagan, Kearsley, and Zelazo, 1978; Lewin, 1975). Some highlights will be presented to illustrate the research directions that have been taken, the types of data that have been gathered and analyzed, and the conclusions to be drawn as to specific biological endowments and biosocial patterns of adaptation of the neonate. Implications for developmental theory will then be considered.

PERCEPTUAL COMPETENCE

Robert Fantz, in a series of studies beginning in the mid-1950s, showed that the newborn infant not only could recognize visual patterns, as determined by length of visual fixation, but showed preferential gazing at such patterns over colored but plain visual stimuli (Fantz and Nevis, 1967). Furthermore, preferential attention was given to complexity, to movement, and to three-dimensionality. Further research in recent years has used human faces as stimuli. "Whether one presents live faces or representaitons, whether the faces are schematic or real, two-dimensional or three-dimensional, appear in the flesh or on film—in every case, infants are fascinated by them, often to the exclusion of all else. The eyes in particular are an important source of attraction. . . . It is as though the infant is biologically 'set' to be triggered by certain quite specific yet primitive stimuli—stimuli found on other human beings" (Schaffer, 1977, p. 37).

Michael Wertheimer (1961) tested the auditory responses of an infant immediately after birth. He sounded a clicker first to the right and then to the left of the infant. In each instance, the neonate turned her eyes to the side from which the sound came. This not only indicated an ability at birth to localize sound but the beginning of intersensory coordination, in which a stimulus in one sensory modality (audition) produced a response in another modality (vision). Other studies indicate that rate of change in sound energy will elicit interest in the newborn, as shown by cardiac deceleration and eye opening, or defensive avoidance, as shown by cardiac acceleration and eye closing (Kearsley, 1973).

The relation between audition and vision in the neonate was also studied by Mendelson and Haith. They found that newborns scan differently in darkness than in light, and that sound affects their visual activity. They suggest that "there is a spatially relevant, functional relation between audition and vision" and that "the newborn is equipped with flexible information-acquisition routines which predispose the infant to learn about the environment" (1976, p. 57).

Neurobehavioral Organization

Traditionally, it was assumed that the newborn functioned only at a brainstem level of organization. Thus, "at birth, the functional ability which ascends from the brainstem up into the brain has not yet reached the cerebral hemispheres" (Peiper, 1963). Recent research has shown that, to the contrary, the neonate shows important evidences of cortical control and responsiveness. Wolff made careful detailed behavioral observations of 12 neonates over a four-day period. Each baby was observed for a total of 24 hours. His findings led to the conclusion that "the frequent occurrence of spontaneous behaviors in restful sleep, their temporal organization as rhythms, and interaction as substitutes for each other . . . suggest that the human brain can instigate temporally organized or rhythmical motor patterns without afferent stimulations, and that it may function as an autochthonous clock for the serial ordering of adaptive functions" (1966, p. 89).

Brazelton (1973, 1978) studied the neonate's range of behavioral integrative processes, variation in state behavior, and responsiveness to various kinds of social stimuli. He found significant evidence of cortical control and responsiveness with 22 behavioral items, which now comprise the widely used Brazelton Neonatal Behavioral Assessment Scale. These items include, among others, response decrement to repeated sensory stimuli, orienting responses to inanimate stimuli and to examiner's face and voice, quality and duration of alert periods, responses to being cuddled, defensive reactions to a cloth over face, consolability and self-quieting activity. Turkewitz and Birch (1971) have also reported a series of studies indicating a wide range to the neonate's level of neurobehavioral organization. The findings included responses to simple and complex auditory stimuli, habituation to auditory and somesthetic stimuli, and correlation between intensity of auditory stimulation and direction of eye movements.

LEARNING COMPETENCE

Learning, as demonstrated by the formation of conditioned reflexes, starts actively at birth. (There is some evidence that conditioning can occur in prenatal life, but reliable data are difficult to obtain.) The capacity for neonatal learning has been demonstrated by a number of investigators (Connolly and Stratton, 1969; Lipsitt and Kaye, 1964; Papousek and Papousek, 1975). Lipsitt (1969) is so impressed by the neonatal competence in learning that he has asserted that newborns can learn better on the first day of life than ever again.

Perhaps the most extensive and complex studies of neonatal conditioning have been done by Papousek and his co-workers (Papousek and Papousek, 1975). Both classical and operant conditioning were demonstrated, using reflex head-turning to an auditory stimulus as the motor response to be conditioned. From a varied series of conditioning experiments the authors conclude that "learning in the neonate is possible when reinforcement is contingent on the child's own behavior and when the nature of the reinforcement corresponds to the biological motivation of the neonatal organism, e.g., when the neonate can satisfy his hunger through learned behaviour" (p. 246). The Papouseks also emphasize that habituation—the decrease in response to a stimulus

with its repeated presentation—is "one of the basic learning mechanisms" and can be demonstrated in the neonate even during
deep sleep (p. 246).

Another basic type of learning in children is through imitation
of others. It is of great interest that this type of learning has been
demonstrated in infants in the first week of life. "If the baby's
mother, or some other adult, sticks out her tongue at the baby,
within a relatively short time the baby will begin to stick his
tongue back at her" (Bower, 1977, p. 28). The same sequence of
imitation can be demonstrated with the adult's fluttering her
eyelashes or opening and closing her mouth. The neonate can
perform these actions spontaneously, but does so to a far greater
extent with an adult model to imitate.

The evidence is thus abundant that the neonate's level of central nervous system functioning makes possible a significant order
of perceptual discrimination and active learning. The extensive-
ness and complexity of learning in the first days of life are vividly
demonstrated in a series of experiments reported by Genevieve
Carpenter (1975). Under standardized conditions, in which the
baby was calm, alert, and in a comfortable position, infants were
exposed to various facial configurations. The discrimination
among the different configurations was measured by the length of
time the infant looked directly at the face. As early as two weeks
of age, the mother's face received significantly more attention
than a stranger's face. Also, each face was looked at longer if ac-
companied by a voice, but the mother's face was a stronger positive stimulus even without voice than the stranger's face accom-
panied by either a stranger's or mother's voice. When the faces
and voices were mismatched, i.e., mother's face and stranger's
voice, or stranger's face and mother's voice, there was a significant
tendency for the infant to turn its gaze away.

These findings indicated an ability to differentiate between two
live female faces during the first weeks of life. Furthermore, the
mismatching experiment indicated that voices were also discrimi-
nated and that associations between face and voice had already
been learned. Carpenter concludes that very young infants are

"able to screen sensory input with reference to information stored from everyday experience. Furthermore, it appears that more than one category may be used in classifying information. . . . More sophisticated information-processing capabilities appear to be operating within the newborn's interaction with its environment than we had thought possible" (pp. 134-135).

SOCIAL COMPETENCE

The capacity of the neonate for social functioning is truly impressive. Her perceptual competence, her patterning of neurobehavioral organization, and her learning competence, as summarized above, are essential assets for an active social relationship with the significant human beings in her environment. Beyond this, recent research has revealed that the newborn is capable of active social communication, that most basic element of social exchange. A remarkable demonstration of this capacity for social communication has been reported by Condon and Sander (1974). In their study, they used a refined technique of microanalysis of sound films of interaction between neonate and caretaker, which made possible detailed correlations between the mother's speech and the infant's body movement. Data were obtained and analyzed on 16 neonates, with the conclusion that "as early as the first day of life, the human neonate moves in precise and sustained segments of movement that are synchronous with the articulated structure of adult speech" (p. 99). The synchrony occurred whether the adult was present or the voice came from a tape recorder, ruling out the possibility that the findings resulted from the adult's synchronization of his speech to the infant's movement. The precise synchrony occurred with both American and Chinese speech, but not with disconnected vowels or tapping sounds. Thus, it required natural, rhythmic speech to elicit these synchronized body movements in the neonate. Condon and Sander suggest that their study "reveals a complex interaction system in which the organization of the neonate's motor behavior is entrained by and synchronized with the organized speech behavior of adults in his environment. If the infant, from the beginning, moves in precise, shared rhythm with the organization of the speech structure of his culture, then he participates development-ally through complex, sociobiological entrainment processes in millions of repetitions of linguistic forms long before he later uses them in speaking and communication" (p. 101).

This interactional synchrony between neonate and caretaker has also been identified in sucking behavior. Kaye and Brazelton (1971) have described the pauses between bursts of sucking as periods in which the mother initiates social interaction by such activities as jiggling and stroking. Schaffer has called these inter-actions between infant and mother "interpersonal synchrony" and considers its establishment to constitute "the primary task of early development. This synchrony is achieved because, on the one hand, the infant, by virtue of his innate endowment, is equipped to participate in social interactions, while, on the other hand, his caretakers offer him the kind of stimulation that will appro-priately enmesh their responses with his" (1977, p. 62). As this interaction becomes established, there is a reciprocal nature to the interpersonal synchrony. The infant's responses act as stimuli to her caretakers, as well as vice versa, and an evolving system of mutual social interaction develops.

Studies of infant communication have paid special attention to the development of the smile, that first clear expression of posi-tive pleasurable feeling by the infant (Spitz and Wolf, 1946; Wolff, 1963; Emde and Harmon, 1972; MacFarlane, 1975). The research data indicate that the neonate already possesses the capa-city for smiling, and this appears to occur spontaneously or to be elicited by a variety of noises. "The first clear indications of a 'social smile' appear during the third week, when a specifically human stimulus elicits the smile more consistently than other stimulus configurations. This specifically human stimulus is the high-pitched voice. . . . By 25 to 28 days, after the silent human face occasionally becomes the adequate stimulus for eliciting a smile, it appears to be specifically the contact between eyes that is effective" (Wolff, 1963, p. 119). Thus, the capacity for smiling, already present at birth, evolves into an active form of social communication over the first month of life. As might be expected, there is evidence that "the time of onset of social smiling and the amount of smiling could be varied with the amount of social stimulation" (MacFarlane, 1975, p. 20).

By contrast to the smile, the infant's cry is an active and effective form of social communication from the moment of birth on. It is through his cry that the infant communicates his needs and distress, and the cry acts as a compelling signal for the caretaker to intervene. The growth of a new mother's self-confidence and assurance as a competent caretaker is perhaps more closely related to her ability to soothe her crying infant than to any other factor.

IMPLICATIONS FOR THEORY

Human existence is social from the moment of birth on. The neonate could not survive without the immediate, active, and continuous involvement of other human beings. (The presumed exception of so-called "feral children" has very dubious validity.) At the same time, the biological endowment of the newborn infant makes this social involvement a mutually interactive and reciprocally influential process from the beginning.

This biological genetic inheritance provides the perceptual and learning capacity for the neonate to begin immediately to claim its cultural nongenetic inheritance. With the first fondling, the first feeding, the first perception of the human face and human voice, the newborn responds to and integrates inputs from the environment which have both cultural and sensorimotor significance. In turn, the active responses of the infant influence the character of the caretaker's attitudes and handling. The nature of this influence is again culturally determined.

The human newborn's social being is, of course, qualitatively different from that of social organisms such as bees and ants, who are born with an elaborate, fixed, preprogrammed, instinctual structure of social functioning. How different the human being is at birth from other mammals can be a matter for debate. What is clear, however, is that the uniquely human aspects of social interaction begin to operate at birth so that the human infant very quickly becomes a different social being from other mammals. From an evolutionary point of view, the perceptual, learning, and social competence of the human neonate is a necessary correlate to the long period of nurturance and dependency of infancy and childhood. These neonatal capacities make possible the maximum transmission of the cultural heritage of humanity, that adaptive mechanism which is so uniquely developed in Homo sapiens.

Previous assumptions about the neonate gave rise to all kinds of speculations and debates as to when the human infant developed from a biological into a psychobiological organism (Mahler, 1968, p. 12). These assumptions regarding the primitive neurobehavioral level of neonatal functioning also led to conclusions that "because the infant's incapacity to communicate at a verbal level . . . data collection [in the newborn] must necessarily be physiologic (including motor development) or biochemical" (Richmond and Lipton, 1959, p. 78). Such speculations and conclusions are now unnecessary. The infant is a psychobiological organism at birth, and his functioning and development can be studied psychologically and culturally, as well as biologically. The only relevant debate is whether psychological processes should be considered to begin at birth or in intrauterine life (MacFarlane, 1975, p. 15). Whether the fetus can be considered a social being, however, is another matter. It is only at birth that the human organism begins to function as an independent biosocial organism capable of active perception and communication and social learning.

The newborn's psychological development does not involve the shedding of such hypothetical presocial and antisocial characteristics—egocentricity, narcissism, omnipotence, etc.—in order to become a human being. The neonate is already a human being in a fundamental sense. The progression through childhood, adolescence, and adult life is rather a process in which maturation and learning continuously intertwine—a biosocial process of continuity combined with quantitative and qualitative change.

Chapter V

The Goals
of Behavior:
Task Mastery and
Social Competence

In the preceding chapters we have examined the special adaptive characteristics of the human brain, its capacity to make possible plasticity and flexibility in behavioral development and the evidence that these attributes are present in the neonate. These considerations lead to the question as to the goals that these human brain-behavior characteristics make possible.

One fundamental characteristic of all living organisms is that their functioning serves some goal. This is a qualitative distinction from the nature of the physico-chemical laws governing inanimate matter. The student of biology has to ask the question "What for?" This question is forbidden to the nonbiological scientist as man-centered teleology, and he is allowed only to ask "How?"—a question the biologist must also ask. "In organisms, but not (in the same sense) in any non-living matter, the adaptation *does* occur. Heredity and muscle contraction do serve functions that are *useful* to organisms. They are not explained, in this aspect, by such answers to 'How?' as that heredity is transmitted by DNA or that energy is released in the Krebs cycle" (Simpson, 1963, p. 87).

In the past, before Darwin provided a natural, objective explanation of adaptation and "did not ignore the teleological aspects of nature but brought them into the domain of science" (Simpson, 1963, p. 86), concepts of purpose in nature necessarily rested on finalistic and vitalistic philosophies. Some students of behavior rejected such ideas and eliminated all consideration of "What for?" from their work. Thus, Pavlov had a standing rule that any worker in his laboratory who offered an explanation of living behavior in terms of purpose had to pay a fine to the laboratory treasury. This tradition has persisted in behaviorism with its focus on the stimulus-response paradigm, and its judgment that goals and motives are hidden in the mind's scientifically unknowable "black box."

Others, however, searched for some purposive agent in living phenomena which would appear to have a scientific basis, in contrast to vitalistic and mystical concepts such as élan vital. Freud, with his concern for the motivational issues in human behavior, sought such a solution in the instinct drive hypotheses so prevalent in his day. Because such concepts were non-Darwinian, Freud's theory of libido as a primary dynamic source of "What for?" in behavior could not escape such a finalistic teleology. Freud's libido theory became a most sophisticated example of the teleological systems, of which the biologist Ernst Mayr remarked, "Even though some of the underlying observations of these conceptual schemes are quite correct, the supernaturalistic

conclusions drawn from these observations are altogether misleading" (1961, p. 1503).

Traditional instinct theory postulates the goal of behavior to
be drive energy reduction. The inadequacy of this concept for
human psychology has been abundantly documented by numerous workers, both within and outside the psychoanalytic movement (Marmor, 1942; White, 1959; Dobzhansky, 1962). Even for
animal behavior, the weight of recent research has contradicted
this concept that drive reduction is a primary goal of the organism's functioning. "Many of the earlier tenets of primary drive
theory have been discredited by recent experimental work. There
is no longer any compelling reason to identify either pleasure or
reinforcement with drive reduction, or to think of motivation as
requiring a source of energy external to the nervous system"
(White, 1959, p. 328).

Consideration of the goals and motives of human behavior has
been a prime concern of the psychoanalytic movement from the
beginning. No other theoretical scheme of development has given
comparable attention to these issues. One of Freud's basic contributions has been this emphasis on goals, with the elucidation
of how much in human behavior that superficially appears to be
aimless or accidental actually involves purposive functioning.
However, Freud's conceptualization of motivational forces always
remained within the framework of drive satisfaction or its frustration. Thus, one of his final comprehensive formulations stated
that "the symptoms of neuroses are exclusively, it might be said,
either a substitutive satisfaction of some sexual impulse or measures to prevent such a satisfaction, and as a rule compromise between the two . . . theoretically there are no objections to sup-
posing that any sort of instinctual demand whatever could occasion these same repressions and their consequences" (1949, p. 85).

In recent years, dissatisfaction with Freud's drive state satisfac-
tion-frustration model have led many psychoanalysts to propose
modifications or radical revisions of libido theory. There does
not appear to be any consensus within the psychoanalytic movement at this time as to which new formulations have validity

and which are speculative. The generally favorable reception by psychoanalysts to Hartman's concept of autonomous ego functions (1950, 1958) and Erikson's scheme of developmental stages (1950) does constitute somewhat of a consensus. However, these formulations do not constitute radical revisions of classical psychoanalytic theory. What is clear is that these various modifications of psychoanalytic theory reflect a recognition of several basic developmental phenomena: A number of psychological characteristics, such as perception, language, and cognition, cannot be encompassed within an exclusively motivational framework; development occurs within a social matrix; and highly significant phenomena, such as exploratory behavior, curiosity, and pleasure in problem-solving, cannot really be explained by instinct and drive reduction theory.

More recently, sociobiologists have given prime importance to the survival of the species as the fundamental behavioral goal of all animals, including humans (Wilson, 1975). In this formulation, even the struggle of the individual for survival is not basic, but a means to the survival of the species. As an overall generalization based on evolutionary theory and the concept of natural selection, there can be no quarrel with this thesis. However, when we come to human behavior, so many exceptions to this concept appear that it is of limited usefulness. All the extragenetic influences of culture, language, thought, and symbolization serve to make human goals extraordinarily varied and complex. Thus, for example, a son may decide to go into his father's lucrative business for many different reasons. He may be genuinely interested and talented in the field; he may view it as an opportunity for easy material success and be willing and able to work hard and to achieve this success; he may be unwilling to commit himself to any new, challenging field of work and go into the family business as a way out, where he can avoid responsibility and stress; he may make the decision because of a strong psychological identification with his father; or he may do it to gain his father's approval. In the first two instances the decision may be considered to further his survival as an individual; in the third instance the decision will not promote this survival; and in the last instance it may or may not do so, depending on the son's abilities and other capacities. Or, the son may refuse to go into his father's business to prove his independence, which, again, may or may not have survival value. To take other more dramatic examples, history is full of instances in which individuals sacrificed their lives for political, religious, ethical or nationalistic ideals, with very little if any evidence that this contributed to the survival of the species. Again, there are many instances in which a person sacrifices a materially comfortable life to pursue scientific or artistic interests, with no assurance that this would equal, let alone better, her life situation. At the other end of the psychological spectrum are the tragically innumerable cases in which the conditions of life are so unrewarding and frustrating that individuals turn to alcohol or other drugs even though they know this will shorten their lives. Or actual mental illness may exist, often largely due to social influences, leading to self-destructive behavior.

Sociobiological theory thus affirms a broad generalization of substantial validity, but one which cannot by itself deal with the richness, complexity and variability which is so characteristic of human psychological functioning.

AN ALTERNATIVE APPROACH

To repeat a fundamental thesis, human developmental theory must base itself on what is *human* in human nature (Eisenberg, 1972). This cannot be done with instinct drive reduction theory, survival theory, or the behaviorist "black box" concept. For an alternative approach, it is very useful to look at the young infant, whose behavior is relatively simple but already human in character. The very young infant shows a remarkable interest in exploratory behavior and ability for the rapid acquisition of motor skills. These characteristics are in sharp contrast to traditional views of the course of child development. As one leading investigator reports, he was highly skeptical of mothers' statements that very young babies could reach out and touch things. "I was so convinced that the textbooks were right and that reaching began at about five months—not five days—that I simply paid no attention to such reports" (Bower, 1977, p. 27). Bower finally convinced himself the mothers were right by carefully observing a one-week-old infant playing with his bell. He had thought that "babies of that age do not play with bells. . . . I realized that my belief that three-week-old babies do not reach out and play with objects was based on observations of three-week-old babies who had never had anything put within their reach. . . . If there are no things within reach, then of course babies will not reach out. If there are, they will" (p. 8).

The manipulatory-exploratory behavior of very young infants has also been studied by Papousek and Papousek. "External change which is contingent on the infant's own activity elicits the most intensive of orienting reactions: approach and manipulatory explorations of various types. These reactions all tend to be remarkably resistant to habituation and usually cease only after trial and error or other operant forms of learning have shown the infant how to get the relevant environmental change repeated" (1975, p. 249).

Piaget has described exploratory and object manipulatory behavior vividly in his own infant son's behavior, together with intense absorption and pleasure in his activity. By the second half of the year, Piaget could describe four stages of response in quick sequence to a new object: visual exploration, tactile exploration, movement of the object in space, and use of a repertoire of manipulation (shaking, striking, swinging, rubbing, etc.), "each in turn . . . as though studying the effect produced" (1952, p. 255). In animal behavior, the ethologist Tinbergen has described analogous patterns of exploratory behavior, "in which the animal sets out to acquire as much information about an object or a situation as it can possibly get. The behavior is intricately adapted to this end, and it terminates when the information has been stored, when the animal has incorporated it in its learned knowledge. This exploration (subjectively we speak of 'curiosity') is not confined to acquisition of information about the external world alone; at least mammals explore their own movements a great deal, and in this way 'master new skills' " (1968, p. 1417) .

White has also emphasized the importance of the exploration and manipulation of objects by the young infant by which the child or animal learns to interact effectively with his environment. His review of the research literature indicates that these behaviors "cannot be successfully conceptualized in terms of primary drives." He proposes the terms *competence* and *effectance motivation* to designate these behaviors which lead "the organism to find out how the environment can be changed and what consequences flow from these changes" (1959, p. 329).

TASK MASTERY AND SOCIAL COMPETENCE

The goal of such exploration and manipulation of objects by the young infant can be designated in a general way as *task mastery*. The tasks to be mastered can be the satisfaction of basic bodily needs, such as food and water, or the manipulation, control, and mastery of objects presented by the environment. Even sucking behavior in the neonate is not accomplished by the action of a stereotyped predetermined pattern of reflex behavior. "The sucking rate can be affected by the rate of milk flow, the size, contour, and compressibility of the nipple, and the type of nutrient. . . . It is by no means a simple stereotyped activity, passively elicited by the mother's stimulation. It is, rather, precisely regulated—and highly sophisticated, not only in its internal organization but also in the way it is synchronized with other physiological functions like swallowing and breathing" (Schaffer, 1977, pp. 33-34).

Thus, the neonate and young infant are biologically equipped for the pursuit of two basic adaptive goals—the development of social relations and the mastery of skills and tasks. These goals can be conceptualized as *social competence* and *task mastery*. Both are specially developed in the human being with his unique capacity for learning. Both proceed developmentally, as the individual's capacities mature, as learning takes place, and as the environment makes successive new demands and presents new opportunities. Both proceed by a constant mutual interaction: Task mastery facilitates social relationships, and increasing social competence promotes the capacity to master the environment. Most activities, such as play, school work, sex, and athletics, contain both social and task features.

Jerome Bruner has defined these two goals in the child in broad terms. "For convenience, the forms of early competence can be divided into those which regulate interaction with other members of the species and those involved in mastery over objects, tools, spatially and temporally ordered sequences of events. Obviously, the two cannot be fully separated, as witness the importance of imitation and modeling in the mastery of 'thing skills' " (1973, p. 1). With his colleagues (Wood, Bruner, and Ross, 1976), he has emphasized the special role of learning and teaching in the process of task mastery in the human child. After pointing out that the child from the earliest months of life "is a 'natural' problem-solver in his own right," they go on to point out that

> . . . his efforts are assisted and fostered by others who are more skillful than he is. Whether he is learning the procedures that constitute the skills of attending, communicating, manipulating objects, locomoting, or indeed, a more effective problem-solving procedure itself, there are usually others in attendance who help him on his way. Tutorial interactions are, in short, a crucial feature of infancy and childhood. Our species, moreover, appears to be the only one in which any intentional tutoring goes on. . . . What distinguishes man as a species is not only his capacity for learning, but for teaching as well (p. 89).

EARLY SOCIALIZATION

The interpretation of the process of early socialization—weaning, toilet training, the establishment of regular sleep and feeding schedules, and the first learning of the rules of social behavior —very much depends on the conceptualization of the goals of behavior. For drive reduction theorists, the period of socialization involves a continuous process of frustration. As Freud puts it, "civilization is the fruit of the renunciation of instinctual satisfaction" (1924, p. 297). In his most influential work, Erikson states of weaning that "even under the most favorable circumstances, this stage leaves a residue of a primary sense of evil and doom and of a universal nostalgia for a lost paradise" (1950, p. 75), and of toilet training that "bowel and bladder training has become the most obviously disturbing item of child training in wide circles of our society" (p. 77). Even investigators who have demonstrated that the level of sucking activity is the consequence of opportunities to suck rather than the expression of an innate oral drive (Davis, Sears et al., 1948) have emphasized that "the weaning process, except under the most fortunate circumstances, is bound to be frustrating to the child" (Sears, Macoby, and Levin, 1957, p. 83).

Quite a different concept of weaning and toilet training emerges when they are viewed as steps in task mastery and social competence. Instead of being the frustrating experiences visualized by drive reduction theory, weaning and toilet training become sources of achievement, satisfaction, and enhancement of social relationships. The use of a cup gives the child a control over the process of liquid intake and swallowing that she does not have when sucking at a nipple. Toilet training gives her control over the time and place of bowel and bladder evacuation. With weaning and toilet training, as with the establishment of regular sleep and feeding schedules, the child takes important steps in her social integration into the family group. The positive reactions of the child to weaning and toilet training are indicated by the data from our own New York Longitudinal Study. In these middle-class families with basically permissive and child-centered child care practices, detailed accounts of each child's behavior preceding, during, and following weaning and toilet training were available. As we have reported previously (Thomas et al., 1961), analysis of the data for the first 50 children in the study showed evidence of disturbance associated with weaning and toilet training in only one child. In this one case, the disturbance reflected overall rigid and inconsistent parental practices and attitudes. In some of the families, weaning was accomplished by the child's spontaneous rejection of the bottle. In some instances the mothers persisted in their efforts to continue with bottle feeding and stopped only when they found their efforts to be of no avail. These attempts of the mothers to delay weaning were due to their fears, which they expressed openly in the interviews, that early weaning or toilet training might be traumatic to the child. These fears were based on the presumably authoritative statements they had heard and read as to the dangers of such early weaning and toilet training. (This was in the late 1950s when such statements were dominant in the child care literature.) Some of the mothers even confessed to feeling uncomfortable and uneasy at the early weaning accomplished by the child, because their friends would interpret this as evidence of rigid, outdated, and harmful child care practices. The findings with toilet training were very similar. Training was not only accomplished without a disturbance (except for one case), but in a number of instances the children themselves initiated the training, usually in imitation of an older brother or sister.

These findings suggest that the process of socialization is a positive and gratifying experience to the child, and not a frustrating and disturbing deprivation. Whether it is walking, weaning, self-feeding, toilet training, self-dressing, or the acquisition of language, the normal child is highly motivated at the appropriate developmental levels to engage in these tasks and carry them through to completion. It is true that the process of mastery is accomplished in many humans by stress and tension, whether in the 10-month-old infant learning to walk and drink from a cup or in the adult artist or scientist struggling with a painting or laboratory experiment. To interpret such stress as undesirable and, if inevitable, regrettable is to misinterpret profoundly the dynamic of healthy psychological development. It is only when demands are made for a level and quality of performance that are excessive and inappropriate for the individual that the stress and tension may become pathogenic. If the demands are not excessive and the stress is resolved by mastery, the consequences are positive. Actually, unfavorable consequences may result if the caretakers engage in misguided efforts to "protect" the child from stress and tension.

THE AUTISTIC CHILD

The crucial significance of the goals of task mastery and social competence for effective functioning and development can be seen in children afflicted with autism. This most malignant mental illness almost always shows definite symptoms by the time the child is two-and-a-half years old and its onset is undoubtedly even earlier. The basic psychopathological features, as originally described by Kanner (1943) and reaffirmed by contemporary authorities (Rutter, 1978), include an inability to develop social relationships with people, an obsessive insistence on the maintenance of sameness, and specific distortions of speech which render it essentially noncommunicative. The insistence on sameness, which is shown in the stereotyped character of play, and the child's extreme disturbance if a familiar element of the environment—even a piece of furniture—is changed, can be considered a basic defect in task mastery ability. Basic to task mastery is the ability to deal effectively with an environmental change. The individual who cannot cope with change will be concerned with maintaining the old and the familiar, to which he has made some level of adaptation. The autistic child's inability to develop social relationships with people is a direct expression of a failure to develop social competence. Some autistic children do develop language, but the lack of social competence makes this language deficient and noncommunicative. Other mental illnesses that develop later in life will show varying degrees of impairment of task mastery and social competence, but not the profound deficiency found in childhood autism. This is in line with the general rule that the earlier in life a disturbance in a pattern of physiological or psychological development occurs, the greater the depth and extent of disability are likely to be.

GOALS OF LATER LIFE

There is every indication that the goals of task mastery and social competence are central to later levels of development as well as to early childhood. Philosophers, writers, and psychologists have consistently made this emphasis. Freud put it in terms of "work and love" as the goals of the healthy adult. For the older child, both goals are intertwined in the central activities of school and play. As it emerges at puberty, sexuality presents the adolescent with a complex new biosocial task which also demands a new level of social functioning. As with sexual functioning, different societies and socioeconomic classes present wide variations in the opportunities and restrictions for school, work, athletics, and family life. The goals are basically the same in all areas; the setting, the complexity, the contradictions, and the degree of facilitation and inhibition of goal achievement which the specific society or class offers to the individual—these may vary, and often tremendously.

One possible exception to the task mastery and social competence model is the truly creative individual, whether as artist, scientist, or philosopher. Creativity is qualitatively different from other cognitive, affective, and social human activities. It may very well involve goal-directed capacities and functions that cannot be fully encompassed within the task mastery and social competence model. Many have pondered over this question, including creative individuals themselves, but this most intriguing issue still rests on a speculative level.

At the other end of the spectrum, we have been impressed in our own longitudinal studies of handicapped individuals by the usefulness of the task mastery and social competence model in the analysis of developmental sequences and crises (Thomas and Chess, 1975; Chess, 1979; Chess et al., 1980). The impact of increasingly complex environmental demands and expectations on these vulnerable individuals has been especially evident. Mentally retarded, brain-damaged, or deaf youngsters may cope more or less adequately with the cognitive task demands and the ground rules for peer social relationships in early and middle childhood. But many, though by no means all, find their limited resources and capacities insufficient to cope with the increasingly complex situations and expectations of later childhood and adolescence.

By contrast, some nonhandicapped subjects in the New York Longitudinal Study showed an opposite developmental sequence. They were youngsters who had difficulties in coping successfully with family, school, and peer relationships in early childhood, to the point where clinical symptoms emerged. In later childhood and adolescence, however, new talents and abilities emerged which dramatically enhanced school and social functioning and the earlier behavior disorders disappeared.

These findings from our longitudinal studies have suggested a wider application of the task mastery and social competence model to the analysis of the dynamics of defense mechanisms and various psychopathological syndromes. This approach will be explored in detail in later chapters.

INDIVIDUAL DIFFERENCES: TASK VERSUS PERSON ORIENTATION

As might be excepted, there appears to be individual differences in the balance between task mastery and social competence goals. Our own data suggest that, as early as three to five years of age, some normal children show a predominant interest in task activities, others in social relationships, and still others a mix in which neither predominates. Preliminary evaluation of behavioral protocols at later age periods in early adult life suggests that such individual differences can be identified at sequential developmental levels. Based on a small longitudinal sample, Abrams and Neubauer have reported similar impressions of individual differences in "the disposition toward human- and thing-orientedness" (1975). They feel that this variant becomes manifest as early as the second month of life. Their review of the literature indicates that similar observations have been made in several other studies of infant and child development.

In our clinical work, this phenomenon of task versus person

orientation has been an important issue in a number of cases. The typical situation has involved parents who requested consultation because of concern over their youngster's behavior pattern. Their distress was occasioned by the child's preference for task activity rather than social interests. This was interpreted by the parents as an ominous sign of behavior disorder, inasmuch as this preference was at such variance with the stereotype of the normal, gregarious, outgoing, all-American youngster. In some cases this behavior did reflect a problem of social inhibition and withdrawal. In many instances, however, detailed inquiry revealed that the child was highly competent at social activities in which he engaged actively when not absorbed in his specific task interests. The distinction between the healthy and pathological variation from the stereotype of normal gregariousness was crucial for counseling and handling of parental concerns.

In other instances, parents came with the opposite concern. Their child was so sociable that he gave insufficient attention to his school work—insufficient, that is, to achieve superior grades. Gregariousness was to be prized, but only if combined with a high order of task activity and mastery. Again, clarification of the difference between normal individuality and pathological deviation was required.

Our research unit has done a cross-cultural study of task orientation with two of our contrasting longitudinal samples (Hertzig et al., 1968). One sample from the New York Longitudinal Study (NYLS) comprised 110 children of native-born middle- and upper-middle-class families. The other sample comprised 60 children of Puerto Rico working-class families (PRWC) living in public housing projects in New York City. Each child was administered the Stanford-Binet, Form L, psychometric test between three and three-and-a-half years of age. An observer kept a consecutive, written record of the behaviors of the child during the test, in terms of the responses made to the specific test demands presented to the child in sequence. The behavior protocols were item-scored in terms of whether the child worked or did not work at the test item and what verbal and nonverbal responses were given—all irrespective of whether the response was correct or not. The NYLS children made a significantly greater proportion of work responses than the PRWC children, as expressed both in the initial responses to the test items and in the ease with which an initial failure to work was converted to a work response on re-presentation of the demand.

These findings were not altered by correction for IQ and birth order. There were also no significant differences in family stability or commitment to child care in the two groups. For the PRWC children, a Puerto Rican psychologist and observer were utilized. The significant differences between the two groups that emerged were in the areas of child-rearing practices and life-style. In the NYLS families, task orientation and task completion in play and in interactions between parents were emphasized. The atmosphere in the PRWC families appeared to encourage social interactions rather than task completion. This difference was reflected not only in relationship to the children, but more generally in expressed attitudes and behavior related to concepts of time and scheduling. As emphasized in the report, the task response patterns of the PRWC children "may easily be interpreted in terms of motivational lacks. These children may be considered by their teachers to be disinterested, unwilling to learn, and inattentive" (p. 46), with teacher responses which can easily lead to self-fulfilling prophecies.

Thus, the importance of these central goals of behavior—task mastery and social competence—for both theory and practice can hardly be overestimated.

Chapter VI

The Structure
of Behavior:
Abilities, Motivations
and Styles

The conceptualization of the goals of behavior represent the
first step in the formulation of the dynamics of psychological development. The next consideration is what might be called the
structural framework of behavior. Freud dealt with this latter
issue with his topographical model of the id, ego, and superego,
in which the id is categorized as the most primitive unconscious
level of the psychic apparatus, the ego as the mediator between

the individual instinctual drives and reality, and the superego as the representative of society and ideal aspirations within the psyche. This model assumes a commitment to the concept of instinct drive reduction as a basic goal of behavior.

Rejection of instinct theory involves the rejection of this topographical model as well. Our own formal structural analysis, which we have found useful in our longitudinal studies, follows the approach of Cattell (1950) and Guilford (1959) in categorizing behavioral attributes in terms of motivations, abilities, and style or temperament. Cattell has identified these "three modalities of behavior traits" as: 1) "dynamic traits or interests . . . [including] basic drives plus acquired interests such as attitudes, sentiments," etc.; 2) "abilities, shown by how well the person makes his way to the accepted goals"; and 3) "temperament, definable by exclusion as those traits which are unaffected by incentive or complexity . . . like highstrungness, energy and emotional reactivity" (1950, p. 35). We would differ from Cattell's formulations by not making a categorical separation between "basic drives" and "acquired interests," and by defining temperamental traits in direct terms and not "by exclusion."

Furthermore, abilities, motivations, and temperament do not operate independently of each other. Quite the contrary. Any item or sequence of behavior will reflect the interactive process of all three, as well as an interaction with other organismic and significant environmental influences. Strong interest in sports and a high activity level temperamentally will promote greater athletic ability. Superior intellectual level and high persistence and attention span temperamentally will increase motivation for academic achievement. Minimal interest in a specific job achievement and relatively low level of motor dexterity required for the job will increase negative mood and slow adaptability temperamentally in that setting.

Though these three structural categories of behavior are functionally intertwined with each other at all times, for purposes of the analysis of psychological phenomena it is convenient to consider them separately.

MOTIVATIONS

There are many definitions of motivations, some of them very broad. Thus, Schneirla, in his consideration of animal behavior in general, states that "Motivation, broadly considered, concerns the causation and impulsion of behavior" (1972, p. 297), and Allport, in his discussion of human psychology, considers that "The problem of motivation is central to the psychological study of personality. . . . By motive we mean any internal condition in the person that induces action and thought" (1961, p. 196).

These definitions formulate motivation as a causative force which underlies and shapes behavior. However, the inclusion of all behavior under this rubric serves to negate the usefulness of the concept of motivation. A formulation which explains everything in effect explains nothing.

We would prefer the definition of motivation as the intraorganismic factor that underlies goal-directed behavior. As David Levy puts it, "What are the motives? The question is directed to the needs of the individual, to his strivings, his goals. The point of view is that of the individual as goal-seeker" (1957, p. 1).

The term purpose is often used synonymously for motivation in humans. It might be more useful to designate those motivations which have a significant conceptualized aspect as purposive. Thus, we speak of someone's "clear purpose," when the goal and the behavior linked with the goal are carefully thought out and planned. By contrast, someone whose purpose "is not clear" has not conceptualized adequately his goals and tactics for achieving them.

As stated in the previous chapter, a fundamental characteristic of all living organisms is that their functioning serves some goal. But not all behavior is goal-directed. Thus, for example, temperamental characteristics, such as high intensity, low persistence, or irregularity in sleep and hunger rhythms, may influence goal-directed activities, but are not in themselves goal-directed. For this reason, we have called temperament "nonmotivational" (Chess and Thomas, 1959). To take another example, a child may react with tantrums as the expression of frustration when prevented from carrying through a pleasurable activity. The tantrum serves no goal; it achieves no end as such. If, however, the parents respond to the tantrum by removing the obstacle to the child's pleasure, then the tantrum may indeed become a conditioned tactic for goal-achievement.

Motives can be as varied as are the goals of different species, from the satisfaction of the need for food of all animals, to the consummation of the sexual drive in sexually differentiated species, to the drive for creative expression, problem-solving or the achievement of material success in human beings. The behavioral mechanisms can vary as widely, from the simple approach or withdrawal pseudopod extensions and contractions of the amoeba, to the intricate "dance" of the bee that communicates the location of food to the other bees, to the suckling behavior of mammals with their young, and to the creative activity of the artist or scientist.

The study of the significance of motivations for psychological development is often confounded by the common tendency to search for meaning and purpose in all behavior. This search is congenial to the human propensity to explain obscure, unclear, and disturbing phenomena in terms of underlying purpose. Primitive man thought that earthquakes, floods, disease, and other tragedies expressed the purposes of the gods. For the young child "the idea of the fortuitous does not exist, causality presupposes a maker, God, the parents, etc., and the questions refer to the intention which he may have had. . . . Organic life is, for the child, a sort of story, well regulated according to the wishes and intentions of its inventor. . . . Causal explanation and logical justification in particular are still entirely identified with motivation" (Piaget, 1932, pp. 178-181).

Chodoff, Friedman, and Hamburg have poignantly described the human search for meaning and purpose in the tragedies of life. Reporting on the psychologic responses of parents of children with malignant disease, they observe:

That their child had been stricken at random by a chance, impersonal blow was very difficult to accept, just as it is generally difficult for human beings to feel that they are living in a meaningless world devoid of norms or of a framework of rewards and punishment for behavior. To combat such an intolerable possibility, the parents sought for an acceptable answer to the question "Why did it happen?", exhibiting as they did so one particular aspect of a universal even existential hunger for a meaningful and understandable explanation of seemingly indifferent events (1964, p. 747).

The emphasis on meaning and purpose in the study of human behavior has been a central concern of the psychoanalytic movement, which can be categorized, broadly speaking, as a psychology of motivations. One of Freud's most important contributions to developmental theory was the systematic study of the motivational aspects of human behavior. However, the study of motivations, or psychodynamics, became more than just the concern of one, albeit very important, aspect of human behavior, but an influential and even dominant ideology in psychiatry and clinical psychology. Many psychiatrists and psychologists habitually assume that there must be an underlying motive to explain every specific item of irrational behavior. They take it for granted that the behavior could not occur unless the individual possessed a purpose and aim, usually unconscious. This assumption has been reinforced by the very nature of psychodynamic formulations, which makes it possible to use almost any item of behavior as presumptive evidence for a motivational explanation. If the behavior corresponds to the hypothetical motive, it represents a "return of the repressed"; if it is contradictory, this is because of "reaction formation." If no behavior which can be related to the motivation is present, it can be evidence that "repression" is still effective; if the behavior is related but does not correspond exactly, this can represent "displacement" or "sublimation" (Thomas, 1970).

Levy, one of the first influential psychoanalysts to challenge the psychodynamic bias, put the issue clearly. "When the need to explain is strong and knowledge is scanty, any explanation may seem better than none. . . . The temptation to favor the motivational answer is a 'natural' one because from infancy onward we live in a world of people and of attitudes. The questions why did so and so do this or that, what did he mean by that, represent necessary adaptational processes in human transactions" (1957, p. 7). He warns of the special pitfalls that result from the motivational bias when the behavior actually reflects "capacity . . . the individual's ability, fitness, endowment, in a general sense the nonmotivational aspects of his behavior" (p. 2), and gives a number of telling examples to document his warning.

With this warning in mind, we can return to our definition of motivation as the intraorganismic factor that underlies goal-directed behavior. We have formulated the goals of behavior for the human being as task mastery and social competence (Chapter V). These goals and motivations can be viewed as reciprocally influential and dynamically intermeshed factors. Motivations such as the satisfaction of hunger, thirst or sexual needs, or the defense against danger, focus and structure the development of task mastery and social competence. These latter goals, in turn, stimulate the emergence and development of a host of motivations.

Thus, as a specific example, the infant is born with genetically determined behavioral mechanisms for the satisfaction of hunger —the hunger cry, the rooting reflex, the sucking reflex, and the swallowing reflex. These behaviors are motivated to obtain and ingest nourishment, and are themselves the beginning of specific task mastery activities. Immediately after birth these behaviors begin to be modified by social experience and maturation. The training and quality of the hunger drive and the patterns of head-turning, sucking and swallowing are progressively altered and changed so that feedings become scheduled at less frequent intervals and include an increasingly wider range of foods. The infant learns to use a cup, to hold the cup and then to feed herself. The hunger motivation has remained the same but an increasingly complex level of task mastery has evolved to satisfy this motivation. Simultaneously, the feeding experience also becomes an active social interaction with the caretaker, then with other members of the family as the child becomes part of the family mealtime gathering, and then with peers and others with whom she shares meals.

The motivation to satisfy hunger thus stimulates enormously the growth of task mastery and social competence. At the same time, the converse also occurs. Task and social activities can become progressively more important as development progresses and can modify feeding behavior. The completion of certain tasks or the pursuit of certain social activities may take precedence over the satisfaction of hunger or modify the kind of food chosen or the surroundings in which it is ingested. Mealtimes may at times become linked with a variety of task and social goals which have little direct relationship to the satisfaction of hunger.

This intermeshing is especially striking with the satisfaction of the sex drive. Sexual pleasure from masturbation for the child is a simple task with little or no social activity in most instances. Sexual activity for the adolescent, however, can become a complex social and task activity leading towards its successful consummation with a partner of the opposite or same sex. For the adult, the activity may become simplified or even more complex. It may also become intertwined with a variety of other motivations—domination, submission, material success, self-assurance, etc.—all of which may modify the character of the sexual task and social activity.

Thus, as development proceeds, motivations become more complex and interrelated. They become conceptualized and even symbolic and abstract, such as "freedom," "my country," "human rights," etc. They take on emotional significance, sometimes lukewarm, sometimes passionate. Hierarchies of importance of different motives are established, but these are hierarchies which may shift with time and circumstance.

The social environment often sets up contradictory goals and expectations—to be cooperative in some settings and competitive in others; to be assertive and yet turn the other cheek; to be self-reliant and yet not afraid to ask for help; to save for the future and yet spend freely in the present, etc. Human motives, as they develop out of life experience, will necessarily reflect these complex and contradictory expectations. A mother may be unresponsive to certain of her youngster's needs and yet deeply nurturant of others. A worker may be highly competitive with certain tasks and yet strongly supportive of his co-workers in others. A husband may be deeply affectionate toward his wife in some situations and grossly inconsiderate and hurtful in others. Such global labels as a "rejecting mother," a "competitive worker," or a "hostile husband," are all too frequently superficial judgments which ignore the complexities and subtleties of human motivation.

Motives are subjective, intrapsychic attributes. They can sometimes be assessed easily by the individual or an observer. But they are often difficult to rate accurately and reliably. Even in intensive psychotherapy with an articulate nonpsychotic individual determined to expose the causes of his disturbed behavior, it may be weeks or even months before the experienced therapist can identify certain significant motivational patterns with assurance. Projective tests, such as the Rorschach or Thematic Apperception Test, are usually of limited help. Simple questionnaires, such as those developed to rate parental attitudes and motives, are less useful and sometimes even misleading (Becker, 1965).

A frequent source of the misjudgment of motives, whether for the individual himself or for the professional observer, is to assume that the consequences of behavior must have been intended as such. If a person behaves in such a way that he consistently fails, it is tempting to judge that he "wants" to fail. If he behaves in such a way that he consistently makes others suffer, it is easy to jump to the conclusion that he wants to inflict suffering on others. These interpretations may sometimes be correct. It may also be true, however, that the individual who consistently fails may want desperately to succeed, but may be dominated by compulsive perfectionist demands on himself which lead to failure instead of success. And the man who makes others suffer may have good intentions, which are nullified by the consequences of his misjudgments of the intentions of others (Thomas, 1970).

All human behavior cannot be attributed to conceptualized

motives. At the same time, any analysis which ignores motivation will be incomplete at best and unable to provide an adequate framework for developmental theory.

ABILITIES

By contrast to motivational patterns, the rating of abilities has a reassuring objectivity and reliability. Quantitative tests have been devised and refined to measure developmental levels in infancy, perceptual skills, intersensory integration, language acquisition, intellectual functioning, cognitive capacity, academic achievement, and vocational aptitudes.

The enormous research literature concerned with objective studies of abilities has contributed greatly to our understanding of many phases of the course of development at successive age periods. A number of the pertinent findings have been cited in the preceding two chapters. Other studies relevant to the exposition of our theoretical position will be summarized in succeeding chapters. At this point a caution will be indicated with regard to the utilization of quantitative measures of abilities.

These quantitative measures with their impressive reliability levels stand in sharp contrast to the inexact qualitative ratings so necessary in the analysis of other psychological attributes. As a result, there is a tendency to isolate the refined quantitative number from other aspects of behavior which cannot be quantified in the same fashion. The number becomes reified, a thing in itself. This trend is most evident with the IQ score, with most serious consequences for innumerable disadvantaged children. Thus, Jane Mercer concludes from her careful eight-year study of school and agency classification procedures for children that "classification systems based on standardized tests have labeled a disproportionately large number of people from minority groups as intellectually subnormal . . . the IQ tests now being used by psychologists are Anglocentric.. They tend to measure the extent to which an individual's background is similar to that of the modal culture configuration of American society. Because a significant amount of the variance in IQ test scores is related to sociocultural characteristics, we concluded that sociocultural factors must be considered in interpreting the meaning of any individual score" (1974, p. 125). Unfortunately, this caveat with regard to the interpretation of IQ scores has been ignored in the recent assertions of a few psychologists that the difference in IQ scores between blacks and whites must have a genetic basis. Though these psychologists are few in number, and their data and analysis have been discredited by leading sociologists, psychologists and geneticists (Thomas and Sillen, 1972), these claims of racial inferiority have received wide public dissemination. (What are we to make of the fraud perpetrated by the eminent British psychologist Cyril Burt, with his fabricated quantitative data "proving" this similar racist thesis! [Dorfman, 1978; Hearnshaw, 1979]).

Even where sociocultural factors have not been involved, the magic authority of a precise number obtained by a poorly administered and evaluated IQ test has condemned many a child to an inferior educational track. Similarly, vocational aptitude testing is another area in which a quantitative score all too often becomes the exclusive basis for counseling and vital decision-making. The test score itself can easily be dangerously misleading unless judged in the context of the individual's motivations, educational background, work record, and social characteristics.

Reliable and valid quantitative data are of special value in the study of developmental processes. But the potential analytic power offered by such data is lost if they are reified, evaluated in a static nondevelopmental fashion, and considered in isolation from other significant variables.

The contrast between the conventional, static, and narrow view of the measurement of abilities and a dynamic approach is demonstrated most vividly in a discussion by the Russian psychologist L. S. Vygotsky (1978). The work and ideas of this most creative developmental psychologist, who died so prematurely at the age of 37 in 1934 (a recent reviewer aptly called him "The Mozart of Psychology"), are only now beginning to receive serious attention in this country. Vygotsky distinguishes between a child's actual and potential developmental level. The first is measured with standard testing techniques in which the child is given credit only for those correct answers he gives independently. "On the other hand," Vygotsky points out, "if we offer leading questions or show how the problem is to be solved and the child then solves it, or if the teacher initiates the solution and the child completes it or solves it in collaboration with other children—in short, if the child barely misses an independent solution of the problem— the solution is not regarded as indicative of his mental development . . . even the profoundest thinkers never questioned the assumption; they never entertained the notion that what children can do with the assistance of others might be in some sense even more indicative of their mental development than what they can do alone" (p. 86). This judgment of psychometric test criteria is as valid today as when Vygotsky wrote this, almost 50 years ago. But Vygotsky goes on to say that two children may show the same actual developmental level on testing, using the above approach, but may show different levels of "potential development as determined through problem-solving under adult guidance or in collaboration with more capable peers" (p. 87). The difference between the actual and proximal level Vygotsky calls "the zone of proximal development" which "permits us to delineate the child's immediate future and his dynamic developmental state, allowing not only for what already has been achieved developmentally but also for what is in the course of maturing" (p. 87). Vygotsky then goes on to indicate the use of this concept of proximal development in the education of both normal and deviant children, in the analysis of the relationship between learning and development, and in the understanding of the process of language acquisition.

In our own clinical and research activities, we have explored impressionistically the usefulness of the determination of potential as well as actual developmental level. For the evaluation of children with learning and/or perceptual problems, we use the Beery and Buktenica Developmental Test of Visual-Motor Integration. After the standard score is obtained by measuring the child's unaided achievement, we give hints and encouragement for those items at which the child appeared almost capable of success. Achievement on these items with such help, as well as the standard score, is reported to the remedial reading teacher to utilize in the formulation of the instructional plan. In the psychometric testing of the deaf children in our congenital rubella longitudinal study, we also give encouragement for the repetition of partially successful items and allow the child to try to complete items even if the time limit has run out. Achievements with this approach are recorded as part of the child's developmental evaluation, though not used in calculating the IQ score.

In our Puerto Rican working-class sample, we also found that the WISC IQ scores were markedly affected by differences in examiner style between two examiners who were equivalent in sex, ethnicity, fluency in Spanish and English, and clinical experience (Thomas et al., 1971). Higher performance level occurred with examiner behavior that encouraged active participation, verbalization, and repeated effort on the child's part. A similar examiner effect was not evident in the NYLS middle-class sample.

It does appear that Vygotsky's concept of "the zone of proximal development" has significant theoretical and practical implications. What is required is the development of systematic protocols for the use of specific cues and assistance under standard conditions, and the formulation of criteria for differentiating responses related to motivation and test attention versus responses related to learning level and task mastery. What is clear is that a test that only measures actual developmental level, no matter how sophisticated, reliable, and refined, is by itself only one step in assessment of capacity and potential.

TEMPERAMENTAL AND BEHAVIORAL STYLE

The study of the significance of motivations and abilities for the course of psychological development has been a major focus of research and clinical interest for almost a hundred years. By contrast, little detailed attention has been given to the stylistic attribute of behavior, temperament, until the past few decades. The

New York Longitudinal Study, which we launched in 1956, represented the first systematic long-term study of this important behavioral variable. A number of reports had previously described individual differences in infants and young children in specific, discrete areas of functioning (see Thomas, Chess, and Birch, 1968, pp. 5-6, for a summary of these reports), but no long-term investigations were conducted on the relationship between these findings in early life and the later course of psychological development.

Our own interest in the study of temperament arose from our dissatisfaction with the one-sided environmentalist view of psychological development, which was firmly in the ascendency by the early 1950s. As parents, we were struck by the clearly evident individual differencies in our children, even in the first few weeks of life. As clinicians, we were repeatedly impressed by our inability to make a direct one-to-one correlation between environmental influences, such as parental practices, and a child's psychological development. There was no question, of course, that these environmental influences played an important role in the child's life, and we, like other clinicians, devoted much effort to trying to persuade parents and others to provide a healthier environment for children. However, we saw many, many instances in which psychopathology in a child occurred even with good parents, or in which a child's development pursued a consistently healthy direction, even into adult life, in the face of severe parental disturbance, family disorganization, and social stress.

The longer we worked with disturbed children and adults, the more we became convinced that many behavioral phenomena which were conventionally attributed to purposive-motivational factors might be better understood if they were viewed as non-motivational behavioral styles. An adult who is shy in new social situations might be anxious and insecure. On the other hand, he might be self-confident but have the temperamental characteristic of adapting slowly to new situations. A child who dawdles in the morning and is chronically late to school might be avoiding school because of a learning problem. He might, on the other hand, be a child with high distractibility and low persistence who is easily diverted from a task or routine by extraneous stimuli. Such differential clinical judgments could have important consequences for psychiatric diagnosis and treatment.

With these considerations in mind, we began to explore various research approaches to a systematic study of individual differences, or temperament, in early infancy and their significance for the developmental process. The NYLS was mounted in 1956 to pursue these objectives. Other longitudinal studies were initiated at subsequent periods to explore the significance of certain other issues, in interaction with temperament, for normal and deviant behavioral development—ethnic and class differences, mild mental retardation, perinatal brain damage, and physical handicap.

Temperament is a general term referring to the *how* of behavior. Two children may dress themselves with equal skillfulness or ride a bicycle with the same dexterity and have the same motives for engaging in these activities. Two adolescents may display similar learning ability and intellectual interests and their academic goals may coincide. Two adults may show the same technical expertness in their work and have the same reason for devoting themselves to their jobs. Yet these two children, adolescents, or adults may differ significantly with regard to the quickness with which they move, the ease with which they approach a new situation, the intensity and character of their mood expression, and the effort required by others to distract them when they are absorbed in an activity.

In its definition, temperament is a categorical term and has no implications as to etiology or immutability. On the contrary, like any other characteristic of the organism—whether it be height, weight, intellectual competence, or perceptual skills—temperament is influenced by environmental factors in its expression and even in its nature as development proceeds.

Our definitions and criteria for categories and constellations of temperamental characteristics, methods of data collection, scoring techniques, methods of quantitative and qualitative analyses, and the functional significance of temperament for normal and deviant behavioral development have been reported over the years in a large number of publications (Thomas, et al., 1963; Thomas, Chess, and Birch, 1968; Thomas and Chess, 1977). The latest volume also reviews some of the rapidly increasing number of studies of temperament by other investigators in recent years.

To summarize briefly, we have been able to identify and score reliably nine categories of temperament as early as two months of age in all the subjects of our several longitudinal studies. These categories have also been rated in other studies of populations of children from diverse national, cultural, and class backgrounds. We are now finding that the subjects of the NYLS can continue to be rated on the same nine categories in early adult life.

The nine categories are: *activity level, rhythmicity* (regularity) of biological functions, *approach or withdrawal* to the new, *adaptability* to new or altered situations, *sensory threshold* of responsiveness to stimuli, *intensity of reaction, quality of mood, distractibility,* and *attention span and persistence.* Each category is scored on a three-point scale: high or positive, low or negative, and an intermediate rating of medium or variable.

Three temperamental constellations of functional significance have been defined by qualitative analysis of the data and factor analysis. The first is characterized by regularity, positive approach responses to new stimuli, high adaptability to change, and mild or moderately intense mood which is preponderantly positive. We have called this the Easy Child pattern, and this group comprises about 40 percent of the NYLS sample.

At the opposite end of the temperamental spectrum is the constellation of irregularity in biological functions, negative withdrawal responses to new stimuli, nonadaptability or slow adaptability to change, and intense mood expressions which are frequently negative. This combination we have called the Difficult Child pattern, and this group comprises about 10 percent of the NYLS sample.

The third noteworthy temperamental constellation is marked by a combination of negative responses of mild intensity to new stimuli with slow adaptability after repeated contact. A youngster with this pattern is referred to as the Slow-To-Warm-Up Child, and about 15 percent of the NYLS falls into this category.

As can be seen from the above percentages, not all children fit into one of these three temperamental groups. This results from the varying and different combinations of temperamental traits which are manifested by individual children. Also, among those children who do fit one of these three patterns, there is a wide range in degree of manifestation. Some are extremely easy children in practically all situations; others are relatively easy and not always so. A few children are extremely difficult with new situations and demands; others show only some of these characteristics and relatively mildly. For some children it is highly predictable that they will warm up slowly in any new situation; others warm up slowly with certain types of new stimuli or demands, but warm up quickly in others.

It should be emphasized that the various temperamental constellations all represent variations within normal limits. Any child may be easy, difficult or slow-to-warm-up temperamentally, have a high or low activity level, distractibility and low persistence, or the opposite, or any other relatively extreme rating score in a sample of children for a specific temperamental attribute. However, such an amodal rating is not a criterion of psychopathology, but rather an indication of the wide range of behavioral style exhibited by normal children.

Graham and his associates (Graham et al., 1973), in a British study of children three to eight years of age, confirmed a number of our findings on temperament and added an additional characteristic, which they labeled "fastidiousness." Buss and Plomin (1975) have recently reported a classification of temperament, utilizing four categories: activity, emotionality, sociability, and compulsivity. The first three categories, as defined by the authors, appear to be contained within our categories of activity level, intensity and quality of mood, and approach-withdrawal and adaptability. The category of impulsivity appears unrelated to any of our nine categories. The authors have not provided data as to the validation of their rating scale or its functional significance, except for significantly higher intra-pair correlation for identical than for nonidentical same-sexed twins. Plomin and Rowe (1977) have very recently reported the development of a new temperament scale derived from a merger of the dimensions suggested by Buss and Plomin and our longitudinal study. Six traits were defined: sociability, emotionality, activity, attention span/persistence, soothability, and reaction to food. A twin study suggested a genetic factor for all the categories except reaction to food.

Kagan (in press) has very recently defined another temperamental dimension in infants, namely, "vigilance." This category is identified as "the disposition to become vigilant and subsequently to display inhibition and even distress in situations of uncertainty." These are the behaviors that parents might call timidity, in contrast to fearless exuberance. Kagan's data indicate a significant relationship between individual differences in heart rate and heart rate variability and variation in the rating of vigilance.

It can be expected that future investigators will identify additional categories which reflect the *how*, rather than the *what* or *why*, of behavior. To avoid confusion of terms, we suggest that *temperament* be used to designate those stylistic characteristics which are evident in the early infancy period, while the broader term *behavioral style* be used for those characteristics which appear in later childhood or adult life.

A number of studies by our own research unit and by other investigators utilizing our formulations of temperament have indicated the significant role of temperament in normal and deviant psychological development (Thomas, Chess, and Birch, 1968; Thomas and Chess, 1977). The major findings to date will be summarized briefly. Children with the Difficult Child pattern are most vulnerable to the development of behavior problems in early and middle childhood. Their intense negative withdrawal reactions to the new and slow adaptability, together with the biological irregularity, make the demands of early socialization especially stressful for these children. Seventy percent of this group in the NYLS developed clinically evident behavior disorders (a mild reactive behavior disorder in most cases) before 10 years of age. With parent counseling and other therapeutic measures where indicated, the great majority recovered or improved markedly by adolescence.

In children with physical handicaps or mild mental retardation, the Difficult Child group is at even greater risk for behavior problem development than are nonhandicapped children (Thomas and Chess, 1977, pp. 49-62). Children with this temperamental pattern are also vulnerable to psychiatric disorder if they have a mentally ill parent (Graham et al., 1973). Infants with colic are also more likely to show the Difficult Child pattern (Carey, 1972).

However, behavior disorders can develop with any temperamental pattern if demands for change and adaptation are dissonant with the particular child's capacities and therefore excessively stressful. Thus, the distractible child is put under excessive stress if expected to concentrate without interruption for long periods of time, the persistent child if this absorption in an activity is prematurely and abruptly terminated, and the high activity child if restricted in his possibilities for constructive activity (Thomas, Chess, and Birch, 1968). Teachers can underestimate the intelligence of the Slow-To-Warm-Up Child or the low activity child, with unfavorable consequences for the learning situation (Chess, Thomas, and Cameron, 1976).

It should be emphasized that these findings do not imply that temperament is *always* a significant factor in the development of *every* behavior disorder. This is also true of motivations, abilities, or specific environmental influences. In any specific instance, the pattern of interaction of factors responsible for disturbed function cannot be assumed a priori, inasmuch as it may vary qualitatively from case to case.

As stated above, temperament is a categorical term, without any implications as to etiology. A number of studies, however, have already provided some data bearing on the issue of the origins of temperamental individuality. These are reviewed in our recent volume (Thomas and Chess, 1977, pp. 132-152) and summarized thus:

The available data suggest an appreciable, but by no means exclusive, genetic role. . . . Prenatal or perinatal brain damage does not appear to influence temperament in any striking fashion. The data also indicate that parental attitudes and functioning, as shaped by the sex of the child or special concerns for a premature infant, at the very most have a modest etiological influence. . . . Special idiosyncratic prenatal characteristics such as chronic anxiety preceding or at least starting in pregnancy may also be significant. . . . It may be that prenatal variations in hormonal activity or other chemical or physiological influences on the developing brain may play a highly significant role in etiology of temperamental individuality. This hypothesis still remains to be tested. . . . A definitive study of the role of the parent also remains to be done (pp. 152-153).

Thus, individual differences in temperament, as they are manifested in early infancy, may be the result of the interplay of genetic, prenatal, and early postnatal factors. In this regard, we question the position of Buss and Plomin that the crucial criterion for temperament is inheritance, that "this is what distinguishes temperament from other personality attributes" (1975, p. 9). Temperament, like nutrition, intelligence, perceptual organization, and other structural attributes of behavior, is best defined operationally and not tied to a theory of origin for which there is only suggestive and presumptive evidence.

Buss and Plomin also give a one-sided emphasis to the role of temperament in personality development. They do recognize that the course of temperamental dispositions "is determined by a complex interaction with the environment" (p. 5), but assert that complex personality patterns, such as psychopathy and hyperkinesis, can be explained on the basis of combinations of several temperamental traits (p. 12). Our own position has always been in opposition to such a viewpoint.

As in the case when any significant influencing variable is identified, there is an understandable temptation to make temperament the heart and body of a general theory. To do so would be to repeat a frequent approach in psychiatry which, over the years, has been beset by general theories of behavior based upon fragments rather than the totality of influencing mechanisms. A one-sided emphasis on temperament would merely repeat and perpetuate such a tendency and would be antithetical to our viewpoint, which insists that we recognize temperament as only one attribute of the organism . . . the relevance of the concept of temperament to general psychiatric theory lies neither in its sole pertinence for behavior disorders, nor in its displacement of other conceptualizations, but in the fact that it must be incorporated into any general theory of normal and aberrant behavioral development if the theory is to be complete (Thomas, Chess, and Birch, 1968, pp. 182-183).

COGNITIVE STYLE

Cognitive style, like temperament, refers to the *how* rather than the *what* of intellectual phenomena.

Ability dimensions essentially refer to the content of cognition or the question of *what*—what kind of information is being processed by what operation in what form? . . . Cognitive styles, in contrast, bear on the question of *how*—on the manner in which the behavior occurs. The concept of ability implies the measurement of capacities in terms of maximal performance, with the emphasis upon level of accomplishment; the concept of style implies the measurement of characteristic modes of operation in terms of typical performance, with the emphasis upon process (Messick 1976, pp. 7-8).

Messick emphasizes that cognitive style (again, like temperament) does not appear to be easily modified by training and that it operates "across a wide variety of situations."

A number of different cognitive style categories have been identified and defined (Kagan, 1971; Messick, 1976). The two categories which have perhaps been most intensively studied are *field independence versus field dependence* (Witkin et al., 1962) and *reflection versus impulsivity* (Kagan et al., 1964) . The first category differentiates persons who experience parts of a field as discrete from the surrounding field, i.e., perceive analytically (field independent) from those whose perception of a field is global (field dependent). Witkin (1973) feels that field independence promotes analytic problem-solving competence, while field dependence promotes social sensitivity and social skills. Reflection versus impulsivity differentiates persons who ponder various possibilities and hypotheses in problem-solving (reflective) from those who tend to accept and report the first hypothesis they formulate (impulse). This category appears to be moderately consistent across problems and relatively stable over time, though it can be modified through training and can be influenced by a teacher's tendencies (Mussen et al., 1979, pp. 270-273) .

Unlike temperament, developmental studies of cognitive style and its functional significance have been limited. Mussen and his colleagues suggest that reflection-impulsiveness may reflect a fear of making a mistake as well as inborn tendencies. It has also been suggested that "cognitive styles are expressions of broader dimensions of functioning that extend into the personality domain" (Witkin, 1973, p. 25) . Messick also feels that cognitive styles are "intimately interwoven with affective, temperamental, and motivational structures as part of the total personality; they provide one aspect of the matrix, as it were, that determines the nature or form of adaptive traits, defense mechanisms and pathological symptoms" (Messick, 1976, pp. 6-7) . Witkin has furthermore suggested an approach to the functional significance of cognitive style similar to our "goodness of fit" concept of the organism-environment interactional process.

In this regard, a scrutiny of the definitions of different cognitive styles given by Kogan (1971) suggests a number of possible relationships to temperament. Field independence versus dependence might be related to distractibility, reflectiveness versus impulsivity to emotional intensity and activity level, scanning to distractibility and attention span, and tolerance for incongruous or unrealistic experiences to approach-withdrawal and mood quality. So far, research studies of cognitive style and temperament have proceeded independently of each other. Specific studies of the relationship of cognitive style and temperament and of their joint influence on the developmental process would indeed be desirable.

ADAPTIVE SIGNIFICANCE OF DIVERSITY

A plausible hypothesis is that temperamental individuality, and perhaps cognitive style differences as well, reflect inherent patterns of neurochemical, neurophysiological, and electroencephalographic differences in neonates and very young infants (Bridger and Reiser, 1959; Grossman and Greenberg, 1957; Richmond and Lustman, 1955; Walter, 1953). Such a biological basis for diversity in response to environmental stimuli demands raises the question of whether this diversity could have evolutionary adaptive significance. Recently, the biologist Bryan Clarke (1975) has reviewed the evidence which shows that most natural populations of plants and animals are genetically heterogeneous to an extent not previously appreciated. Moreover, he emphasizes, "there is strong evidence that the diversity of forms exists because natural selection favors it, that is, because the variants themselves affect the survival and reproduction of the individuals carrying them" (p. 60). He points out that human beings show wide diversity genetically and biochemically and that polymorphism not only characterizes the human species, but is desirable.

Specifically, as it relates to behavioral style, it is clear that each individual's pattern of temperament will be optimal for one particular constellation of environmental demands and less so for other environmental constellations. Thus, for example, high distractibility and low sensory threshold may be desirable where vigilance and watchfulness are required, while low distractibility and high threshold are preferable where sustained concentrated attention to one activity is needed. Or, quick adaptability may be optimal at times in situations when rapid change is optimal, while low adaptability may be preferable at times when stability and slow change are more productive. In any community as a whole, there will be individuals who can respond effectively, no matter what the specific environmental stimuli and demands may be.

Viewed from this evolutionary perspective, the wide range of diversity in human infants in temperament and in patterns of psychophysiological responses—which may be related—may not be some accidental and meaningless phenomenon. We would expect to find such individuality in all populations, though not necessarily across populations. And, indeed, this is what the research studies of temperament in different classes and cultures are beginning to suggest.

Chapter VII

The Process of
Development:
Interaction and
Goodness of Fit

In previous chapters we have considered the various attributes
of the brain and mind—the genetic endowment which makes the
transmission of culture possible, the capacity for plasticity and
alternative pathways in development, the goals of task mastery
and social competence which are evident from birth onward, and
the categories of motivations, abilities, and temperament. These
various attributes do not function separately and in isolation from
each other. How can we then conceptualize the dynamic process

which serves to integrate, coordinate and unify psychological development and functioning?

In the past, concepts of development were dominated, as were other areas of thought, by Aristotelian categories, in which opposites were mutually exclusive. Behavioral phenomena were ascribed either to heredity or to environmental influences, depending on which theory was dominant at the time. Biology and culture were separate and distinct. Where opposites operated together, as heredity and environment in shaping an individual's phenotypic characteristics, it was presumed that the contribution of each category could be parcelled out—so much for heredity and so much for environment, so much for biology and so much for culture.

As indicated earlier, this model has proven to be an inadequate theoretical framework. "For an adequate perspective in the methodology of research and theory, we cannot accept an a priori definition of behavioral development either as an unfolding of the innate, with gains through learning presumably superimposed in superior phyla, or as a continuum expanding mainly through the pressure of environmental forces, with the genes merely contributing an initial push to the process. Rather, a defensible generalization is that a species' genetic constitution contributes in some manner to the development of *all* behavior in *all* organisms, as does milieu, developmental context, or environment" (Schneirla, 1957, p. 79). Dubos states the same principle: "Whether the organism be microbe, corn plant, fruit fly, or man, all its characteristics are hereditary, and all are also determined by the environment. This apparent paradox applies to human health and disease as well as to all other manifestations of life" (1965, p. 10).

Thus, development becomes a dialectical process, in which opposites interact with each other to produce an organic unity of opposites. The need for such an approach has led Tinbergen, a leading ethologist, to question some of the formulations of Lorenz, the prime authority in ethological theory.

Lorenz tends to classify behavior types into innate and

acquired or learned behavior. Schneirla rejects this dichotomy into two classes of behavior. He stresses that the developmental process of behavior as well as other functions should be considered, and also that this development forms a highly complicated series of interactions between the growing organism and its environment. . . . But I now agree (however belatedly) with Schneirla that we must extend our interest to earlier stages of development and embark on a full program of experimental embryology of behavior. . . . When we follow this procedure the rigid distinction between "innate" or "unmodifiable" and "acquired" or modifiable behavior patterns becomes far less sharp. This is owing to the discovery on the one hand, that "innate" patterns may contain the environment, and, on the other hand, that learning is, from step to step, limited by internally imposed restrictions (1968, p. 1416).

For human psychological development, both Freud and Pavlov formulated the beginnings of an interactionist approach. One of the major achievements of the psychoanalytic movement has been the demonstration of how much that had previously been labeled as hereditary or constitutional was really the result of the interaction between the young child and his effective environment. Pavlov, on his part, showed how biology and life experience are integrated in the formulation of the conditioned reflex. But neither Freud nor Pavlov could develop the logic of a dynamics of interactionism. With the limitations of their biological positions, only the first steps were possible.

In subsequent years, a number of developmental psychologists suggested conceptualizations which gave some emphasis to an interactional model (Stern, 1927; Lewin, 1935; Murphy, 1947; Sears, 1951). The most definitive statement came, perhaps, from Vygotsky in the early 1930s. "We believe that child development is a complex dialectical process characterized by periodicity, unevenness in the development of different functions, metamorphosis or qualitative transformation of one form into another, intertwining of external and internal factors, and adaptive processes which over-come impediments that the child encounters" (1978, p. 73).

However, the dichotomization of biology and culture continued to dominate much of the psychiatric and psychological thinking until very recently. There has been a dramatic change in the last 10 years, however. Leading research workers in developmental psychology and longitudinal behavioral studies (Bell, 1968; Kagan, 1971; Rutter, 1972; Sameroff, 1975; Murphy and Moriarity, 1976; Clarke and Clarke, 1976; McCall, 1977; Vaillant, 1977; Spanier et al., 1978) have helped to bring a dynamic interactionist view-point into the mainstream of psychological and psychiatric theory. Based on their own studies and reviews of the literature, these workers have all emphasized that developmental processes cannot be understood in terms of linear, static models. All affirm the ne-cessity of "a dynamic interactional conception of individual and social changes across the life-span, social contexts, and history" (Spanier et al., 1978, p. 328).

This interactionist view of behavioral development has been re-inforced by data from the fields of neurobiology and neurochem-istry on the reciprocal relationships among brain, behavior, and environment. Mammals raised without exposure to patterned vis-ual stimuli are subsequently deficient in the ability to learn vis-ual discrimination habits (Riesen, 1960). Rats kept in a lively environment show distinct changes in brain anatomy and chem-istry compared with animals kept in isolation (Bennett et al., 1964). Psychosocial processes can influence the susceptibility to some infections, to some neoplastic processes, and to some aspects of humoral and cell-mediated immune processes, and these psy-chosocial effects may be related to hypothalamic activity (Stein et al., 1976). There is impressive evidence that behavioral events can alter neurochemical function and that altered neurochemical function can change behavior (Barchas et al., 1978). These find-ings of necessity come primarily from animal studies, but they do affirm the validity of the interactionist conceptualization of de-velopment.

Eisenberg (1977) has recently reviewed the evidence that the expression of a large number of metabolic disorders reflects an intimate genetic-environmental interactional process.

> Attempts at quantitative partition of phenotypic variance into genetic and environmental components require the assumption of linear models, single causes and additive effects, assumptions which ignore the ubiquity of interactions and correlations between genotype and environment. . . . For a given genotype, a particular environmental variable may have only trivial effects, whereas it may be decisive for the expression of a second. . . . In other instances environmental effects produce a curve shaped like an inverted U with the phenotypic trait maximal at midrange. . . . In still other instances, the genotype that is superior in survival value in one environment will be disadvantageous in a second and relatively neutral in a third (p. 226).

In our own data from the New York Longitudinal Study and our other longitudinal studies, intimate organismic-environmental interactional process has been highly evident, with the same range of variability of relationships as detailed by Eisenberg above for metabolic disorders. From the beginning of our study of the functional significance of temperament, it was clear to us that conceptually an interactionist approach was required. Thus, in our first paper (Thomas and Chess, 1957), we suggested that "total personality characteristics at any age-period develop out of the interaction of the specific reaction pattern with all other determinants of psychological development" (p. 356). (We had initially used the term "primary reaction pattern," but because this formulation had undesirable implications, we began to use the term "temperament.") By 1961 we had spelled out this approach definitively: "Behavioral phenomena are considered to be the expression of a continuous organism-environment interaction from their very first manifestations in the life of the individual. This overall approach may be designated as interactionist" (Thomas, et al., 1961, p. 723).

We have found that, while certain temperamental traits or constellations may put a child at greater risk for behavior disorder development, "a given pattern of temperament did not, as such, result in a behavioral disturbance. Deviant, as well as normal, development was the result of the interaction between the child with given characteristics of temperament and significant features of his intrafamilial and extrafamilial environment" (Thomas, et al., 1968, p. 182). High activity level rarely became a source of disturbance for middle-class children with ample living space, but was excessively stressful to such highly active lower-class children with restricted space for freedom of movement. Middle-class native-born parents, as a group, demanded regularity of bedtime and sleep schedules of their preschool children, which was stressful for those youngsters with irregularity of biological functions. The Puerto Rican working-class parents did not make this demand, and their biologically irregular preschool children did not develop sleep problems (Thomas et al., 1974).

Temperamental patterns which deviated from the middle-class stereotype of the "normal," such as the difficult or slow-to-warm-up constellation, often created anxiety, guilt and impatience in the parents, resulting in excessive and rigid demands on these children (Thomas, et al., 1968). Conversely, changing environmental circumstances in some instances heightened the expression of some aspects of temperament at one period and in other aspects at other times (Thomas and Chess, 1977, pp. 165-167).

The emergence of new abilities in a child can alter the attitudes of parents and teachers and change the developmental course significantly (Thomas and Chess, 1977, pp. 169-170). Motivational patterns and conceptions about oneself and the nature of the environment affect behavior, and the environmental response to the behavior reciprocally influences these motivations and conceptions of oneself and the environment (Bandura, 1978). Attitudes of hospital staff to the mentally ill can influence the behavior of these patients dramatically (Goffman, 1961). New and more complex environmental demands in adolescence can drastically alter the previously established adaptive level of handicapped youngsters (Chess et al., 1980). The prevalence of intellectual retardation, behavioral deviance and psychiatric disorder is significantly correlated with social class and disadvantaged school (Rutter et al., 1976). Stereotyped expectations and the differential responses they elicit are major factors for cognitive and personality differences in male versus female children that lead them to fulfill different roles (Birns, 1976).

THE INTERACTIONIST APPROACH

We could expand on such examples at great length from the recent developmental literature. They all emphasize the need for the interactionist view that behavioral attributes must at all times be considered in their reciprocal relationship with other characteristics of the organism, and in their interaction with environmental opportunities, demands, and expectations. The consequences of this process of interaction may in turn modify or in its turn modify or change recurrent or new environmental in-change selective features of behavior. The new behavior may then fluences. In addition, new environmental features may emerge independently or as the result of the previous or ongoing organism-environment interactive process. The same process may modify or change abilities, motives, behavioral style, or psychodynamic defenses.

Development thus becomes a fluid dynamic process which may reinforce, modify, or change specific psychological patterns at all age periods. Such a concept of development can be called *homeodynamic*, in contrast to those formulations which conceptualize the interplay of organism and environment as achieving one or another form of *homeostatic* equilibrium.

As indicated above, the past 10 years have witnessed an increasing commitment by leading figures in developmental research to an interactionist theoretical position. (Some workers, such as Sameroff, prefer the term *transactional* to *interactional*, but the latter term is more generally used.) Yet, as pointed out by Spanier and his co-workers (1978), the interactionist model presents complex and demanding methodological issues of data collection and analysis as compared to simple conceptual models: "Current statistical techniques, based on linear mathematical models and buttressed by Aristotelian logic, are not fully appropriate to analyze continual reciprocities. Circular statistical models, based on dialectical logic . . . will have to be devised" (pp. 329-330).

The factors responsible for the acceptance of the interactional model, in spite of the formidable methodological problems it presents, come from a number of directions. The philosophical formulations of dialectics by Hegel and Engels in the nineteenth century provided a creative conceptual scheme. The resolution of the age-old debates over heredity versus environment in biology through interactional formulations played a part. The firm commitment to an interactional framework by the important group of comparative psychologists led by Schneirla (Schneirla, 1957; Lehrman, 1953; Birch, 1945; Tobach and Schneirla, 1968; Schneirla and Rosenblatt, 1961) was influential. But most compelling has been the repeated demonstration in one research project after another, and especially in long-term studies, that simpler models are inadequate to conceptualize sequences of human development and the transformations of psychological attributes over time.

Psychoanalysis offers one such simpler theoretical model, with its formulation that psychological attributes of later life arise directly out of early life conflicts, drive stage fixation, drive object specification, and the evolution of related defense mechanisms. Interestingly enough, Freud himself questioned the predictive adequacy of this psychoanalytic scheme in a rarely quoted statement: "So long as we trace the development [of a mental process] backwards, the connection appears continuous, and we feel we have gained an insight which is completely satisfactory and even exhaustive. But if we proceed the reverse way, if we start from the premise inferred from the analysis and try to follow up the final result, then we no longer get the impression of an inevitable sequence of events, which could not have been otherwise determined. We notice at once that there might be another result, and that we might have been just as well able to understand and explain the latter" (1950, p. 226). The stimulus-response model of behavior has certainly been unable to encompass the mutually reciprocal influences of abilities, motivations, temperament, cognitive style, psychodynamic defenses, and the influences of the family and the larger social environment.

Child development research, for its part, has focused on correlation studies, to a large extent in terms of experimental situations with controlled quantitative measurements. This model has now been subjected to a definitive critique in a seminal paper by Robert McCall (1977). He points out that developmental psychologists in the last 15 years have preferred to ask "can" questions, rather than "does" questions, "because the former issues are amenable to manipulative, laboratory research methods" (p. 325). But the demonstration in an experimental study, for example, that children "can" learn certain responses by operant conditioning does not in any way prove that they "do" learn in this fashion in real life. "Adults can learn nonsense syllables, but they rarely do; children can be classically conditioned, but this may not be the process by which they learn most or even many behaviors" (p. 334).

McCall further points out that the establishment of correlations between two phenomena in the naturalistic environment can give valuable data, but that "causality cannot be inferred from correlation" (p. 335). Also, creating experimental deprivations to determine necessary causes of development is ethically impossible. "We must simply accept the fact from logical and practical standpoints that we will probably never prove the sufficient or necessary causes for the naturalistic development of a host of major behaviors, some of which represent the essence of our discipline" (p. 336). McCall recommends following the example of epidemiologists, who "do not have a history of deifying the manipulative experimental method above all others" and who marshall evidence from as many approaches as possible. Each approach may be "inadequate by itself, but each makes a vital contribution to the conclusion." In adopting such a model, developmental psychologists must include approaches "we have maligned or ignored in the past—the description of naturalistic events, the use of longitudinal methods, and the willingness to employ procedures sensitive to diverse types of developmental progressions and multiple causal and moderating factors" (p. 336). Such a commitment, McCall emphasizes, requires the development of a multivariate, longitudinal approach to data collection and analysis, appropriate to a concept of the ontogeny of behavior that "emphasizes a complex and interacting set of environmental and organismic determinants that change over age" (p. 342). This is a clear and precise statement of the logic of interactionism.

The *interactionist* approach must be distinguished from the simpler and essentially static *interactive* model. (The apparent similarity of the two words is one reason some workers prefer the term transactional to interactional.) The interactive model attempts to overcome a unidimensional approach, in which, for example, only heredity-constitution or environment is emphasized, by creating a two-dimensional structure of an additive nature. Good constitution plus good environment leads to a good outcome; poor constitution plus poor environment leads to a poor outcome. Intermediate outcomes are the result of a good-poor combination. As Sameroff (1975) points out, this model "is insufficient to facilitate our understanding of the actual mechanisms leading to later outcomes. The major reason behind the inadequacy of this model is that neither constitution nor environment is necessarily constant over time. At each moment, month, or year the characteristics of both the child and his environment change in important ways. Moreover, these differences are interdependent and change as a function of their mutual influence on one another" (p. 281).

On an entirely different level of conceptualization, von Bertalanffy (1962) has formulated a general systems theory approach to the study and analysis of phenomena from different disciplines and systems. Boulding describes this approach thus: "General systems theory is . . . a level of theoretical model building which lies somewhere between the highly generalized construction of pure mathematics and the specific theories of the specialized disciplines. . . . It aims to point out similarities in the theoretical constructions of different disciplines, where these exist, and to develop theoretical models having application to at least two different fields of study" (1956, p. 11).

Some behavioral scientists have found general systems theory useful in their work (Grinker, 1975). However, by and large, the broad generalizations of this theoretical approach have not as yet been helpful in organizing and analyzing the phenomena of the field of developmental psychology.

GOODNESS OF FIT

In analyzing the nature of the organism-environment interactional process we have found the concept of "goodness of fit" and the related ideas of consonance and dissonance to be very useful. Goodness of fit results when the properties of the environment and its expectations and demands are in accord with the organism's own capacities, motivations, and style of behaving. When this *consonance* between organism and environment is present, optimal development in a progressive direction is possible. Conversely, poorness of fit involves discrepancies and *dissonances* between environmental opportunities and demands and the capacities and characteristics of the organism, so that distorted development and maladaptive functioning occur. Consonance is never an abstraction, but is always goodness of fit in terms of the values and demands of a given culture or socioeconomic group.

It should be emphasized that goodness of fit does not imply an absense of stress and conflict. Quite the contrary. These are inevitable concomitants of the developmental process, in which new expectations and demands for change and progressively higher levels of functioning occur continuously as the child grows older. Demands, stresses, and conflicts, when in keeping with the child's developmental potentials and capacities for mastery, may be constructive in their consequences and should not be considered as an inevitable cause of behavioral disturbance. The issue involved in disturbed behavioral functioning is rather one of *excessive* stress resulting from poorness of fit between environmental expectation and demands and the capacities of the child at a particular level of development.

The concept of goodness of fit has also been applied by Dubos as a measure of physical health. "Health can be regarded as an expression of fitness to the environment, as a state of adaptedness. . . . The words health and disease are meaningful only when defined in terms of a given person functioning in a given physical and social environment" (1965, pp. 350-351).

The goodness of fit concept does not in any fashion imply some modification of the basic interactionist position. Rather, it is a formulation which facilitates the application of the interactionist conceptual model to specific counseling, early intervention and treatment situations. The formulation structures a strategy of intervention that includes an assessment of the individual's motivations, abilities and temperament, his behavioral patterns and their consequences, and the expectations, demands and limitations of the environment. The specific potential or actual dissonance between individual and environment can then be proportioned. Thus, for example, if consultation is requested for a girl who stands passively at the periphery of a group, and if assessment reveals a slow-to-warm-up temperamental pattern, then attention can be focused on whether the parents and teachers are making a demand for quick active group involvement. If a boy disrupts his class with bizarre behavior, the assessment may show a severe reading difficulty, with defensive avoidance behavior. If we know that the handicapped youngster may have special difficulties in mastering new complex demands and expectations in adolescence, this can provide a guide to preventive intervention to ensure continued goodness of fit.

The continued application of the interactionist model to developmental study at all age-periods will certainly result in progressively increasing knowledge of the behavioral outcomes of the interaction of specific characteristics of the individual with specific features of the environment. As this happens, it will make the application of the goodness of fit formulation to preventative intervention, counseling and treatment increasingly useful.

IMPLICATIONS OF THE INTERACTIONIST APPROACH

The fundamental thesis of the interactionist approach is that behavioral phenomena at any age-period are the expression of a continuous organism-environment interactional process. "The problem of development is the problem of the development of new *structures* and activity *patterns* from the resolution of the interaction of existing ones, within the organism and its internal environment, and between the organism and its outer environment. At any stage of development, the new features emerge from the interactions within the *current* stage and between the *current* stage and the environment. The interaction out of which the organism develops is *not* one, as is so often said, between heredity and environment. It is between *organism* and environment! And the organism is different at each different stage of its development" (Lehrman, 1953, p. 345).

This conceptualization raises questions with regard to a number of the important formulations of various developmental theories. How crucial is early life experience to later behavioral outcome? How significant are the phenomena of "imprinting" and "critical periods"? How can we best approach the issue of continuity versus discontinuity in development? How invariant or variable are the sequential stages of development?

Subsequent chapters will take up these questions. At this point, we would like to emphasize that for human development the interaction of the organism, from birth onward, is most significantly with the *social* environment. This basic principle is all too often overlooked. As Michael Lamb puts it, "I cannot help being disappointed by the propensity of the developmental psychologists to ignore the fact that neither individual persons nor individual dyads exist apart from their social context. The index unit (whatever it is) is irretrievably anchored in its social context. The nature and relevance of the interactions within any target system are determined by the societal structure and its demands—in short, the unit can be *understood* only in its social context" (Lamb, 1978, pp. 156-157). And, we might add, this propensity

to ignore social context is just as rife among psychiatrists as among developmental psychologists.

Social context is most obviously overlooked in those theories which conceptualize the developmental process as the unfolding of invariant sequences of maturation. Whether the emphasis is on the maturation of instincts, neuromuscular patterns, cognition, or subjective psychological attributes, the assumption of an invariant and inherent sequence must of necessity ignore or minimize the role of the social environment in the developmental process.

More common is the formulation which narrows the social context to an individual, the family, or some special aspect of society at large. In this regard, a recurrent theme in all too many studies is the dominant or even exclusive focus on the mother-child dyad. Whether the phenomenon at issue is the development of social bonding and attachment behavior in the infant, task mastery and academic achievement in the older child, delinquent behavior, neurosis, or schizophrenia in the adolescent or adult, the responsibility is heaped on the mother's head (Chess, Thomas, and Birch, 1965; Thomas and Chess, 1977). We have labeled this preoccupation with the mother's presumed role as a pathogenic agent for the child as the "mal mère syndrome (Chess, 1964).

Finally, there are those formulations which distort the social context by assuming one psychological norm—that of the white, male, middle-class—with deviations from this norm being ipso facto evidence of pathology. (An exception is made for the upper class, where behavioral differences from the middle-class norm are tolerantly labeled as "eccentricity.") Such distortions feed on the social ideologies of sexism and racism, as we witness in all the professional pronouncements on the inferiorities and pathologies of women, underprivileged minorities, and the poor (Miller, 1976; Chess, Clark, and Thomas, 1953; Thomas, 1962; Thomas and Sillen, 1972). In this context, it should be emphasized that our goodness of fit model does not imply an acceptance of *all* environmental demands that appear consonant with the individual's capacities as desirable. A subculture may expect alcohol or other drug use from its members. This may appear consonant with an individual's capacities, i.e., he suffers no apparent ill effects and even seems to thrive. However, in a larger sense, the drug use will interfere with the optimal use of his mental abilities, and will therefore represent poorness of fit. Or, a white male may accept the dominant racist and sexist attitudes of his group, and take pleasure and comfort in the attitudes of superiority this gives him. But, again, this apparent consonance will make a deeper dissonance, with impairment of his capacity for close human relationships.

If the social context of development is not to be ignored or distorted, behavioral data must at all times be gathered and analized within the specific content of the environmental situation in which it occurs. A priori hierarchical judgments of the relative importance of specific behavioral styles, norms, individuals, family constellations, or sociocultural judgments must be avoided. Specific characterizations of behavior in specific contexts are necessary, rather than global labels and ratings, whether of the child, the parent, the family, or individuals in the larger social environment. What is required for the evaluation and analysis of behavioral constellations at any age period is "the delineation of those *specific* attributes of parental attitudes and practices and of other intra- and extrafamilial environmental factors that are interacting with the *specific* temperamental and other organismic characteristics of the child to produce *specific* consequences for psychological development" (Thomas, Chess and Birch, 1968, p. 184).

Chapter VIII

Early Life Experience and its Developmental Significance

Is early life experience of decisive importance for later psychological development? The answer to this question has profound importance both for developmental theory and for practical issues of prevention and treatment of mental disorders.

If early experience is indeed decisive, then the task of theory-building is enormously simplified. A simpler linear model is sufficient, and different outcomes in later life can be traced back directly to variations in the causative factor or factors in early childhood. Debate can rage, as it does, as to whether the crucial childhood factor is mother love, types of child care practices, family characteristics, patterns of conditioned reflex formation, sociocultural influences, or some combination of these factors. But whatever challenges are raised to the proponents of any one theoretical position, the assumption in this debate is that further research findings or clinical data will validate one or another childhood variable as decisive.

On the practical side, the mental health professional's task is simplified and his judgments take on authority once he operates from the conviction that some aspect of early life experience does determine the course of psychological development. He can give parents, teachers, and social agencies clear categorical guides which will ensure the child's future mental health. Treatment of the disturbed child and adult can be structured from the beginning so as to uncover and change the pathogenic influences carried over from early life.

As Clarke and Clarke (1976) emphasize, "The allegedly crucial importance of the preschool years for future development is reflected throughout the whole history of Western thinking" (p. 4). Their quotes from Plato, Quintilian, Barbaro, Locke, and Mill spell out this thesis in varying forms, and provide a background to the positions taken by psychoanalysis and behaviorism. Freud (1949) put it in his last overview volume that "neuroses are only acquired during early childhood (up to the age of six), even though their symptoms may not make their appearance until much later. . . . The events of the first years are of paramount importance for . . . [a child's] whole subsequent life" (p. 83). Watson (1928) stated a similar view even more dramatically from the behaviorist standpoint. "But once a child's character has been spoiled by bad handling, which can be done in a few days, who can say that the damage is ever repaired? . . . Some day the importance of the first two years of infancy will be fully realized" (p. 3). Psychoanalytic and behaviorist theories, as much as they might disagree otherwise, are thus united in insisting on the decisive role of early life experiences.

This thesis has been buttressed in recent decades by the reports and formulations of a number of influential figures. Perhaps most important was the study done by John Bowlby (1951) for the World Health Organization on the mental health of homeless children. In this report he concluded that "mother love in infancy and childhood is as important for mental health as are vitamins and proteins for physical health." Though he has modified some of his early formulations, in a more recent volume (1969), Bowlby has reaffirmed his conviction that the loss of the mother figure in early life is capable of "generating responses and processes that are of the greatest interest to psychopathology" and that continue into adult life (p. xiii).

Other formulations have come from different conceptual frameworks, but each has subscribed to the thesis that individual psychological characteristics and structures are determined in the first few years of life. The psychosocial life cycle concepts of Erikson (1950) emphasize the decisive attributes that are found in the preschool period. Family pathology and dynamics are considered by others to determine the ontogenesis of schizophrenia in the young child, as well as other pathological developments (Ackerman, 1958; Lidz et al., 1965; Wynne and Singer, 1963). Concepts of minimal brain dysfunction (Wender, 1971) and a continuum of reproductive causality (Pasamanick and Knobloch, 1966) focus on the later and permanent consequences of early brain damage. Early malnutrition is seen as producing irreversible psychological effects (Stoch and Smythe, 1963). Socioeconomic influences on the disadvantaged young child are presumed to cause profound, permanent behavioral and cognitive consequences, usually subsumed under the labels of "cultural deprivation" (Hess, 1970) and the "culture of poverty" (Lewis, 1966). The ethologists have emphasized the decisive permanent effects of early life experience through the concepts of "imprinting" and "critical periods" (Lorenz, 1952; Hinde, 1966). Bloom (1964) and White (1975) have asserted the all-important significance of the first few years of life for later cognitive levels of functioning.

CHALLENGES TO THE THESIS

These formulations of the special, even unique, importance of the first few years of life did not go unchallenged. Bowlby's thesis of the devastating effect of early maternal deprivation met "severe methodological and other criticisms" even though it "gained very wide currency" (Rutter, 1972, p. 13). A number of research reports challenged the view that maternal child care practices and attitudes were responsible for the development of simple behavior disorders, delinquency, and schizophrenia (Thomas and Chess, 1977).

Yet, until recently, the thesis of early fixation of psychological characteristics appeared invulnerable to all challenges. Certainly, similarities between the young child and the adult are often noticeable and even striking. In physiognomy, musculoskeletal structure, aptitudes and interests, IQ level, cognitive style, perceptual skills or difficulties, temperamental characteristics, psychodynamic defense mechanisms—consistency from early childhood may be apparent and measurable. The child often does seem to be "father to the man." Kagan (1978) has suggested a number of other reasons for the easy general acceptance of the doctrine of early infant determinism: "the influence of liberal egalitarian philosophy; the maxim that one must prepare for the future," (p. 135) so that "parents prepared their children for psychological salvation when they were young" (p. 136); the psychobiological concept that psychological experience presumably causes fixed changes in the neurons and their synapses; and the deep-rooted tendency in our descriptive language to use categories such as "passive, irritable, intelligent, or emotional for infants, children, and adults as if the age of the person described were irrelevant to the meaning of the terms" (p. 68).

In addition, the influential psychodynamic developmental concepts make it possible to identify later behavior with earlier behavior even when they appear to be strikingly dissimilar. The passive, clinging three-year-old has not really changed if he becomes an aggressive adult who refuses all help. He is only displaying a reaction formation against the same unconscious dependency needs which determine his behavior now as they did in the past. The youngster who behaves cruelly toward his younger sibs and peers and then becomes a dedicated surgeon is only sublimating his sadistic drives. Within this closed conceptual scheme, continuity over time is guaranteed. Similarity in behavior from childhood to adult is ipso facto evidence. Change in behavior is interpreted as the effect of a psychodynamic mechanism, and not as a qualitative alteration in psychological characteristics. If the IQ level changes, this does not mean that the individual's intellectual capacities have changed. These capacities are the same, fixed from infancy but modified in their expression by anxiety, avoidance reactions, or compulsive needs for "overachievement."

The Present Scene

In the past 10 years, however, there has been a progressive shift in the weight of professional judgments and evaluations of the significance of early life experiences. Rutter (1972) has reassessed the whole issue of maternal deprivation through a masterly comprehensive review of the entire literature, including his own important studies. His volume, which has already become a classic, observes that "Perhaps the most important recent development in 'maternal deprivation' research has been the emphasis on individual differences in children's responses to 'deprivation.' " It concludes with the authoritative judgment that

> The concept of "maternal deprivation" has undoubtedly been useful in focusing attention on the sometimes grave consequences of deficient or disturbed care in early life. However, it is now evident that the experiences included under the term "maternal deprivation" are too heterogeneous and the effects too varied for it to continue to have any usefulness. It has served its purpose and should now be abandoned. That "bad" care of children in early life can have "bad" effects, both short-term and long-term, can be accepted as proven. What is now needed is a more precise delineation of

the different aspects of "badness," together with an analysis
of their separate effects and of the reasons why children differ
in their responses (p. 128).

As Rutter says, bad care of children in early life is highly undesirable. Bowlby's 1951 report did have "many humane effects,
sensitizing the public to the needs of children" (Clarke and
Clarke, 1976, p. 272). A "bad" environment is also highly undesirable for older children, adolescents, or adults of any age. But
bad care in early life does not necessarily cause permanent irre-
trievable damage. The Clarkes have brought together an impressive array of reports documenting this fact with regard to isolated
and neglected children, mentally retarded youngsters, abused infants, children reared in deprived environments, and young children suffering death of a parent. Given a positive change in care
and overall environment, these studies consistently find an amaz-
ing resiliency and dramatic improvement in later functioning.

In a similar vein, Winick and his associates (1975) studied the
development of a group of adopted Korean children who had
suffered early malnutrition. They found that the effects of such
malnutrition, even when severe, could be overcome by the environmental enrichment resulting from adoption. The successful
nutritional rehabilitation was documented by measures of physical growth, school achievement, and IQ. The authors suggest that
previous findings of the permanent effects of early malnutrition
may have resulted from the persistence of an unfavorable environment, or the failure to provide an enriched environment for a
sufficiently long period. Similar conclusions are reported by Richardson (1976) in an extensive study done in Jamaica on the effects
of early malnutrition.

An acute episode of acute malnutrition in the first two
years of life has differing consequences for intellectual impairment depending upon the background history, the characteristics of the child's guardian, the economic conditions
of the household, and the kinds of social experience the child
has had. . . . If severe malnutrition in infancy occurs in the

context of a life history which is generally favorable for intellectual development, the early malnutrition appears to have a negligible effect on intellectual functioning. If early malnutrition occurs in an unfavorable general ecology for intellectual development, the severe episode of malnutrition has a clear relation to later intellectual impairment (p. 269).

Sameroff and Chandler (1975) have reviewed the literature concerned with the relationship between pregnancy and delivery complications and later deviancy, and have concluded that "prospective studies . . . have, however, not succeeded in demonstrating the predictive efficiency of these supposed risk factors. Most infants who suffer perinatal problems have proven to have normal developmental outcomes" (p. 236). They emphasize, as Winick does, the crucial role of the environment in minimizing or maximizing early developmental difficulties.

In the cognitive area, the validity of the widely quoted statement (Bloom 1964) that 50 percent of a child's intelligence is developed by the age of four has been sharply criticized (McCall, 1977; Clarke, 1978) as showing an imperfect understanding of the meaning of correlation coefficients. Furthermore, the statement is clearly incompatible with the weight of evidence from the numerous studies of significant change in intellectual functioning from early childhood to later life (Kagan and Klein, 1973; Clarke and Clarke, 1976; Hindley and Owen, 1978).

A new look has also been taken at some of the concepts derived from animal behavior studies. Reversal of imprinting in newly hatched ducklings has been reported (Hess 1972). Wolff (1970) has reviewed the studies related to the critical period hypothesis and concluded that the "available evidence does not support" this concept. In another review, Connolly (1972) has also advocated that the term "critical period" be abandoned. He emphasizes that "early experience has far-reaching consequences for an organism's development" but that "development is an extremely complex set of processes which are often oversimplified" (p. 711). The stereotyped and bizarre social behavior shown by monkeys reared in isolation for the first six months of life has also been shown to be reversible (Suomi and Harlow, 1972). The isolate monkeys were placed with younger female monkeys over a 26-week period, following which the behavioral levels of the previously isolate-reared monkeys were virtually indistinguishable from those raised normally.

Significant data bearing on the significance of early experience for later development come from the major long-term longitudinal studies. Such studies are specially suited to the analysis of naturalistic developmental processes. "If a primary mission is to discern ontogenetic change within individuals, the sequence and timing of developmental transitions, and the changing social and environmental factors that permit development to occur, then we must use longitudinal, not cross-sectional, approaches to our subject matter" (McCall, 1977, p. 335). With an impressive unanimity, these studies have reported the unpredictability of later functioning from early life experience and behavior.

Thus, in a review of the 30-year Berkeley Study, MacFarlane (1964) notes that "many of our most mature and competent adults had severely troubled and confusing childhoods and adolescences. Many of our highly successful children and adolescents have failed to achieve their predicted potential. . . . We did have several small groups whose adult status fulfilled theoretical expectations" (p. 124) (that is, the investigators had expected to find significant linear continuity from childhood to later life). From the Topeka Study, Murphy and Moriarty (1976) report that "the relations between earlier and later forms of experience and behavior are too complex to warrant our thinking of simple causal relations between what came first and what came later. . . . Our conclusion is that development is not merely due to the effect of either simple heredity or environmental forces; at any time the child's response to and ways of coping with these and their complex interactions involves unpredictable emergents" (p. 150). From a recent analysis of the Fels Longitudinal Study data, Kagan (1976) concludes that "there was little relation between important aspects of the mother's treatment of the child during the first three years of life and a variety of psychological dispositions displayed during adolescence or adulhood" (p. 120). Vaillant (1977) summarizes some of the findings of the Harvard Grant Study thus: "Successful careers and satisfying marriages were relatively independent of unhappy childhoods" (p. 300). "When the childhoods of Best and Worst outcomes in the Grant Study were compared, there were many surprises. When identified in advance, fingernail-biting, early toilet training, the 'tainted family tree,' even that old standby—the cold, rejecting mother—failed to predict emotionally ill adults" (p. 284). "The life cycle is more than an invariant sequence of stages with simple predictable outcomes. The men's lives are full of surprises, and the Grant Study provides no prediction tables" (p. 373).

An interesting long-term single case report is the well-known case of Monica, a girl born with an esophageal stricture which prevented normal feeding. Numerous hospitalizations and operations were necessary throughout infancy, until surgical establishment of the integrity of the gastrointestinal tract at 22 months. Extensive studies of Monica were done by Engel and his associates (1967), with emphasis on the severe prolonged psychological distturbances resulting from the highly traumatic infancy experiences. Yet now, at age 25, Monica is reported as married with three children, an active sex life, an absence of any significant symptoms and an overall favorable functioning, in which she "appears to be a responsible and reliable woman" (Viedemar, 1979, p. 118). When these finding were reported at a psychoanalytic meeting, several analysts commented that "the unexpectedly good outcome did violence to what we might predict from analytic theory" (Viedemar, 1979, p. 122).

In our own longitudinal studies the evidence is clear from a number of directions that simple linear prediction from early childhood to later childhood, adolescence and early adult life is not possible. The evolving child-environment interactional process was affected by many emerging unanticipated influences—changes in basic function, new talents, new environmental opportunities or stresses, changes in family structure or attitudes, and possibly late emerging genetic factors. In some cases the sequence of behavioral development was affected quantitatively; in many other instances the changes were qualitative and even dramatic.

In the NYLS sample, a clinical diagnosis of behavior disorder was made in 43 cases in childhood. Most, though not all, were mild in severity, and over 70 percent had onset of symptoms before five years of age. By adolescence, almost 50 percent had recovered. There was no significant correlation between the severity of the original disease and outcome in adolescence. These recovered cases have appeared to function as well in adolescence as those subjects who did not show behavior disorder in childhood (Thomas and Chess, 1976). In a follow-up into the early adult period (20 to 23 years), the recovery has been maintained in almost every case. In those few cases that have relapsed, new environmental stresses have appeared etiologically significant. Five new clinical cases have been identified in the adolescent period which could not have been predicted from the early childhood data. While our analysis of these data is still in progress, there has been a clear qualitative relationship evident in a number of the cases between change in environment and change in clinical course and between consistency in environment and consistency in behavioral course (Thomas and Chess, 1977).

In our congenital rubella sample, an extraordinarily high incidence of the very serious mental illness, autism, was found in early childhood (Chess, 1971). As many as 10 children showed a complete syndrome of infantile autism, and eight more a partial syndrome, out of a total sample of 243 children. This rate of 741 per 10,000 was 100 times greater than the prevalence rate reported in surveys of the general population. Beyond this, four additional cases of autism were identified in the middle childhood period, and three of the original 10 cases of the complete syndrome diagnosed in early childhood have recovered. No intra- or extrafamilial family influences could be found to account for this marked change in mental status in this latter group from early to later childhood. The most plausible hypothesis is that the slow virus encephalitis, which is known to exist in some cases of congenital rubella, was responsible for this unpredictable psychological change (Chess, 1977).

In both the rubella sample and our mildly retarded longitudinal study, there was clear evidence that the new environmental demands and expectations of early adolescence could influence qualitatively the developmental sequences of handicapped children. A number of the deaf and mentally retarded youngster who had made favorable behavioral adaptations in school and in the community in early and middle childhood could not maintain this level in adolescence. The new behavioral, social, and academic expectations of this period changed a child-environment goodness of fit to a poorness of fit, and substantial behavioral difficulties and maladaptation ensued (Chess et al., 1980).

ATTACHMENT AND WARINESS OF STRANGERS

It is a common observation that most infants begin to show evidence of specific attachment to the mother or other primary caretaking adult during the second six months of life. At about the same time, negative reactions to strangers also appear. In recent years the study of these phenomena has been a major interest of child development research. The positive reaction to the mother and the distress at separation from her usually represents the first expression of a specific structured social response pattern with clear emotional content. The negative response to the stranger indicates an ability to discriminate between and respond differently toward different categories of humans. As such, it suggests the beginning of the development of cognitive competence.

Furthermore, both attachment behavior and the reaction to strangers can be identified through the infant's overt behavior, described objectively, and rated reliably. The stimuli which produce the behaviors can also be manipulated systematically and experimentally—the manner and timing of the mother's leaving and returning, the nature of the infant's activities and surroundings during the mother's absence, the characteristics of the stranger, his manner of approach to the child, etc.

It is no surprise, therefore, that studies of attachment behavior and reactions to strangers have become a major area of interest for a number of research workers in child development. An increasing body of data, theory and controversy has resulted from these studies. Spitz's original concept of "eight-month anxiety" (1965) has been found wanting, as the behaviors may appear as early as the fourth month or as late as the fifteenth month (Rutter, 1975, p. 65). The assumption that the negative reaction represents anxiety is speculative, and the more appropriate term is "wariness" (Sroufe 1977). There is great individual variation in the strength and distribution of attachments, and the bonds may be multiple (Rutter, 1972). Infants may show strong positive reactions to strangers as well as wariness, and both may occur in the same exposure (Sroufe, 1977). Some workers question the actual usefulness of the concept of stranger wariness because of its inconsistency and instability (Rheingold and Eckerman, 1973); others feel strongly that it remains an important construct in spite of its inconsistency with contextual and procedural variability (Sroufe, 1977).

Bretherton (1978), in a recent study indicating the complexity and variability in an infant's responses to strangers, highlights a basic issue: "I have taken the position that a baby's friendly interaction with a specific responsive adult would, in the course of time, lead to the formation of a social bond. Just in what way such a bond could be said to differ from an attachment to the primary caretaker and, indeed, the point in a developing relationship at which one can begin to speak of a bond is a question which we cannot at present answer and which deserves further research" (p. 50). We would add, in an extension of Bretherton's comments, that the infant starts life as a social being and that by the second half of the first year is already capable of organized differentiated social interractions. The complexity and variability of his reactions to familiar and strange adults at this age, as well as to other children, give dramatic testimony to this developing social competence. Attachment behavior and reactions to strangers, as they develop in infancy, should be considered as one stage in the constantly evolving process of social interaction with other humans. The specific characteristics of this stage of emotional and cognitive development in any individual child undoubtedly reflect the interplay of genetic factors, temperamental attributes, and life experience. "All of the discrete behaviors that have been proposed as indices of attachment serve many other behavioral systems as well. . . . While a measure based on discrete behaviors may *look* like a useful measure of looking, or distance interaction or attachment, it is more likely that the major consistent influence across unselected instances of a discrete behavior will be the ubiquitous dimensions of temperament" (Waters, 1978, p. 492) .

Attachment behavior and the pattern of response to strangers might be considered a measure of developing competence, as Sroufe and his co-workers suggest (Matas, Arend and Sroufe, 1978) . Of course, there are a number of other measures of competence in six- to 18-month-old infants—self-feeding, assistance in dressing, manipulation of toys and other play patterns, and motor skills. Whether social competence in attachment behavior is predictive of later competence in problem-solving and task performance, as Sroufe and his group hypothesize, remains to be tested. The data from the major longitudinal studies, as summarized above, suggest that such a linear predictive relationship is unikely.

THEORETICAL CONSIDERATIONS

It should be no surprise that the research data from many sources converge to discredit the concept that the child's early life fixes decisively the course of his subsequent psychological development. Interactionist theory postulates that behavioral characteristics can change at any age-period, and even change qualitatively, if a significant change in organism or environment alters the dynamics of the developmental process. The unique capacity of the human brain for learning and for plasticity in developmental pathways would be wasted if the individual's potential for mastery and adaptation were frozen, or even severely limited, by his early life experiences. Emde (1978) makes this same point

in commenting on the infancy studies using the Brazelton Neonatal Behavioral Assessment Scale, which have reported lack of
predictive power with regard to developmental outcome.

> Is it not likely that what is especially adaptive is a *vari-
> ability and range of behavior?* In other words, would not
> these features provide selective advantage during evolution
> and therefore be preprogrammed in our species? I would
> think that an individual newborn characterized by sufficient
> variability of behavior would be favored, with more op-
> portunities for matching or synchronizing such behavior with
> a caretaking environment—an environment which to a con-
> siderable extent would be unpredictable. Indeed, the vulner-
> able infant may be one who is consistently "modal" or who
> otherwise has a narrow range of behavioral variability over
> time (p. 136).

From an evolutionary natural selection point of view, it also
makes sense that attachment bonds in infancy should be multiple,
and that there be wariness combined with positive approach reactions to strangers. If the young child needed to attach himself
specifically to only one person, as Bowlby (1969) believes, then
loss of that one person by death or otherwise would be disastrous.
Multiple bonding, of which the infant is actually capable, guards
against such a danger. The approach of a stranger can signal a
desirable or an undesirable outcome; the adaptive capabilities of
the infant should be able to encompass both contingencies.

Furthermore, as Lewis and Feiring (1978) point out, "If only
nurturant protective functions are considered, then the mother
as the most important (and only) social object to be studied makes
some sense. However, other functions exist as needs in the infant's
life, including, for example, play and exploration" (p. 53). This
makes the issue of social bond development to sibs and peers and
other adults, and not just to the mother, of high significance.

The belief in the deterministic influence of the early years dies
hard. We meet it constantly in the formulations of clinicians who
remain committed to traditional psychoanalytic or behaviorist

theory. Even among some sophisticated and knowledgeable researchers in child development, the evidence does not change theoretical viewpoints, as typified by Bronson's position (1974): "Along with some others, I see our apparent inability to make empirical predictions about later personality from the early years as so much against good sense, common observation, and the thrust of all developmental theories that I can take it only as an indictment of established paradigms and methods rather than as evidence of a developmental reality" (p. 276). But "good sense" and "common observation" have never been reliable criteria for the validity of a scientific theory. The "good sense" of natural selection actually dictates the desirability of adaptive accommodation to unpredictable environmental changes in the process of psychological development. And "the thrust of all developmental theories" is now more and more influenced by interactionist formulations which challenge the possibility of finding simple linear correlations between the early years and later personality.

Our "inability to make empirical predictions about later personality from the early years" does reflect a "developmental reality." This in no way negates the importance of early life experience for later psychological development. But there is a fundamental distinction between *importance* and *determinance*. An analogy with physical development is pertinent. A young child who experiences good health and is well-nourished has a better start in life than does a sickly, poorly nourished youngster. But we would never assume that the healthy six-year-old is invulnerable to future illness, or that the undernourished, frail youngster is doomed to a life of chronic disease. Physical medicine has long since freed itself from simplistic linear developmental models. Developmental psychology requires the same freedom. Edward Zigler (1975), former director of Head Start, puts it well:

> I, for one, am tired of the past decade's scramble to discover some magic period during which interventions will have particularly great pay-offs. Some experts emphasize the

nine months *in utero;* Pines and White, the period between eight and 18 months; others, the entire preschool period; and yet others emphasize adolescence. My own predeliction is that we cease this pointless search for magic periods and adopt instead the view that the developmental process is a continuous one, in which every segment of the life cycle from conception through maturity is of crucial importance and requires certain environmental nutrients.

PRACTICAL CONSIDERATIONS

On the practical side, the judgment that early life experiences are all-important has had serious far-reaching consequences. The mother, as the most important influence on the young child, became the all-powerful determinant of her infant's future. Her every move, her every gesture, her every thought or feeling was considered to be fraught with dangerous possibilities for her child. By the mid-1950s, this ideology and its consequences were firmly entrenched in this country, to the great concern to some of us (Chess, Thomas, and, Birch, 1965). This concern was well expressed at the time by Dr. Hilde Bruch (1954), a prominent child psychiatrist: "Modern parent education is characterized by the experts' pointing out in great detail all the mistakes parents have made and can possibly make. . . . An unrelieved picture of model parental behavior, a contrived image of artifical perfection and happiness, is held up before parents who try valiantly to reach the ever receding ideal of 'good parenthood' like dogs after a mechanical rabbit (p. 723). . . . The new teaching implies that parents are all-responsible and must assume the role of playing preventive Fate for their children" (p. 728). Bruch quoted Millicent McIntosh, then President of Barnard College: "All the experts seem to be saying to young parents 'Even the most innocent appearing act or a carelessly spoken word may "harm" a child or "damage" his future happiness. You hurt them by comparing them and praising them for being special. You hurt them by being too affectionate to them and by not being affectionate enough'" (p. 727).

Those of us who had to come to the rescue of parents tormented by the guilt, anxiety, and confusion produced by the "experts'" pronouncements can testify to the great harm and suffering this ideology produced for so many. With the increasing challenge to the concept of early life determinism in recent years, the influence of the parental guilt stereotype has begun to recede—but only just begun! Sad to say, one aspect of the stereotype has taken a new lease on life. This is the pronouncement that a young child needs the full attendance of his mother at all times, that if the mother goes out to work she is risking the emotional health of her child. By the mid-1960s the research data clearly indicated the fallaciousness of this assertion, which had put mothers who had to work in a terrible dilemma (Chess, Thomas, and Birch, 1965, Chap. 19). Subsequent studies have abundantly confirmed these earlier reports. As summarized by Rutter in a recent review (1978c), "Children of working mothers develop just as well as those whose mothers remain at home and there are no differences between these two groups in rates of psychological disorder." A study of special interest is that reported by Kagan and his associates (Kagan et al., 1978). Thirty-three infants attended a day-care center created and administered by the research team. The infants were enrolled at three to five months, and studied until 29 months. A control group of 37 infants with no day-care experience and matched for age, sex, ethnicity, and social class was also set up. Extensive data were gathered and carefully analyzed, with the overall conclusion that "Day-care, when responsibly and conscientiously implemented, does not seem to have hidden psychological dangers. . . . The assessment of language, memory and perceptual analysis failed to reveal any obvious advantages or disadvantages to the day care experience" (pp. 260-262).

Yet, just recently a respected child care professional has resurrected the old shibboleth that a working mother harms her children and has received wide publicity for this statement (Fraiberg, 1977). And another popular child psychologist, who also advises mothers not to work, when asked about the research evidence to the contrary, is quoted in a newspaper interview as saying "I don't

believe those studies. . . . You can prove anything in a study"
(*New York Daily News,* 1978). One hardly expects such an anti-
scientific bias from professionals whose authority presumably derives from their scientific experience and knowledge.

Finally, another variant on the theme of early life determinism
has been played out recently. In the 1960s, the Head Start program was launched to provide the disadvantaged preschool child
with an enriched and stimulating intellectual experience. This
program was oversold by a number of professionals as providing
a permanent cognitive effect for these children, again based on the
hypothesis that early life experiences were all-important determinants of subsequent development. When it became apparent that
these children, who then went on to their inadequate slum public
schools, showed no significant permanent rise in IQ, this was used
as "proof" of the uselessness of the program and of the genetically
determined intellectual inferiority of black children (Jensen,
1969). But, as Kagan (1969) pointed out, to presume that a brief
childhood program of stimulation could override subsequent as
well as previous deprivation is the same nonsense as "to assume
that feeding animal protein to a seriously malnourished child for
three days would lead to a permanent increase in his weight and
height, if after 72 hours of steak and eggs he was sent back to his
malnourished environment" (p. 276).

To conclude this discussion of the significance of early life
experiences it is pertinent to quote a recent statement (Chess,
1979):

> As we grow from childhood to maturity, all of us have to
> shed many childhood illusions. As the field of developmental
> studies has matured, we now have to give up the illusion
> that once we know the young child's psychological history,
> subsequent personality and functioning are *ipso facto* pre-
> dictable. On the other hand, we now have a much more
> optimistic vision of human development. The emotionally
> traumatized child is not doomed, the parents' early mistakes
> are not irrevocable, and our preventive and therapeutic in-
> tervention can make a difference at all age-periods (p. 112).

Chapter IX

Continuity, Change and Predictability

All psychological attributes show both continuity and change over time. This is true at all stages of the life cycle. The developmental study of any behavioral phenomenon requires a conceptualization of the dynamics of continuity and change, their interrelationship and relative significance at any age-period, and the criteria for their identification and measurement.

The first few years of life are characterized by rapid and dramatic changes. The qualitative variability in the sequences of

113

change from child to child does not permit the application of an a priori formula which will predict beforehand the specific direction of behavioral development in any individual infant. But this process of change is orderly and organized. As the young child develops increasing experience and competence in social functioning and task mastery, stable behavioral patterns are formed.

By what age can we anticipate that a child's psychological characteristics will have sufficient stability to make some degree of prediction possible? Certainly, this will vary from child to child, and in any one child certain characteristics may achieve stability before others do. Kagan's judgment places this development in the middle childhood years. "We suspect, but have not yet documented, that the late childhood and adolescent personality traits we are fond of—like self-confidence, intellectual ability, motivation, hostility—do not become firmly established until the child is six to 10 years old, after attitudes toward self have become structured as a result of identification with parents, class, and ethnic groups, and following opportunities to arrive at conclusions regarding one's competences and reliabilities relative to peers" (Kagan et al., 1978, p. 28). Our own impressions from our research and clinical experience support Kagan's judgment.

It is of interest that many different cultures have identified the child of six or seven as competent to assume a new level of functioning (Shapiro and Perry, 1976). During the Middle Ages, children became pages at court at this age, and in a later period, children were apprenticed away from home at seven years. In modern society formal schooling usually begins at six or seven years. This consensus undoubtedly reflects an awareness that stability in psychological functioning does become evident at this age.

In psychoanalytic developmental theory, the period between six and 12 years is considered a time of "latency" between the passage of the oedipal stage and the beginning of adolescence, with a kind of "psychosexual moratorium in human development" (Erikson, 1968). The term "latency" tends to imply that the child is marking time and waiting for puberty, and even if originally formulated as a period of psychosexual quiescence, it has been criticized by many writers, both within and outside the psychoanalytic movement (Thomas and Chess, 1972). From our own longitudinal study data, it is clear that the middle childhood period is one of continued developmental and psychological change. Children with onset of behavior problems in the preschool years showed active change in severity and symptoms, while some problem cases only emerged between six and 10 years. Sexual interest and activity were evident in the vast majority of the school-age children, but were without any pathologic significance. We concluded that "the term latency, therefore, would appear to be a confusing and inappropriate way to designate and characterize children between the ages of six and 12. We would suggest that this term be abandoned and that simple descriptive designations, such as middle childhood and elementary school age, which imply no a priori assumptions or theories about the dynamics and course of psychologic development, be used in its place" (Thomas and Chess, 1972, p. 340).

One can presume that Freud had recognized that a significant transitional point occurs at age six to seven years, at which time the child becomes capable of a new level of psychological functioning. Inasmuch as this new level is not uniformly characterized by psychosexual activity, from the point of view of psychoanalytic theory this appeared "latent" rather than "active."

DIALECTICAL UNITY OF CHANGE AND CONTINUITY

Once stable patterns are formed, subsequent development is by no means static. On the contrary, change and continuity become intermeshed in a dialectical unity of opposites. Continuity emerges from change, but can itself become an agent of further change. The stable behavior, because it operates consistently over time, can influence significant features of the environment, and the resulting environmental alteration can in turn modify behavior. For example, a five-year-old boy may develop temper tantrums as an effective technique of gaining his immediate desires with easily intimidated parents. The same tantrums may then alienate him from his peer group. Their rejection may then lead him to develop ingratiating techniques, such as buying their favor, to reinstate and maintain himself with his peers. A six-year-old girl may learn to accept help cheerfully from her parents, older sibs, and nursery school teachers. The consistent task mastery which then ensues may lead to self-confidence in approaching new demands and challenges and to her becoming a constructive leader in her peer group, to whom others turn for help.

Depending on the nature of the individual-environment interaction, change or continuity may be dominant over time. If the environment remains stable, and if the individual's behavior serves to reinforce those environmental influences which were instrumental in shaping this behavior to begin with, then continuity will be maintained. The continuity may even appear immutable, determined, and fixed by some presumed intrapsychic state, if the dynamics of the interactional process are overlooked.

> I suggest that we err when we attribute the apparent consistency and continuity in personality to internal psychological structures alone. What determines the similarly between my behaviour last year and what it is likely to be during the next is not nearly so much a matter of that which is "I" as it is of the social fields of force in which that "I" moves. That is, having acquired a repertoire of behaviours, I maximize their adaptive utility by seeking out the familiar and avoiding the strange in the social world around me. The apparent consistency in the self is the result, not merely of what has gone before, but the continuation into the future of the same social forces that have given rise to it (Eisenberg, 1977, p. 233).

If new characteristics emerge in the individual, and especially if they also serve to change significant features of the environment, then modification or even dramatic change in basic behavior patterns may occur. Change can also result if new features emerge in the environment and modify significant aspects of the individual's psychological functioning. Once change occurs, the interactional process may stabilize with a new continuity of behavior. Or the change may promote successive shifts in the individual and/or environment, so that a new stability in behavior is not quickly achieved.

In the NYLS we have seen examples of all these types of interactional sequences. Consistency can be favorable, with consonance between the individual's temperamental pattern and other characteristics and environmental expectations, demands and opportunities. In these cases, the children developed adequate and even superior competence in social functioning and task performance at succeeding age-periods and had strongly positive feedback from parents, teachers, and peers. They are now young adults who have self-confidence, a strongly positive self-image, clear goals, healthy coping mechanisms, and active social and sexual functioning. At the same time, they are quite different from each other in personality attributes, interests, and way of life.

Consistency can also be unfavorable as a result of dissonance between the individual and the environment. When this dissonance was not corrected, excessive stress led to disturbed functioning which then intensified the situation, leading to more stress and disturbed functioning.

In the middle-class achievement-oriented families of the NYLS, this kind of stubborn dissonance occurred most typically with children who were temperamentally distractible and nonpersistent (Thomas, Chess, and Birch, 1968). For the parents, these traits were dissonant with their standards that persistence is essential for both success in life and personal "good character." As a result, our guidance effort with the parents of such children was uniformly unsuccessful, although it was moderately or highly successful in the majority of other cases. The guidance procedure demanded that the parents truly accept the individuality of their child's temperament pattern, a demand that these parents could not meet.

Poorness of fit between individual and environment which is not easily changed may arise from factors other than parental attitudes and demands. The maladaptive consequences of brain damage, mental retardation, or mental illness may require special

efforts, which in many cases may be at best only partially successful. An area of special concern is the failure of the school and the
economic system to meet the needs of disadvantaged children,
with resulting perpetuation of the disadvantage and its consequences. Edmund Gordon, a leading authority in the field of compensatory education, makes the point that

> . . . schools have made little progress in achieving a match
> between the developmental patterns, learning styles and tem-
> peramental traits of learners and the educational experiences
> to which they are exposed. . . . Our research data indicate
> wide variations in patterns of intellectual and social function
> across and within subpopulations. These variations in func-
> tion within privileged populations may be less important be-
> cause of a variety of environmental factors that support ade-
> quate development and learning. Among disadvantaged pop-
> ulations, where traditional forms of environmental support
> may be absent, attention to differential learning patterns
> may be crucial to adequate development (Gordon and
> Green, 1974, p. 14).

In the NYLS population, marked and even dramatic psychological change has been evident in a number of cases, initiated
through the emergence of new abilities, or deviations in the individual, or new opportunities or demands in the environment.
Whether initiated in the individual or the environment, psycho-
loigcal change required a significant alteration in the preexisting
individual-environment interactional process. As an example, one
girl had a typical Difficult Child temperamental pattern from infancy, to which the father responded with unrealistic, rigid, and
punitive demands, and the mother with vacillation and confusion.
This interaction resulted in an increasingly severe behavior disorder in the youngster. In middle childhood unexpected musical
and dramatic talents blossomed, and the girl became an outstanding performer in school plays and assemblies. Teachers and other
parents praised her to her parents, who, fortunately for the girl,
also held her new abilities in high esteem. For the parents, the

daughter was transformed from a "rotten kid" to a highly talented individual with "artistic temperament." The youngster's inter-action with parents, teachers, and peers now became progressively benign, her symptoms disappeared, and her psychological com-petencies blossomed. Now, at age 22, she still has stormy initial adaptations to some new situations, but she is self-confident, has had substantial academic achievement, has good friends, success-ful sexual relationships, and constructive life plans.

A contrasting example is another young woman whose early developmental course was benign and favorable. She was an Easy Child temperamentally, though her mood expressiveness was in-tense, including intense, albeit infrequent, negative reactions. However, with her predominance of positive mood, easy adapta-bility, and quickness of movement, she received consistently fa-vorable feedback from parents throughout early and middle child-hood, and easily fulfilled all their expectations and demands. There was a dramatic change at adolescence, however, as a result of the pressures of new sexual drives, academic demands, and peer group standards. The need to exercise self-control over her im-pulses and to postpone immediate gratification of her desires con-flicted with her quick intense emotional reactions. Impulsive be-havior with defensive denials, tantrums, and lying began to domi-nate her functioning. Family and friends were progressively alien-ated, which only aggravated her intense impulsive responses. By age 19, she had dropped out of a number of schools, had a series of promiscuous sexual affairs, and a succession of marginal jobs. As of now, two years later, there is some evidence of beginning self-control, with more sustained commitments and improvement in her social relationships. However, the dramatic negative change from the promise of her childhood years is still the dominant phenomenon of this young woman's developmental course.

IDENTIFICATION OF CONTINUITY AND CHANGE

The identification and categorization of continuity and change in individual psychological development are by no means simple. Do we look for similarity in observable behavior from one age to another? Do we look for similarity in abilities, motivations, or temperament which may be expressed in different behaviors at succeeding ages? Or do we look for continuity in the individual-environment interaction, one that promotes self-esteem and a positive sense of identity, or the reverse, but which may result both in change in overt behavior and in abilities, motivations, and temperamental characteristics?

The issue is complicated by the fact that the same behavior can result from different causes, and the same cause can produce different behaviors. Thus, a person who is aloof in a group of strangers may be slow-to-warm-up temperamentally, or anxious about his social competence, or waiting for the right moment to impress and dominate the group, or expressing an attitude of superiority and arrogance. On the other hand, any of these motives of anxiety, competitiveness or arrogance might, in other individuals, lead to immediate involvement with the group as a whole or selective attention to one or several of its members.

Furthermore, behavioral continuity or change in any individual is not a global phenomenon. Some patterns may remain stable over a certain period of time, while others are changing. At subsequent age-periods, one or more previously stable traits may undergo change, while some previously changing patterns may now show stability.

Kagan (1971) has suggested a classification of continuity into three types: homotypic, heterotypic, and complete. Homotypic continuity refers to stability over time in the same overt behavior, such as in tested IQ during adolescence and adult life. Heterotypic refers to stability in the behavioral structure or process which is manifested in different overt behaviors at different ages. Thus, anxiety at separation from the mother might be manifested in excessive clinging behavior at three years and in a school phobia at seven years. Complete continuity refers to stability in both the underlying psychological process and the manifest behavior. This last type is "most likely to occur after puberty when the rate of change of basic components of psychological organization is slowing down. . . . The 13-year-old boy who is competitive and involved in athletics because of a desire to match behavior to a sex role standard is likely to display similar behavior a decade later" (Kagan, 1971, p. 17). This classification, whether one uses these labels or not, provides a useful framework for studying developmental sequences in behavior.

Sameroff (1975), on his part, emphasizes that the continuity which is basic to development is not in behavioral characteristics or environmental influences considered in isolation, but in the interactional process itself. "The constants in development are not some sets of traits but rather the *processes* by which these traits are maintained in the transactions between organism and environment."

In this interactional process, continuity and change show a dialectical unity of opposites, as we find with the heredity-environment interactions. Continuity in behavior leads to change, and change to continuity, as discussed earlier in this chapter. Continuity in the social environment fosters stability of behavior. On the other hand, environmental rigidity may frustrate the pursuit of adaptive goals and force the individual to modify or change his goals, adopt a new perspective on himself and his relationship to society, and generate new coping mechanisms and defenses. Change in the social environment often fosters change in behavior. On the other hand, environmental change which the individual cannot master may lead to reactive and defensive rigidity instead of adaptive change. From this vantage point, in which continuity and change form a dialectical unity of opposites, the current debate among some personality theorists over a trait versus a situation model (Magnusson and Endler, 1977) appears unnecessary. Trait or person factors are the main determinants of behavior, and so are situational or environmental factors. Any behavioral trait always manifests itself within specific environmental situations and is influenced by the situation. Conversely and simultaneously, the effect of the environment is shaped by the behavioral characteristics of the specific individual, and these traits also actively influence the situation itself.

DISCONTINUITY IN CONTINUITY

A special problem in tracing continuity of behavior derives from the intermittent, discontinuous expression which is so typical of stable behavior patterns. This phenomenon is clearly evident when one can monitor the psychological functioning of an individual over an extended period of time, as in long-term psychotherapy. With such treatment, a previously fixed neurotic pattern may be ameliorated and then seem to disappear completely. To all intents and purposes this previously stable psychological constellation will seem—to patient, family, friends, and therapist—to be gone forever. Yet, a new environmental situation may arise —a week later, six months later, five years later—which will trigger off this same neurotic response, with all the behavioral chararteristics it had manifested in the past. As a simple example, a man may have been burdened with an automatic reaction of threat and danger when working with other men who appeared assertive, aggressive, and highly competent. The sense of danger produced anxiety, with defensive reactions of appeasement, ingratiation, and, where possible, withdrawal. These reactions resulted in inferior performance, which served to confirm this individual's conviction that he could not compete successfully with other vigorous men. With treatment, the nature and dynamics of his neurotic pattern were exposed, its irrationality and dangerous consequences clarified, and successful methods of mastery developed. The man's level of work functioning improved, his defensive reactions disappeared, and he became convinced that he had nothing to fear from competition with his co-workers. Yet, two years later he returned with a full-blown recurrence of his neurosis, with the same symptoms and behavior. Several months before he had been promoted to a more demanding position, in which several of his superiors were in reality aggressive and hypercritical, not only to him, but to all their staff. For this man, however, this new situation created not a realistic discomfort and uneasiness, but a full-blown reaction identical to his previous neurosis, which had presumably vanished. Such relapses are so common as new life events make their impact with the passage of time that we have routinely cautioned patients as to this possibility at the successful conclusion of a course of psychotherapy for a neurotic problem. (Recovery from the relapse in this case took only a short series of review discussions, as is often true in such situations.)

One of us (A. T.) saw this same phenomenon in simpler form during army service in World War II. Typically, a pilot or other air crew member had been through a series of harrowing life threatening experiences in air combat, developed severe acute anxiety symptoms, returned to the United States for recuperation, with disappearance of his anxiety symptoms. He was then reassigned to routine duty at an air base in the Midwest. As soon as he sat down in a combat airplane, safe and sound, and the motor started, his anxiety symptoms returned with the same manifestations and intensity as in combat in Europe or the Far East.

In ordinary life, similar phenomena are not unusual. An adult appears to have completely "forgotten" a skill acquired in childhood. Yet, on returning to the same activity, the ability and even specific manner of performance return quickly, indicating that the early learned behavior pattern had by no means been forgotten.

The analogy of these behavioral phenomena with memory is striking. How often have all of us thought we had forgotten completely some past situation or event in our lives, only to have some stimulus—a remark, a sensation, a new event—trigger off a flood of recollection in which this past memory comes back to life vividly and in detail. And perhaps the analogy is not a superficial one. Perhaps the neurobiological mechanisms involved in the storage and retrieval of memories are functionally the same as for behavior patterns.

CONTINUITY-DISCONTINUITY OF TEMPERAMENT

As we ourselves originally began to observe clinically and impressionistically the phenomenon of temperament, we were struck by the many dramatic evidences of continuity in individuals we knew, sometimes from early childhood to adulthood. It was tempting to generalize from these instances to the concept that an older child or adult's temperamental characteristics could be predicted from a knowledge of his behavior style in early childhood. However, such a formulation would have been at complete variance with our fundamental commitment to an interactionist viewpoint, in which individual behavioral development is conceived as a constantly evolving and changing process of organism-environment interaction.

The determination of consistency of temperament over time is, first of all, beset by a number of specific methodological problems. Rutter (1970) has pointed out several of these: reliance on adjectives used by parents or observers in describing children's behavior; the possibility of selective bias in deciding which episodes of behavior the parent or other observer reports; and the problem of separating the content from the style of behavior. Most important, he feels, is the effect that the changing context of the child's behavior might have on the temperament ratings.

In addition to these issues raised by Rutter, several other methodological problems regarding the determination of consistency over time have been apparent in the NYLS. A child's characteristic expression of temperament may be blurred at any specific age-period by routinization of functioning. Thus, an infant who shows marked withdrawal reactions to the bath, new foods, and new people may, a year or two later, show positive responses to these same stimuli because of repeated exposure and final adaptation. If at that time he experiences few new situations and stimuli, the withdrawal reaction may not be evident. Adaptation and routinization of activites may, in the same way, blur the expression of other temperamental traits, such as irregularity, slow adaptability, and negative mood expression. Limitation of opportunity for physical activity may lead to frequent restless movements which may be interpreted as high activity or even hyperactivity. The procedures for quantitative scores necessarily rely on routine judgments and scoring approaches which can preclude the identification of meaningful subtleties in the developmental course of individual children. Specific single items of behavior may sometimes be significant in indicating temperamental consistency from one age to another, but quantitative scoring methods can hardly give proper weight to the importance of such functionally significant items.

Finally, the issue of consistency of temperament over time cannot be studied globally. One or several temperamental traits may show striking continuity and the other attributes may not. Alternatively, the original consistent traits may not show the correlations, whereas other attributes may now do so. The factors affecting the identification of continuity over time are so complex and variable as to create all kinds of permutations in the patterns of correlations.

In the NYLS, we determined the degree of consistency for each of the nine categories over the first five years of life. Pooled weighted scores were used for each year, and inter-year product-moment correlations calculated. As reported earlier (Thomas and Chess, 1977), statistically significant correlations were obtained between most categories for adjacent years. As the time span for the comparison was increased, the number of significant correlations decreased, the greatest number being for activity level and adaptability. For years one to five, only threshold was significant (.25 at the .05 level of confidence). These findings probably reflect a combination of methodological problems and actual change in functioning.

We are currently engaged in a quantitative assessment of temperament in the early adult age-period. When this is completed, levels of correlation for the group as a whole with the preschool years will be determined.

As the subjects in the NYLS were followed from early infancy through adolescence, a number of qualitative longitudinal studies were done. These qualitative studies made it possible to trace the consistency of temperamental characteristics in individual children over time (Thomas and Chess, 1977). In general, five patterns were defined: 1) clear-cut consistency; 2) consistency in some aspects of temperament at one period and in other aspects at other times; 3) distortion of the expression of temperament by other factors, such as psychodynamic patterns; 4) consistency in temperament but qualitative change in temperament-environment interaction; and 5) change in a conspicuous temperamental trait. Any individual child may show a combination of several of these possibilities.

Carey and McDevitt (1978) have recently reported a study of stability and change in the temperamental clusters of Easy Child, Difficult Child and Slow-To-Warm-Up Child, by comparison of the rating established once at four to eight months and once at three to seven years. Data were obtained on 187 children, using the Carey Infant Temperament Scale and the Behavioral Style Questionnaire developed by the authors for the three- to seven-year period. At the older age period, 30 percent of the 187 children remained in the same cluster rating. This was consistently more evident for the three- to five-year group (39.2 percent) than for the later period of five- to seven-years (20 percent). A disproportionate number of children with the Difficult Child pattern or intermediate high ratings at four to eight months remained so at three to seven years (17 out of 43; $p < 0.01$).

The data indicate clearly that temperament, like other psychological characteristics, cannot be expected to show linear continuity over time. The categorization of temperament in any individual is derived from the constellation of behaviors exhibited at any one age. These behaviors are the result of all the influences, past and present, which shape and modify these behaviors in a constantly evolving interactive process. Consistency of a temperamental trait or constellation in an individual over time, therefore, will require stability in these interactional forces, such as environmental influences, motivations, and abilities.

However, in some instances environmental stability may actually serve to change the character of a temperamental trait, rather than enhance its continuity. This is specifically true of the difficult and slow-to-warm-up temperamental patterns, in which the conspicuous responses of withdrawal, negative mood and slow adaptability are evident in new situations, i.e., with environmental change. With environmental stability, the absence of new situations will result in minimum or absent withdrawal, negative mood and slow adaptability responses. Given a significant environmental change, the same person who had previously been positively and smoothly adapted to a stable life situation may again revert to the previous pattern. We have seen this sequence repeated a number of times in individuals in the NYLS sample with these temperamental constellations. Again, this is another illustration of the significant phenomenon of *discontinuity in continuity* discussed earlier.

Developmental Stages: Invariant and Variant

It is clear, even to casual observation, that much of development proceeds in definite invariant stage sequences. With few exceptions the infant sits first, then stands, and then walks. He cannot run or hop before he can walk. Mastery of language almost always proceeds from single simple words to phrases and sentences. Motor skills, social behavior, task mastery, and cognitive functioning all evolve sequentially from lower to higher levels of competence.

It is tempting, therefore, to look for a similar pattern in behavioral development, in which one stage would follow another in some fixed sequence. Such invariance would introduce a basic structure of continuity and stability in the process of behavioral change from one age period to another, and confirm the ever-present assumption of continuity in the developmental process from infancy to adulthood.

The studies of Jean Piaget on cognitive functioning have provided the most substantial and solid conceptualization of a single sequential scheme of development. Out of his empirical studies, Piaget (1963) has postulated sequential periods of cognitive growth, which follow each other in an invariant order: sensorimotor (birth to two years), preoperational (two to seven years), concrete operations (seven to twelve years), formal operations (twelve years and on). The age-periods are not fixed; the sequences are.

Piaget's description of successive cognitive stages has been verified in numerous investigations among dissimilar groups (Modgil, 1974). These studies have also indicated that the rate of progression from one stage to another may be different in various groups and under different circumstances, a formulation Piaget has himself accepted (Piaget, 1972). However, a serious question has been raised as to the validity of a "linear, sequential, unidirectional conception of cognitive behavior and development" (Flavell, 1972, p. 341). Flavell reports studies of learning in college students which showed that "Acquisition of the higher level material did not require having achieved a high degree of mastery of the lower level prerequisites. . . . In an even more telling experiment . . . students seemed to learn and retain the material just as well whether the instructional sequence was randomized or not, even in the case of the most hierarchically-organized of the three subject matters" (p. 343). Flavell concludes that most cognitive activity and development may be characterized by a process that is "tortuous and spiral-like, cyclical and recursive, sequence-violating and sequence-transforming" (p. 343), which, as he points out, is similar to the continuous process of reciprocal interaction that is such a general phenomenon of psychological development.

Questions have also been raised as to the validity of Piaget's formulation of the dynamics of development from one developmental stage to another (Mussen et al., 1974, pp. 314-318). Furthermore, in his considerations of cognitive development in infancy, Piaget concentrates on the infant's innate motor and sensory reflexes and sensorimotor activities. In the process, he ignores the social matrix within which these and all other activites occur, and which have such importance in shaping all developmental process. Also, although he does take a basically interactionist approach, Piaget has studied and conceptualized cognition in isolation from emotion, while in reality cognitive and emotional processes always profoundly influence each other. However, "regardless of the results of future research . . . it is obviously true that Piaget's contributions have been epochal and his influence on developmental psychology without parallel" (Mussen et al., 1979, p. 284).

Freud, like Piaget, also conceptualized development in terms of invariant sequential stages, in which progress from one stage to the next depended on the mastery of the demands and tasks of the earlier stage. As Piaget ignored emotions, Freud ignored cognition, and both gave scant attention to the social matrix of development. For both, also, the consideration of developmental stages stopped essentially at adolescence.

Piaget's concepts, however, are formulated so that they can be categorized and rated reliably and tested by empirical data collection. Freud's concepts, to the contrary, lack such operational definitions, and this presents great obstacles to the development of independent research designs (Baldwin, 1968). The dissatisfaction within the psychoanalytic movement with classical Freudian formulations of developmental stages in terms of orality, anality and genitality has led to many proposed modifications of this conceptualized scheme of sequential stages. The most influential formulation is that of Erik Erikson (1963). While accepting Freud's outline of instinctual transformation and the genetic stages of psychosexual development, Erikson has attempted to incorporate a social dimension with this outline, and emphasized that each stage of development is influenced and directed by some basic elements in society. In his developmental chart, the first five stages (basic trust, autonomy, initiative, industry, and identity) have their corresponding phases in Freudian theory. His last three stages (intimacy, generativity, and ego integrity) reach into adult life and go beyond traditional psychoanalytic formulations. "Erickson's developmental system represents in essence an elaboration of the stages of psychosexual development proposed by Freud, with a notable amplification at the adult end" (Wohlwill, 1973, p. 195).

Like Freud's conceptualization of developmental phases, Erikson's stages also lack operational definitions and criteria which can be applied to research or clinical studies. (Erikson himself has opposed the construction of scales and ratings to measure and test his formulations of developmental stages.) Erikson's system has also been criticized as neglecting personality attributes that may be just as important as his selection, and for remaining committed to a system of psychosexual stages based on shifts in libido (Lidz, 1968). The sociologist Jules Henry (1967) has also pointed out how much Erikson's formulations, such as "industry" and "initiative," reflect the middle-class ideology of Western industrial society.

Mention may be made of two recent efforts at the elaboration of systems of invariant sequences of psychological developmental stages. Loevinger (1969) has proposed a model of "ego" development as proceeding through a series of sequentially ordered stages in an invariant order. She defines the ego as "above all a process, not a thing. . . . The striving to master, to integrate, to make sense of experience is not one ego function among many but the essence of the ego" (Loevinger, 1969, p. 85). Her formulation of seven stages and three transitional phases has been constructed with operational definitions and assessment techniques, in contrast to psychoanalytic ego concepts. As a result, it is possible to use her constructs for systematic empirical research, and this has been done in a large number of diverse studies. Hauser (1976) has recently reviewed these studies comprehensively. He concludes that "in reviewing the validity studies, it became clear that there was meager support for two critical assumptions made by Loevinger: a) The sequence of ego development stages has an invariant order and b) The stages correspond to a range of character types, each with a structural coherence of diverse personality dimensions" (p. 952).

Kohlberg (1964) has proposed the concept that moral judgment develops through "invariant" sequences. Also, "the use of a more advanced stage of thought depends upon earlier attainment of each preceding stage" (p. 404). Kohlberg (1978) further claims that "the stage sequence in moral development is universal; the same sequence is found in all cultures, subcultures or social class structures" (p. 210). Such a complex psychological phenomenon as moral reasoning must reflect social values and standards, and be influenced by the individual's socioeconomic position, family characteristics, and idiosyncratic life experiences. It appears highly unlikely that moral reasoning could show an invariant developmental pattern, and even more unlikely that its development could be independent of culture and social class. Wolff (1978) has sharply challenged Kohlberg's formulations and Vaillant (1977) has reported that the data from the Harvard Grant Longitudinal Study indicate that "ego development is far more reversible than Kohlberg's model" (p. 343). On the methodological side, Wohlwill's analysis of Kohlberg's data leads him to doubt whether "there is any systematic interrelationship between the responses to his set of moral judgment items that would warrant the use of the stage concept with regard to them" (1973, p. 198).

DEVELOPMENTAL STAGES: AN OVERVIEW

Development does proceed sequentially. Learning, maturation, and continuing genetic influence (Wilson 1978) all serve in their mutual interaction to shape the emergence of new, more complex psychological attributes over time. Whether in overt behavior, affect, language, or cognition, as development proceeds, simpler levels are replaced by more highly organized and complex patterns of psychological organization. Piaget's delineation of sequential stages of cognitive development, in which more complex and more effective levels succeed simpler levels as the result of maturation and experience, provides a model for conceptualization of change over time.

Emde and his co-workers (1976) have identified, in their developmental studies, sequential periods of biobehavioral change from early infancy to seven years. In our own NYLS (Thomas, Chess, and Birch, 1968), we have identified "the shift from symptoms expressed primarily on an overt behavioral level in the preschool years to those reflecting complex subjective states, attitudes, distorted self-images and psychodynamic patterns of defense by school age. These shifts appeared to reflect the normal transition from action to ideation that characterizes the course of development from infancy to adulthood" (p. 163).

It is also clear that development does not stop with adolescence and that new psychological stages emerge in adult life. Erikson (1963) has emphasized this point with his general broad characterizations of adult life in terms of generativity versus stagnation, and ego identity versus despair. Levinson (1978) has recently made a beginning with a systematic inductive study of mid-adult life. Data from larger samples, but ones studied less intensively than Levinson's group, have also indicated that active development characterizes adult life as well as childhood and adolescence (Gould, 1972; Stein et al., 1978; Neugarten, 1979).

The identification of sequential developmental stages can provide important insights into the nature of the general laws that govern the processes of development from the simple to the more complex. However, several caveats are necessary. Individual differences in the quality, timing, and speed of transition from one stage to another for any psychological function are substantial and widespread. As Emde and his co-workers (1976) emphasize, "Our research also directs attention to the lack of invariant sequences among different sectors of development within a given infant" (p. 148). Given the degree of individual variability that exists in biological capacities, vicissitudes of genetic influence, temperament, maturation, life experience, environmental demands and expectations of different cultures and social classes, as well as the complexities of the interactional process among these variables, it is not possible to expect predictable, invariant linear sequences of development for any behavioral pattern. Group trends can be defined for a population of similar sociocultural background, but marked individual variability that is normal will still be evident.

Beyond this, it is questionable whether stable sequences of development can be defined, even for specific group trends, for behavioral categories that do not show a clear hierarchical progression from the simpler to the more complex. Thus, in Freud's scheme "orality" is not necessarily a simpler pattern than "anality," though the first is assumed to precede the second. The same is true of Erikson's formulation, in which the earliest stage of "basic trust" is not necessarily simpler than "autonomy," and the latter is again not necessarily simpler than the presumed later stages of "initiative" and "industry." It is much more likely that Freud and Erikson's characterizations reflect sequences of demands and expectations of a specific environment rather than any pre-programmed maturational sequence.

A striking illustration of group differences at the same developmental level has become evident in the comparison in adolescence of our NYLS subjects with the handicapped subjects in our congenital rubella and mentally retarded longitudinal samples. The more complex level of peer relationships and academic demand, the beginnings of active sexual functioning and the progressive change in parent-child relationships which characterize this new developmental stage were evident for all the populations, normal and handicapped. Except for the small minority with substantial behavior disorder, the NYLS group coped adequately with these new demands and expectations, and in many cases with little evidence of the traditionally described adolescent "storm" and "turmoil" (see Coleman [1978] for an overview evaluation of this traditional view). Much greater stress and uncertainty have been evident in this group at the subsequent early adult stage, when they face the more complex and challenging demands of career choice and implementation, economic independence, and the establishment of emotional depth in their sexual relationships.

For the physically handicapped or mentally retarded child, by contrast, the new demands and expectations of adolescence were typically highly stressful. Even where previous levels of adaptation in the community had been excellent, and where families were highly supportive, a deaf or retarded adolescent often could not cope with the demands which were encountered at this new developmental stage (Chess et al., 1980).

CONCLUSIONS

Certain fundamental theses are impressively documented in the research literature. Development is characterized by both change and continuity, and one cannot occur without the other. Development necessarily proceeds from the simpler to the more complex, and sequential stages can be identified in this process. But such sequential stages are the categorizations of group trends for specific populations with specific sociocultural backgrounds. Individual variability between and within groups is significant and widespread, and the search for invariant linear developmental stage sequences which are valid for all individuals is indeed a search for "fool's gold."

Developmental research can concern itself with the identification of patterns of change *and* continuity, as they coexist, as they interact dynamically at the same age-period, and sequentially, as their manifestations are similar or different between individuals and between groups, and as change turns into continuity, and continuity into change. From such studies we can hope to elucidate progressively the general laws that govern development, rather than be imprisoned in the blind alley search for linear continuity and invariant stage sequences.

The evidence that early experience is not irreversible, that change is characteristic of the infancy period, still appears unsettling to many. As eminent a psychologist as William Kessen (1978), reviewing Kagan's most recent volume, worries that "if early experience matters so little what difference does it make how we treat our infants?" It does make a difference, just as it makes a difference how we treat our older children, our adolescents, our adults. An interactionist view of development considers that experience at any age-period is *important* but not *all-decisive* for later functioning. Vaillant puts it well in his comment on the Harvard Grant study findings on linear continuity and predictability: "The life cycle is more than an invariant sequence of stages with single predictable outcomes. The men's lives are full of surprises, and the Grant Study provides no prediction tables. Rather, the study of life times is comparable to the study of celestial navigation. Neither a sextant nor a celestial map can predict where we *should* go; but both are invaluable in letting us identify where we *are*" (Vaillant, 1977, p. 373).

Chapter X

Language and Its Developmental Significance

The acquisition and use of language have profound significance for the dynamics of human psychological development. Learning a language represents a demand for complex task mastery. Language has "rules of phonology, which describe how to put sounds together to form words; rules of syntax, which describe how to put words together to form sentences; rules of semantics, which describe how to interpret the meanings of words and sentences,

135

and rules of pragmatics, which describe how to participate in a conversation, how to sequence sentences and how to anticipate the information needed by an interlocutor" (Moskowitz, 1978, p. 93). The average child masters most of these rules by five years of age, plus learning and storing a vocabulary of many hundreds of words. Many young children learn two languages, and some even three.

Learning language also requires a substantial level of social competence. Language acquisition always takes place in a social context, and a child who hears no language learns no language (Bruner, 1978; Moskowitz, 1978). The young infant's ability to engage in precise sustained movements that are synchronous with the caretaker's speech may very well represent, as Condon and Sander (1974) suggest, the beginning of language development. Bruner (1978) also emphasizes that the process of sequential and increasingly sophisticated caretaker-child patterns of communication is of primary importance in language acquisition.

Language development in the human being is unique in its scope and quality and in the competencies and active role which the young organism brings to bear in its acquisition. Many animal species have extensive systems of communication (Tavolga, 1970). Bees have an elaborate method of movements by which they announce the direction and distance of available food (von Frisch, 1950). Chimpanzees have been taught sign language, up to one or two hundred words (Gardner and Gardner, 1967). However, the acquisition of language by the child is a uniquely human accomplishment. "No animal society has ever developed a language with the diversity and complexity of human language or one that makes possible the transmission and understanding of an infinite variety of messages. Every human society, however primitive or isolated, has a language" (Mussen et al., 1979, p. 197). And it is spoken and written language which makes possible the unique human capacity for the transmission from one generation to another of our extragenetic cultural inheritance.

The truly incredible ability of all normal young children to master the many complex and interlocking rules of language use and to learn and store an extensive vocabulary—and to do this within the space of five years or less—strongly suggests the existence of some built-in mechanism in the brain to make this possible.

Such a biological basis is further indicated by the evidence that "it seems to be virtually impossible to speed up the language-learning process" (Moskowitz, 1978, p. 94), i.e., language acquisition cannot be purely a phenomenon of learning. Furthermore, there are the children with developmental aphasia who have serious difficulties in either comprehending or expressing words, or both, in spite of good intelligence. No emotional factors can account for this developmental deviation, which must have a biological basis. Natural selection would favor the development of such a biological base, inasmuch as language brings so many adaptive advantages. The accumulated knowledge and experience of any culture is transmitted from generation to generation by language; problem-solving, cooperative group activities, communication of opportunities and dangers—all are decisively enhanced through the use of language.

To account for the highly creative and extraordinarily rapid mastery of the complexities of language by the young, Noam Chomsky (1957) has postulated an innate preprogrammed brain mechanism for the processing of language. Chomsky's ideas and work in defining the complexities and depths of language structures have provided a major stimulus to the rapid development of the field of psycholinguistics in the past 20 years. How to define the biological component of language development, what neurophysiological mechanisms are involved, how the biological interacts with the social in language acquisition—all these issues are currently the subject of lively debate and extensive research (deVilliers and deVilliers, 1978). (This volume by the deVilliers can be highly recommended as a comprehensive scholarly review of current research data and concepts of the sequences and dynamics of language acquisition.)

The Use of Language

The acquisition of language requires task mastery and social competence. As language becomes established, it then becomes a key instrument for the progressive expansion of task mastery and social competence. "The child does not describe events in a social vacuum. Instead he is using language for a variety of social purposes, such as demanding, questioning, blaming, denying, and the like" (deVilliers and deVilliers, 1978, p. 278).

It is not unusual to see a one-year-old reach a hand toward a forbidden object, such as an electrical outlet, hold his hand suspended, say "No, no!", and withdraw the hand. Language here is already being utilized in learning a safety rule. The two-year-old is eager to be given tasks to master in imitation of those around her. She will listen gravely to directions as she puts away groceries or places the eating utensils on the table, asking "like dis?" Socialization and task mastery are commingled—she is at one and the same time learning the social customs and carrying out jobs. The actions are partly learned by observation, partly by following the spoken directions, partly by questioning.

The nature of the world about her must also be understood; the three-year-old already uses the ubiquitous "why" for this purpose. Success in carrying through a task from verbal directions alone becomes a cause for triumph and pride. This is already evident in many two-year-olds, and becomes an important source of self-esteem in the succeeding years.

The reciprocal influence of language, task mastery and social competence on each other is even more striking in the older child, adolescent and adult. Increasing environmental expectations for the mastery of the more elaborate and symbolic aspects of language go along with the skillful use of language for learning, for problem-solving, and for social communication.

Dysphasia

The crucial role played by language is revealed dramatically in those children who suffer from developmental disturbances in language acquisition. Previously labeled developmental aphasia, this condition has more recently been termed *dysphasia*. Children with dysphasia have adequate intelligence and organized thought processes, as shown by their nonverbal functioning, but they show significant deficiencies in the usual rate and/or sequences of language acquisition. The cause or causes are still unclear, but the difficulty in language development is undoubtedly the reflection of a biological disturbance, most probably in the auditory cortex of the dominant hemisphere. Dysphasia may be mild and temporary, so that its consequences will usually be transient and minor. The language problem may be severe and protracted, however, in which case the psychological consequences are very likely to be widespread and serious.

The child with severe dysphasia has difficulty in discriminating between language sounds and their sequencing. He shows unpredictable word loss, unstable syntactic structure, and inconsistent grammar. There is semantic confusion in the use of words, and parts of speech other than noun and verb are frequently missing or underutilized. A combination of auditory inaccuracy and approximation of word meanings results in jargon or meaningless words.

Basically, the dysphasic child manifests a specific difficulty in the task mastery of language, with no evidence of other task mastery problems. Social competence and intellectual capacity are unaffected at first. The marked impairment in language acquisition, however, has later consequences for the child's development, in terms of both task mastery and social competence functioning. Thus, for example, one such three-year-old could not communicate his food preferences to his mother at mealtime, and had to resort to elaborate and time-consuming pantomime to make his simple wishes known. At an older age, the same boy was highly motivated to master the use of carpentry tools, and had the necessary perceptual and neuromotor skills to achieve this task. However, his difficulty in comprehending verbal instructions made it impossible for him to pursue this goal effectively. He could only learn painfully and slowly, except when he could watch and then imitate others.

The social consequences of dyphasia are usually even more drastic than the problem with task mastery. As early as three or four years of age, the child with language difficulties may become the object of ridicule by his peer group. This can become more intense as he grows older and the gap between his use of language and age expectation increases. Social communication with others may also suffer severely. To take a simple example, a 10-year-old boy and his mother had just finished supper. She was washing the dishes and asked him, "Do you want to dry the dishes?" He said "No." The mother continued washing, and then turned to find the boy standing ready with a dish towel. Annoyed at his apparent teasing, she said, "Well, make up your mind, yes or no!" The boy replied with evident puzzlement, "I don't know." This brought to the mother's mind innumerable prior instances in which the child had said one thing, but done another. When he was younger, she had thought this normal. As he grew older, she had automatically resorted to teaching him tasks by demonstration, but with frequent reactions of annoyance at having to do so. With professional consultation, the mother became clear as to her boy's problem, took notice of the recurring incidents which revealed the great discrepancy between his ability to carry out complicated tasks through observation and imitation, as compared to difficulties with verbal instruction alone. Her annoyance disappeared and was replaced by constructive understanding and concern. Unfortunately, the boy's teachers and schoolmates responded to his confused language use with irritation and ridicule.

Inevitably, children with severe dysphasia adopt various defensive strategies to minimize the consequences of dysphasia. They avoid situations which will expose their difficulties to others; they try to learn by surreptitiously watching and copying others; they try to rationalize away or even deny the existence of their problem. Some are fortunate enough to have supportive families and sympathetic teachers to help them cope until spontaneous acceleration of language acquisition occurs. Others are not so fortunate, and remain psychologically crippled for life. Poorness of fit between the dysphasic child and environmental demands and expectations can indeed have drastic effects. Goodness of fit, in which parents, sibs, teachers, and friends appreciate the nature of the problem, empathize with the child's struggle for task mastery and social competence, and are supportive and helpful of the youngster's efforts, can, by contrast, minimize and even eliminate the unfavorable consequences of dysphasia.

WRITTEN LANGUAGE

As with oral language, skill in reading and writing requires a high level of task mastery and social competence and this, in turn, leads to expanded horizons in learning, task performance, problem-solving, and social communication.

The mastery of written language demands a high order of perceptual and cognitive functioning, in which an auditory stimulus which has assumed specific meaning becomes equated with a complex, abstract, and unfamiliar visual stimulus. It is therefore no surprise that difficulties in learning to read, or developmental dyslexia, are relatively common. The cause of this problem is unknown, and the relationship between perception and written language in general is the subject of considerable debate and controversy (Chess and Hassibi, 1978; Belmont, in press).

The difficulties of the dyslexic child do not appear as early or as obviously as those of the dysphasic child. However, once reading and writing become essential tools for learning and important for social communication, the consequences of failure to achieve these skills at the expected rate can be serious. In many cases of severe dyslexia, the problem is compounded by difficulties in mastering mathematics, resulting from the basic sequencing and perceptual disturbance. Defensive strategies of clowning, avoidance of homework and other written tasks, and elaborate rationalizations and denials can exacerbate the original defect in learning, and may persist even after reading and writing have improved to the point of being only minor problems in themselves. Here again,

as with dysphasia, the flexibility or rigidity of environmental demands and expectations, and the understanding—or lack of it—
from parents and teachers determine goodness or poorness of fit
for the dyslexic child, with all the differential consequences for
developmental outcome.

LANGUAGE, THOUGHT AND EMOTION

In considering the developmental significance of language, its
close relationship to thought and emotion is evident. As indicated
above, difficulties in the mastery of oral or written languages can
have serious consequences for cognitive and emotional development. Conversely, cognitive or emotional disturbances can impair
the process of language acquisition.

The relationship between language and thought is an especially
important one. "A word does not refer to a single object but to
a group or to a class of objects. Each word is therefore already a
generalization. Generalization is a verbal act of thought and reflects reality in quite another way than sensation and perception
reflect it" (Vygotsky, 1962, p. 5). (This is true, of course, when
the word is used with meaning, and not when used without meaning, as with the echolalia of schizophrenia or brain-damaged individuals.) Thus, it is not uncommon for a child with developmental aphasia to be judged to have a thought disorder and mis-
diagnosed as schizophrenic. At the same time, the severe thought
disorder in primary autism was considered by some research
workers to reflect a severe developmental aphasia.

But it is evident with careful study that aphasic children, even
with very severe difficulties in naming or comprehending words,
can have otherwise normal cognitive functioning (Chess, 1944).
Autistic children have problems of behavior and communication
which cannot be designated as the consequences of aphasia (Wolff
and Chess, 1964; Wolff and Chess, 1965; Rutter, 1978; Cohen
et al., 1976). From his own studies of 50 years ago, Vygotsky
criticized the then common assumption of an identity of speech
and thought, asserted their separate ontogenetic roots, which then

intermeshed, "whereupon thought became verbal and speech rational" (1962, p. 44).

Recent research has documented this intimate interaction between language and thought, but not their identity. "Although these results are convincing evidence that language facilitates memory, thought and problem-solving, they do not demonstrate that language is necessary for these cognitive functions. For some children, other kinds of mediators—images, pictorial representations, or nonverbal symbols—may serve the purpose that words do for verbal children (Mussen et al., 1979). The lack of any simple one-to-one relationship between language and thought is dramatically evident in deaf children. Thus, Furth (1971), in an authoritative review of language and thought in deaf subjects, comments that "the general conclusion seems abundantly clear that thinking processes of deaf children are similar to hearing children" (p. 70), in spite of the fact that "with few exceptions persons profoundly deaf from birth are severely deficient in linguistic skills in spite of many years of schooling" (p. 58).

By contrast, attempts to teach sign language to nonverbal, autistic children have been disappointing (Cohen et al., 1976). Unlike the otherwise normal deaf child, the autistic child has some profound biological disturbance which distorts behavior, thought, and language. Sign language cannot circumvent this disorder, as it can the handicap of the deaf child.

Piaget has also emphasized the separateness of language and thought. For Piaget, as Flavel points out, "It is not the acquisition of language which gives rise to the symbolic function. . . . Thought is nonetheless far from being a purely verbal affair, neither in its fully formed state nor, above all, in its developmental origins." At the same time, Piaget does stress "the enormous role which a codified and socially shared linguistic system plays in the development of conceptual thinking" (Flavell, 1963, p. 155).

In contrast to the extensive research and theorizing devoted to the relationship between language and thought, little attention has been given to connection between language and emotion. This undoubtedly reflects the focus of developmental research on cognitive rather than emotional phenomena. And yet the relationship between language and emotion, as between language and thought, is indeed an intimate one. We use language to express our feelings and to hide them. The form and content of our language can heighten, diminish, or modify our feelings, as the poets know so well.

The interplay and association between disturbances in language and in emotions have always been a focus of interest for clinical psychiatrists and psychologists. Whether interpreted psychoanalytically or in terms of some other theoretical or empirical framework, a patient's speech patterns and emotionality provide valuable data for the practicing clinician. But for developmental psychology, the systematic study of language and emotion over time presents formidable unsolved conceptual and methodological issues. As discussed in the next chapter, reliable criteria for rating norms and changes in specific emotional states at sequential stages of development are much more difficult to establish than for language or cognitive processes. Promising explorations of these issues are in progress (Lewis and Rosenblum, 1978) and should create a basis for the systematic consideration of the role of emotion in language acquisition.

INDIVIDUAL DIFFERENCES IN LANGUAGE DEVELOPMENT

As with temperament and cognition, normal language acquisition and use are characterized by a wide range of individual differences. "Just as they vary in physical growth and temperament, children show substantial variation in their language development. For reasons of biological maturity as well as experience, children differ in the age at which they begin to talk, in the rate at which linguistic development proceeds, and in the strategies they may adopt at various stages of development. Marked individual differences are also reported in the prevalence of the typical errors that children make: phonological omissions and substitutions, overgeneralization of syntactic rules, and over- and under-extensions of word meanings" (deVilliers and deVilliers, 1978, p. 228).

Nelson (1973) has reported significant individual differences in the types of words children learn first. Some youngsters first learn and use words that name objects; others learn words for personal desires or aspects of social interaction. The first group Nelson has called *referential* children, the second *expressive* children. Other youngsters fit into a continuum between these two opposite categories. In a follow-up study, Nelson (1975) has reported that, at 30 months of age, the referential children in their language use appeared more concerned with objects and their properties, as contrasted to the interest of expressive children in people and their relationships. No reports of these children's language characteristics at later age periods are available.

It is a plausible supposition that these individual differences in language style, as well as others which remain to be identified, can exert a significant influence on the course of psychological development. Long-term longitudinal projects will undoubtedly be required, as with temperament studies, to test such a hypothesis.

SOCIOCULTURAL ISSUES

The ideology of "cultural deprivation" has postulated that lower-class children suffer from restricted language acquisition and consequent deficiencies in cognitive development. This presumed sequence is then offered as an explanation for the inferior achievement scores in language and verbal facility of lower-class children as compared to middle-class and upper-class children (Bernstein, 1961; Bereiter and Engleman, 1966).

Certainly there are evident differences in language use and development in middle- and upper-class children as compared to lower-class children. But differences between groups do not necessarily mean that one group has a deficit and the other an abundance of the quality at issue. As a number of linguists (Labov, 1970; Stewart, 1969; Baratz and Baratz, 1970; Houston, 1970) have pointed out, an ethnocentric bias lies behind the assumption that linguistic competence is synonymous with the development of standard English. They cite convincing data that lower-class black children have a fully ordered, fully structured language, different from standard English, to be sure, but not inferior. Careful studies of "Black English," for example, indicate that this presumably impoverished language is "a fully developed, highly structured system that is more than adequate for aiding in abstract thinking" (Baratz and Baratz, 1970, p. 49). And as Houston (1970) points out, "there is no such thing as a primitive language . . . some societies with unsophosticated technology have incredibly complex languages" (p. 51). Modern English is less highly inflected than Anglo-Saxon, but we do not regard our speech as inferior to Old English because we drop more of our noun endings to indicate case and our verb endings to indicate tense. Houston (1970) also points out that users of nonstandard English may have different styles or "registers" of language use, depending on the social context. Thus, in one of her own studies, black children in a rural area showed two distinct registers. One was used in school settings, with teachers, with other persons in authority, or with those engaged in studying the children. The characteristics of this "school" register "include most of the observations given as indications of disadvantaged fluency, notably foreshortened utterances, simplified syntax, and phonological hypercorrection. It should be added that the content expressed in this register tends to be rather limited and non-revelatory of the children's attitudes, feelings, and ideas" (pp. 952-953). Unfortunately, "most investigations and research carried out among these children involve situations in which the school register is almost certain to be used, especially when the children are black and the researcher is both white and unknown to them—and this register does give an impression of nonfluency and strange language use" (p. 953), but is in no way "representative of their linguistic competence" (p. 953). By contrast, these children, when not in the school setting, had a "non-school" register which showed a complete set of syntactic patterns normal for children their age. Their play involved "constant language games, verbal contests, and narrative improvisations far removed from language disability" (p. 953).

Labov (1970) reports similar findings in which a black boy's language in a constrained and formal interview situation appeared impoverished and inarticulate. When the situation was changed to a relaxed informal setting, with the boy's best friend present, the youngsters' speech became lively, vivid, with "no difficulty in using the English language to express themselves." Labov makes the cogent observation that "the social situation is the most powerful determinant of verbal behavior and that an adult must enter into the right social relationship with a child if he wants to find out what a child can do. This is just what many teachers cannot do" (p. 163).

This does not mean, as some have argued, that the lower-class child should not be taught standard English. On the contrary, failure to teach it is another form of discrimination. It is a sociolinguistic fact that in our society some forms of language are an impediment to academic success and securing employment. What must be challenged is the failure of social scientists and educators to recognize, respect, and utilize existing cultural forms of the lower-class black community. Otherwise, these differences are labeled as restricted language which is inadequate for abstract thinking and makes the lower-class child unprepared for education, a judgment which easily becomes a self-fulfilling prophecy (Thomas and Sillen, 1972).

OVERVIEW

This discussion of language has in no way attempted to review current data and concepts on the mechanisms or sequences of language acquisition. As important as those issues are, they are not germane to the central concern of this volume with the dynamics of development. Rather, we have emphasized the dialectical unity of the biological and the social, the active role of the child, the beginnings of language development in the neonate's patterns of communication with the caretaker, the intermeshing of language with thought and emotion, the individual differences in language style, the significance of task mastery and social competence as both an antecedent and a consequence of language acquisition, alternative developmental pathways in the deaf child, and the usefulness of the goodness of fit model in tracing the consequences of perceptual, cognitive and sociocultural difficulties in language acquisition and use. These issues are dramatically highlighted in the widespread and curious effects of developmental language problems, which serve to emphasize the crucial role of language in healthy human psychological development.

Chapter XI

Emotions and Thought

Traditionally, emotion and thought have been counterposed to each other as opposite, even contradictory attributes. In recent centuries, and into the present, rational thought has been most highly prized (what Kagan calls the "modern West's symbolic substitute for virtue" [1978, p. 20]) and philosophers like Kant and Spinoza have viewed strong emotions as a danger to the intellect. The emotionality of the creative artist is tolerated and excused as "artistic temperament," but not admired. Thought and

149

reason appear as unique human characteristics (as they are), flowering with the individual's maturation and life experience from childhood into adult life. Emotions, by contrast, appear to be shared with other animal species, and are already fully evident for the most part in childhood. Unlike reason, emotional maturation appears to involve learning control and restraint. (How often we reproach an adult's expression of passionate feelings with the injunction "Don't behave like a child.")

The dichotomy of emotion and thought is evident in the work of Freud and Piaget. Freud's focus was on emotional life, with only secondary attention to cognition. Piaget, on the other hand, has concentrated on the study of cognitive processes, with little concern for the role of emotions. Behaviorism, for its part, could not really fit either emotion or thought, with their basic subjective intrapsychic components, into its stimulus-response model. It is of further interest, given the tendency to prize thought over emotion, that Freud's studies of emotional phenomena derive largely from emotionally disordered and mentally ill individuals, while Piaget's data on cognitive processes come from the study of normal children.

The terms thought and cognition tend to be used synonymously, and will be in our discussion. Emotion and affect will also be used as synonyms. Various attempts have been made to distinguish mood from affect. Sroufe (1978) considers mood as "a more enduring affective state." In a review of the literature, Owens and Maxmen conclude that the definitions of mood, emotion, and affect have been unclear and show much confusion and considerable overlap. They suggest that the main distinction is that "inferences about affect usually pertain only to current observations," and, therefore, they view "mood as a disposition persisting over time" (1979, p. 99). It may thus be desirable to restrict the term "mood" to affects or emotions that are more than transient. (However, the new official psychiatric DSM-III system retains the term "affective disorders" for persistent mood disturbances.)

Conceptually and methodologically, emotion and thought are also on sharply different levels. Cognitive processes can be classified, labeled and rated quantitatively, subcategories defined, and developmental changes and sequential patterns identified and studied. Thus, there is Piaget's scheme of cognitive development which is carefully elaborated, with a systematic formulation of progressive age-stage development from simpler to more complex patterns of functioning. Each stage has been defined operationally, specific methods for identifying and rating each stage precisely elaborated, and the dynamics of transition from one stage to another identified. As another example, the processes involved in problem solving have been formulated on the basis of specific objective studies (Scheerer, 1963).

By contrast, the study of emotional attributes, their subcategories, their sequential age-stage characteristics, and the dynamics of evolution and change in their patterning have been impressionistic and speculative. Satisfactory and reliable objective methods of study and rating have been conspicuous by their absence. The same labels are applied to specific emotions in the preschool child, school-age child, adolescent and adult—joy, anger, pleasure, fear, etc.—and criteria are absent for their differentiation at successive developmental stages.

By the same token, there is no disagreement as to the vital significance of cognition for human psychological functioning, but there is a great range of opinion with regard to emotions. Thus, Izard, in his review of this issue, emphasizes the "wide range of scientific opinion regarding the nature and importance of the emotions" (1977, p. 1). He further points out that there are those who assert that definitions of emotion are confusing and lack explanatory power, should be discarded, and replaced by concepts of activation and arousal. At the opposite end of the spectrum are those who consider emotions as crucial determinants of motivated behavior. For example, Bleuler once stated that "affective influences play such a dominant role in psychopathology . . . that practically everything else is incidental" (cited in Cichetti and Sroufe, 1978, p. 311). Some maintain that emotions are only transient phenomena, others that there is no action without emotion. Some emphasize the role of emotions in psychopathology, others in normal behavioral functioning (Izard, 1977).

The lack of precision in the definition, evaluation, and ratings of emotion has been reflected in the paucity of systematic developmental studies. Edward Zigler states:

> Until the mid-1950s, American behaviorism held sway, and thought was considered by many to be a secondary phenomenon not worthy of investigation. . . . Indeed, it was considered bad form even to ask a child why he was doing what he was doing, since such "subjective reports" were considered highly suspect. . . . When enthusiasm for behaviorism waned, however, American researchers decided that thought and cognition were phenomena worthy of investigation, and Piaget in particular was discovered with a vengeance. . . . An inappropriately small amount of effort is being expended in illuminating the nature of emotional and motivational development. . . . Just as thought and cognition were considered unworthy of investigation by many child psychologists during the 40s, so emotional and motivational development became unworthy of investigation during the 60s (1973, p. 6).

INTERACTION OF EMOTION AND THOUGHT

To debate the relative importance of emotion and thought in psychological development appears as fruitless and irrelevant as the argument over heredity and environment. Both emotion and thought are basic attributes, which in the human being are intimately meshed in a dialectical unity. Every emotion has a cognitive component, and every thought is influenced by emotional factors. "Unfortunately, our tendency has been to separate the affective and cognitive domains from each other. Yet, we cannot separate the two, whether for study, or emphasis, or for instructional purposes. They are so integrally related that it makes no sense to talk about one independent of the other" (Gordon, 1975, p. 11).

However, there has been little systematic study of the interaction between affect and cognition (Cichetti and Sroufe, 1978). Again, the emphasis has been one-sided, in terms of cognition (Lewis and Rosenblum, 1978). Theories of emotion do, in the main, recognize cognitive aspects, but little attention has been given in cognitive theory to the role of affect. Lewis and Rosenblum propose an interactive model to correct this lopsided approach. "The relationship between cognition and affect is dependent on the point of entry into the observation. If, for example, one's observation starts with the cognition, then an affect will be seen as a consequence of this cognition. If, on the other hand, one starts with the detection of an affective response, cognition will appear to be a consequence of that affect. For us, neither is right; rather, there is a flow between both factors: affects giving rise to cognitions that give rise to new affects and in turn to new cognitions" (1978, p. 9).

Thus, the distress of many eight- to 12-month-old infants at separation from the primary caretaker is conceptualized by most investigators as having an emotional origin (Bowlby, 1969; Ainsworth and Bell, 1974). Kagan, however, has argued convincingly from the research data that the emotion of separation distress has a cognitive basis. "Our view is that distress to separation is the result of the new ability to generate a question or representation concerning the discrepant quality of the separation experience coupled with the temporary inability to resolve it" (1976, p. 189)'.

When we come to the more differentiated psychological traits of older children and adults, it is clear that both emotion and thought are involved in a mutually interactive process. Whether it is empathy or scorn, altruism or selfishness, benevolence or aggression, love or hate, cooperativeness or competitiveness, all involve definite emotions toward another person or persons and simultaneous thoughts about those persons. The feelings reinforce the ideas, and the ideas reinforce the feelings.

This intimate relationship between emotion and thought is strikingly evident in individuals with a cyclical manic-depressive pattern. To the best of our knowledge, the mood disturbances are primary, and most probably have a neurochemical basis. In the manic phase, the mood of elation and expansiveness is associated with ideas of grandiosity and expectation of great achievements. Reciprocally, if others do not share the manic's feelings and ideas, he easily develops paranoid ideas and feelings of irritability. In the depressed phase, ideas of guilt and self-derogation develop and then serve to deepen the depressed mood. Thus, whether manic or depressed, the special emotional state stimulates specific ideas, which in turn influence the mood and its expression.

A dramatic vignette to illustrate this intimate connection between emotion and thought comes from a personal communication from a young Frenchwoman. During World War II, she was a member of the French underground in Nazi-occupied France. She traveled one day by train, smuggling forged passports hidden in a basket of fruit. The Gestapo came through the train checking the passengers' belongings. If they had searched her basket she would have been doomed. For some reason, they passed her by. At the time she felt no anxiety. Ten years later, relating this experience at a New York dinner party, she was overwhelmed with severe anxiety. It was evident that during the actual experience her thoughts were completely focused on avoiding detection, hence no anxiety. At the dinner party, she was thinking of her extreme danger in the situation, hence the severe anxiety.

As indicated in the quotation from Zigler above, emotion and motivation tend to be linked and contrasted to thought. This undoubtedly reflects the influence of the psychoanalytic theory of instinctual drive states, which are goal-directed and also generate emotional states, whether directly or through the dynamics of conflict. Without question, motivations typically have an emotional component, in turn influencing emotions and are then influenced by them. A student with a strong motivation for learning and academic achievement will take great pleasure in her scholastic success and become frustrated and angry in relationship to indifferent and incompetent teachers. The enthusiasm and excitement generated by expansion of her intellectual horizons will in turn intensify her academic motivations. A young man caught up in a passionate love affair will be highly motivated in many ways in relationship to his beloved; success or difficulties in pursuing his goals will certainly influence his feelings directly and intensely.

However, a similar close interrelationship between motivation and thought is also evident. Ideas shape and modify goals; passionate ideas can become primary driving forces in the life of the individual. And there is nothing that can stimulate a person's thinking and ideas quite like the pursuit of a strongly desired goal. Whether it is the creative artist or scientist determined to master the project which absorbs him, the parents concerned for the welfare of their children, the student or young adults pursuing his ambitious goals, the adolescent looking for acceptance in the peer group, or the child trying to master reading or a new athletic activity—emotion, thought, and motivation are always involved, intermeshed with each other and mutually interactive.

ORIGINS OF EMOTION AND THOUGHT

In line with the basic thrust of our developmental concepts, we look to the beginnings of both emotion and thought in the newborn infant. Social relatedness and task mastery begin at birth and both these goals always have affective and cognitive components. The emotional aspect of the young infant's psychological functioning is evident in his overt behavior—he cries, he smiles, he grimaces and spits out some new foods, he startles at a sudden loud noise, he squirms and twists when forcibly restrained to change his diaper. By contrast, the very young infant appears to lack any cognitive activity. Thus, for Piaget, in the first month of life "the child shows little besides the reflexes with which he is provided at birth" (Flavell, 1963, p. 88). The Papouseks, however, point out that operant conditioning studies have demonstrated learning in the neonate, and can also be considered as problem-solving situations. "The integration of muscular activity may well be analogous to or may be one of the real bases for cognitive integration of single experiences and perceptions" (1975, p. 248).

In Piaget's developmental scheme, cognitive processes may be said to begin in the second month of life, when the infant begins to coordinate and integrate sensory data and motor experiences through the complementary processes of "assimilation" and "accommodation" (Flavell, 1963). Thus, Piaget calls this period extending through the second year of life, the stage of *sensorimotor intelligence*. Piaget's data for this conceptualization of the early stage of cognitive development come almost entirely from his detailed observations of his own three children, and lack precision as to the dynamic mechanisms involved. Kagan (1971, 1972) has reported extensive cognitive studies in infancy, from which he has formulated certain dynamic concepts. He emphasizes the ability of the young infant, from birth on, to give selective attention to objects showing stimulus contrast or changes. By the second month the infant begins to acquire mental representations of events, which Kagan calls "schemata." (Piaget uses the term *schema* differently, to connote action sequences, such as the schema of sucking, of prehension, of sight, etc. [Flavell, 1963, p. 53].)

Kagan enunciates what he calls "the discrepancy principle: events that are moderately different from an infant's schema elicit longer spans of attention than either totally familiar events or totally novel events" (1972, p. 74). If the infant can cope with the discrepant event by assimilation of the new stimulus, successful mastery of the event occurs. If this is not possible, the infant is likely to become fearful. Kagan makes the generalization that "the greater the variability of the varying environment, the less vulnerable to fear the organism will be when discrepant events are encountered. A highly variable environment provides the organism with discrepant experiences, permits the development of a set for discrepancy, and furnishes opportunities to learn ways of coping with it" (1971, p. 9). Kagan further reports data showing that the infant's duration of attention to masklike representations of a human shows a U-shaped curve from two to 36 months. From two to nine months the attention time decreases as the schemata for a face matures and the mask becomes less discrepant. However, at nine months this changes, and from then to 36 months the duration increases. Kagan found this sequence true not only for American children, but for samples of Guatemalan and rural African children. To explain the U-shaped curve, Kagan postulated the emergence at nine months of a "new cognitive structure or hypothesis. We call this presumed structure a hypothesis. The child, we suggest, tries to mentally transform the discrepant event into the form with which he is familiar, the familiar form being the schema" (1972, p. 78).

Kagan finds further support for this postulate in the specifics of separation distress from the primary caretaker that many infants in varied cultures exhibit between eight and 15 months. Kagan suggests that so-called separation anxiety reflects the infant's ability to conceptualize "hypotheses that cannot be resolved involving the immediate future. What will happen to me? Will my parents return? What will the stranger do?" (1972, p. 80).

If Kagan's formulation is correct, it would indicate that by nine months of age or thereabouts the young infant has already developed the capacity for symbolic thought. This would place the beginning of this special human cognitive capacity long before Piaget's formulation. Wolff also makes this same issue: "Research over the past 20 years has demonstrated that the newborn infant is far better equipped with prefunctional mechanisms ('reflex schemata') to perceive the physical, linguistic and social world than Piaget's description of the sensorimotor phase would lead one to suspect" (1978, p. 259).

In Kagan's formulation, if the infant is presented with an environmental change in the form of a discrepant schema, assimilation and cognitive growth occur if the discrepancy is not extreme. If the discrepancy is marked, distress, which can also be categorized as excessive stress, ensues. This is in keeping with our own formulation of goodness and poorness of fit and consonance and dissonance.

Thus, the emergence and development of cognition in the young infant have been the subject of extensive systematic and productive study. By contrast, the analysis of emotional categories, which appear so much more obvious and striking in the young infant's behavior, has proven much more difficult. "Too often psychologists' attempts to pin down the age of onset of various emotional reactions have led to tedious exercises in operational definition, controversies over terminology, disputed results, and, all too frequently, dismissal of the very construct under study" (Cichetti and Sroufe, 1978, p. 345). Psychoanalytic formulations of emotional development have not provided a useful model for systematic studies, because of their reliance on hypothetical, untestable constructs such as libido and id, and the commingling of affect and motivation in the concept of drive states. Paradoxically, while on the surface an emotion may appear clear and evident, it is actually a complex phenomenon. It comprises at least three aspects: "a) the experience or conscious feeling of emotion; b) the processes that occur in the brain and nervous system; and c) the observable expressive patterns of emotion, particularly those on the face" (Izard, 1977, p. 4). The relationship to cognition is intimate, and Kagan proposes that "affect is a phenomenon that emerges from the operation of cognition on information" (1978, p. 31). He further suggests that "the term *emotion,* like the concept *weather,* must be analyzed if it is to have any meaning" (1978, p. 38). In a similar vein, Sroufe cautions against "endless argument and confusion about when various affective reactions emerge (or throwing out affective concepts entirely)" and recommends a strategy of being able "to say by what criteria, at different developmental points, can we say an infant is afraid or is capable of anxiety, or is capable of moods" (1978).

A DEVELOPMENTAL APPROACH TO EMOTION

Our ability to construct developmental sequences in the infant and young child for any psychological category involves inferences from observable behavior. For emotion this requires a higher order of inference than for other categories. Thus, by contrast, criteria for levels of neuromotor functioning can start with the reflex patterns of the neonate, and proceed to increasingly complex phenomena of muscle coordination and control, fine movements, etc., all of which can be objectively and precisely defined.

Perceptual criteria can start with fixation and habituation responses to simple stimuli and proceed to the measurement of responses to increasingly complex ones. The development of speech can be traced from the characteristics of the earliest babbling, to word recognition and expression, to increasingly complex mastery of language. Cognitive criteria can begin with conditioning in the neonate, proceed to the identification of Kagan's schemata, then to the task performance and problem-solving items used by Piaget, starting with the earliest sensorimotor level and proceeding to the more complex levels of cognitive functioning.

For emotion, on the other hand, we cannot as of now construct such a developmental sequence based on precise objective behavioral data. Emotions are categorized by adults in terms of feelings states linked with specific cognitive meanings. The labels become subdivided and refined with increasing self-awareness and cognitive sophistication. Happiness becomes contentment, gladness, joy, delight, exultation, ecstasy. Anger becomes annoyance, displeasure, distaste, hatred, outrage, fury. But the identification of these emotions requires self-report or report to others of a combination of subjective feeling and cognitive state, supplemented by inferences from facial expression, tone of voice, and gestures. These data are even at best inexact, and lack the preciseness and objectivity of information on neuromotor, perceptual or cognitive functioning.

For the infant we do not and cannot have even these reports of subjective feeling and cognitive state. His developmental level and limited life experience do not give the basis for the elaboration of complex emotions. In the very young infant the objective data consist of vocal, facial and body movement expressions of positive or negative moods. From these we can infer the existence of subjective distress or comfort (Dunn, 1977), as the first emotional states in the neonate. As learning proceeds, starting at birth, these simple emotions quickly become selective and differentiated. By six weeks of age, many crying babies will not be comforted when picked up by a stranger, but will stop crying and snuggle as soon as the mother does so. By six months, the elaboration of mood has progressed much further. Here is a mother's report of her daughter's expressiveness at that age: "When I am dressing Winnie after her bath, she may look toward the door and start to kick her legs, reach her arms up and gurgle. I know she must have recognized the sound of the front door opening, or heard footsteps, because sure enough her father comes into the room and starts tossing her up in the air. It's a daily game." This description bespeaks a complex pattern of positive mood expression with a well-defined cognitive element.

Overall, emotional development from infancy onward can be characterized in two ways. Initial simple emotions become increasingly differentiated and elaborated, and new, complex emotions appear. The global label attached to emotions ignores the first developmental issue. Terms such as pleasure, distress, joy, anger, fun, etc., are all too often applied to animals, to four-month-old infants, to adolescents, and to adults without consideration of the qualitative differences in the meaning of these labels at different developmental stages. The three-year-old who is angry at his mother for refusing him ice icream may threaten "I'll cut you up and flush you down the toilet." Is the anger expressed in that outburst the same as that of the frustrated adolescent or the injured adult who threatens violent reprisal? We call all of them anger, yet they are manifestly not identical. For cognition, we have differentiated categories that reflect differences at successive developmental stages, thanks to the work of Piaget, Bruner, Kagan and others. For emotion, we do not have a comparable systematic scheme to distinguish differences in emotional states with the same labels developmentally. Until we do, we must at least not confuse identity of label with identity of meaning.

New complex emotions that appear as learning and cognitive development proceed are readily distinguished from earlier simpler affects. Pride and guilt as they begin to crystallize in the preschool period are clearly different from the pleasure or distress of the young infant. Still other emotions with a highly developed cognitive component, such as empathy, may not appear until middle childhood or adolescence. But here, too, no systematic study of the developmental sequences involved in the formation and expression of complex emotions has been reported. For the time being, we have to be content with empirical and impressionistic formulations. The same was true for considerations of cognition before Piaget opened the way to systematic analytic studies, both conceptually and methodologically.

TEMPERAMENT AND EMOTION

Gordon (1973) has suggested that temperament, as we have defined and categorized it, can be considered as the individual style of emotional or affective response tendency. His term, "affective response tendencies/temperament" emphasizes this close relationship between temperament and affect. In this connection our nine categories of temperament can be subdivided empirically as follows:

1) Categories in which emotion is expressed directly. These include approach/withdrawal, quality of mood, and intensity of reaction.
2) Categories which influence emotion directly. These include activity level, adaptability, and sensory threshold.
3) Categories which influence emotion indirectly. These include distractibility and persistence/attention span. The ease of distractibility may in many instances affect the ease with which an extraneous environmental stimulus produces an emotional response.

The persistent individual who succeeds in a difficult task will have a positive emotional response. Interference from the outside with such persistent activity may cause intense emotional reactions of frustration. The individual with low persistence and short attention span will usually tolerate such interference with mild or no frustration. It is also a plausible speculation that persistence and distractibility may be related to the ease or difficulty with which an emotional state will take hold or be transient.

The prolonged involvement with an activity or idea of the persistent, non-distractible individual may permit stable long-term linkage of the accompanying emotion with that activity or idea, which may not occur as easily with the shorter involvement of the non-persistent, highly distractible person.

The ninth temperamental category—rhythmicity of biological functions—does not show an obvious relationship to emotion. It may be possible that the degree of rhythmicity may be an expression of degree of ease of physiological habituation, which in turn could be related to ease in development of a consistent pattern of emotional response. The available data are insufficient to test this speculation.

It appears a reasonable hypothesis that the origins of temperament may be closely related to the origins of emotion. Also, it is not unlikely that temperament may play a significant role in the evolution of specific emotional patterns in the course of psychological development. Systematic data, however, are not at hand to test these hypotheses or to formulate them operationally.

GLOBAL MISJUDGMENTS OF EMOTION

All too frequently, the empirical and impressionistic rating of emotion leads to global characterizations. Individuals are given an emotional label which is presumed to typify their behavior in any and all situations. The "angry" person is angry at all times, the "kindly" individual can always be counted on to be benevolent, "selfishness" is a general trait, the "hostile" mother always feels that way toward her child, etc.

Personality characteristics in general, no matter how stable and enduring, can never be characterized globally. An individual's behavior, thinking, and emotions will vary from situation to situation, depending on its meaning to him, his goals, past experiences, and coping mechanisms. This is most certainly true of emotions and their expression. Someone may always appear angry or on the edge of anger to his co-workers and subordinates, but ingratiating and pleasant to his superiors, and thoughtful and charming to the woman he is courting. A mother may be indulgent or indifferent to her child's behavior in certain settings, but forceful and demanding in others. The violent adolescent may have generalized aggressive antisocial emotions and ideas, or he may not (Chess, 1953). A case vignette from our own experience illustrates this issue vividly. A 16-year-old boy from a slum area came to the mental hygiene clinic at his mother's request. His younger brother was already being treated at this clinic. The older boy had been arrested during gang practice with zipguns for an expected war, and placed on probation for six months. At the clinic he expressed appreciation for the remedial and psychiatric services being given his younger brother, who would thereby be spared his own history of school failure. As for himself, he faced a dilemma for which there was no help. His probation required that he not carry a weapon. But if unarmed on his neighborhood streets, he would have to step aside and let other youths have the right of way, something his pride would not allow him to do. His only solution, therefore, was to stay out of sight in his own apartment so as to avoid such a confrontation with members of other gangs. But in doing so, he could not get to school and back, and he was concerned that he would be arrested for breaking parole because of failure to attend school. He rejected the offers for help from the clinic staff as impractical. His hope was that if he could somehow survive his parole period without landing in jail, he could enlist in the army and learn a useful trade as soon as he became 17. (As it turned out, the school was indifferent to his absence, an all too typical situation in city slum schools. He completed his parole uneventfully and enlisted in the army, where perhaps he gained the education and training the school system had failed to provide.)

Certainly, this adolescent boy was capable of positive emotions which he could experience and express in relation to certain people and settings. His feelings toward his mother and brother were empathic and affectionate; his gratitude to the clinic for the help given to his brother was real; his sorrow at his own fate was poignant. Yet, had the gang war gone on as scheduled, he would have engaged in violent, aggressive behavior with no sense of guilt. As with so many individuals, whatever their age or position in life, this youngster's emotional characteristics could not be reified with some general abstract label.

It is thus unrealistic to expect that an individual's "typical" affect can be tapped by observation of behavior in a single setting or by responses to a single questionnaire. For each situation one might even obtain a consistent and durable categorization of affect, but one could then only be justified in concluding that the affect was typical in that setting and interactive sequence.

Cognitive Consistency and Change

The search for simple linear models that can predict later outcome from early childhood data has influenced many cognitive studies. Researchers have sought measures of infant development that would predict later intellectual functioning. The IQ score has been reified into a fixed entity, leading to reports that 50 percent of a child's intelligence is developed by the age of four (Bloom, 1964). Children raised in institutions have been thought to suffer irreversible cognitive damage (Bowlby, 1951; Goldfarb, 1945). Ethologists and others have asserted that there are "critical periods" in early childhood in which learning must take place if the child is to reach his full intellectual potential. White (1975) has made the sweeping generalization that the capacity for intellectual achievement is irrevocably fixed in the first three years of life.

Again, as with overall behavioral development, the weight of research challenges conclusively these attempts to find linear predictive models for cognition. Infant tests are not reliable predictors of later intellectual levels (Lewis and McGurk, 1972; McCall et al., 1972). "The data are strong in their denial of simple continuity of general precocity at one age with general precocity at another age during the infancy period. . . . Moreover, to label as 'mental,' performances at every age perpetuates the belief in a pervasive and developmentally constant intelligence. . . . The network of transitions between skills at one age and another is likely more specific and complex than once thought, and not accurately subsumed under one general concept" (McCall et al., 1977, p. 745).

Hindley and Owen (1978) report that in a British long-term study of 109 subjects from varied social backgrounds, between three and 17 years, the IQ scores of 50 percent of the sample changed by 10 points or more, and in 25 percent by 22 points or more. Between eight and 17 years the changes were almost as widespread, and from infancy even greater. The findings are similar to those from an earlier California study (Pinneau, 1961).

Tizard and Rees (1974) found no evidence of cognitive retardation, verbal or otherwise, in a group of four-year-old children institutionalized since early infancy. At age two the children were somewhat retarded; by age four and one-half years, this retardation had disappeared. Those children adopted at three years into middle-class families showed the greatest improvement; next came those still in the institution. Least improved, though still significantly better, were those returned at three years to their own working-class mothers and homes with adverse living conditions. Winick et al. (1975) have reported a study of 141 Korean children placed for adoption in the United States before two years of age, of whom 42 were rated as malnourished, 52 moderately nourished and 47 well-nourished. At school age, all three groups had surpassed the expected mean for Korean children in both height and weight. The mean IQ of the originally malnourished group was 102, of the middle group, 106, and of the originally well-nourished group 112. Academic achievement scores were similar to those for IQs. Thus, the effects of early malnutrition produced no permanent impairment of intellectual functioning, when overcome by the environmental enrichment resulting from adoption.

As to the concept of critical periods, Wolff sums up a review of the pertinent evidence: "In conclusion, we state with some assurance that there is no evidence for biologically fixed critical periods of cognitive development . . . and no evidence that acceleration in the acquisition of specific sensorimotor skills augments the child's ultimate intellectual attainment" (1970, p. 87). For cognition, as for emotions, language, or behavior, there is no magical period in which the individual's fate is decided. It would indeed be most disadvantageous for the human being from an evolutionary adaptive viewpoint if such an irrevocable period did exist. Magic can cut both ways, and the child's future would be settled by a toss of the dice.

"Primary Process Thinking"

A special categorization of thought processes made by Freud has had a significant role in psychoanalytic formulations of the dynamics of psychological development. This concept of primary process versus secondary process thinking was proposed by Freud in one of his earliest and most important works, *The Interpretation of Dreams* (1900). Primary process thinking in this formulation occurs unconsciously, as opposed to secondary process thinking which occurs consciously and is reality-oriented. Unconscious thought, to Freud, was primary, because it reflected the activity of the id which he designated as "the core of our being" (1949, p. 108). Primary process thinking is expressed most clearly in dreams, with the characteristics of "condensation," "displacement," and absence of logical thinking. "Impulses with contrary aims exist side by side in the unconscious without any call being made for an adjustment between them" (1949, p. 53). Primary process thinking is concerned with the satisfaction of instinctual drives, irrespective of logic and reality. It is the ego and logical secondary process thinking which keep these primitive primary processes under control and maintain a rational orientation toward reality.

Freud developed his formulation of primary process thinking as an explanation of dream characteristics. In line with his theory of dream states, primary process thinking was linked integrally with instinctual drive states. The illogical, primitive, cognitive characteristics he postulated for primary processes were congruent with his description of the primitive asocial emotional characteristics of these unconscious id drives. With his own prime focus on emotional phenomena, Freud did not pursue the study of cognition beyond his formulation. "Although Freud discovered the primary process, he did not pursue the study of the cognitive mechanism of the primary process" (Arieti, 1975, p. 233).

As can be seen with this formulation, almost any severe thought disturbance can be explained as the result of the weakening of secondary process controls and the emergence of primary process thinking. And, indeed, one finds the term "primary process thinking" used freely and loosely in all kinds of psychiatric case discussions, even though some psychoanalysts do state that "the study of unconscious or primary process mentation is a complex matter and highly conjectural" (Lidz, 1968, p. 252).

If the development of cognition is approached as a social reality-oriented process from birth onward, as Piaget, Bruner, Kagan and others have done, then irrational reality-disoriented thinking can in no way be considered "primary." Rather, such disturbances in thinking are *secondary,* that is the reflection of some underlying psychopathological process. Irrational, disturbed ideation can thus have many causes and its significance will vary with the nature of the psychopathology which produces it. Such disturbed thought processes must also be distinguished from the special characteristics of thinking expressed in normal dreaming and normal fantasy.

The terms "primary process" and "secondary process" thinking derive from and require the theoretical concepts of an id and of basic instinctual drive states. The terms also offer an appearance of an explanation for pathological thought processes, when in fact they obscure the need for systematic specific analysis of each constellation of abnormal ideation. No benefit can ensue from maintaining these terms, and their use should be abandoned.

In summary, it appears from the research evidence that emotional and cognitive development begin at birth. Both are crucially involved in the growth of social competence and task mastery. Much more is known of the dynamics and sequential stages of cognitive as compared to emotional development. It is clear that emotion and thought evolve through a continuous interactive process with each other and with all other influential factors in psychological development. Consideration of one without the other can lead to mechanical simplistic formulations. As an example, in education it can lead to the view of the child as "some sort of disembodied cognitive system" (Zigler, 1973) or to a preoccupation with emotional communication which deprives the child of the essential experience of successful mastery of cognitive tasks (Gordon, 1975).

For emotion and cognition, as for behavior in general, there are no magical periods where relationships, experiences, and events are all-decisive for subsequent development. Each age-period is important, and can contribute positively or negatively to emotional and cognitive growth.

Chapter XII

Defense
Mechanisms

A major contribution of the psychoanalytic movement to developmental theory has been the identification and analysis of psychodynamic defense mechanisms. These mechanisms often play a significant role in both normal and deviant psychological development.

Defense mechanisms can be defined operationally as behavioral strategies which attempt to cope with stress or conflict which the

169

individual cannot or will not master directly. This definition does not assume, as Freud did, that defense mechanisms are necessarily unconscious. Nor does it assume any a priori theoretical formulations of the ontogenesis of stress and conflict. Thus, although derived originally from psychoanalytic theory and practice, the concept of defense mechanisms, as here defined, can be used in the analysis of behavioral dynamics independently of the psychoanalytic framework.

Specific defense mechanisms can also be defined operationally and identified by simple inference from empirical data, again without commitment to any one theoretical scheme. *Suppression-repression* represents the attempt to extinguish feelings or ideas; *denial,* the posture that the stressful environmental demands are really insignificant and unnecessary of attention; *avoidance,* the detachment from the stressful situation; *reaction formation,* the attempt to cope by transforming the motivation into its opposite; *rationalization,* the ascription of a socially acceptable motive to behavior which has other motivations; *displacement,* the involvement with a less meaningful but less stressful object or situation than the one at issue; *projection,* the ascription of motives, feelings, or ideas to others that are really one's own; and *fantasy,* the retreat into intrapsychic thoughts and feelings as a substitute for confronting external reality. *Sublimation,* or avoidance through a socially desirable activity, and *humor* are generally more constructive defense strategies. *Delusional thinking,* the reconstruction of reality to eliminate stress and threat, usually occurs in severe mental illness. Fantasy and humor are not always defensive maneuvers; they may even be prominent features of healthy and creative functioning.

Some professionals argue that, inasmuch as the original formulation of defense mechanisms was developed in the psychoanalytic movement, the term should only be used by those committed to that theoretical position. To do so would require inventing a new label for the phenomenon. It seems to us preferable to retain the term defense mechanism with its clear operational meaning, rather than to proselytize for some neologism.

Direct Mastery Versus Defensive Strategies

We have postulated that social competence and task mastery represent the basic goals of psychological functioning. Furthermore, the achievement of these interrelated goals at any age-period depends on the goodness of fit between organism and environment—that is, the consonance between the capacities and abilities of the individual and the demands, expectations and opportunities presented by the environment. Where such consonance exists, growth of social competence and age-appropriate task mastery is possible by direct interaction between individual and environment. Of course, goodness of fit and consonance are rarely global. The pattern of organism-environment interaction at any age-period in any individual is most likely to show striking consonance in some areas, partial consonance in others, and varying degrees of dissonance in other areas.

From infancy onward, the human being is faced with demands for social and task mastery; positive adaptation necessarily creates a certain degree of stress. The psychologically healthy individual can tolerate this stress and engage directly in the effort required for new mastery, without resorting to any defensive strategies. The success of his efforts increases his sense of competency and self-esteem and adds one more experience to the awareness that stress can be a desirable challenge and not a dangerous threat.

Even where the new demands and expectations are only partially consonant or even somewhat dissonant with capacities, and the stress is therefore greater, direct mastery and positive adaptation are still often possible. These are the situations in which the individual's direct engagement with the issue results in sufficient modification of the environmental demand or growth of his capacity, or both, so that direct mastery and positive adaptation can occur. For example, a boy with clumsiness of neuromuscular development may find that he cannot meet the expectations of his peer group as a ball player. However, he may stick to the group in spite of their initial criticisms and teasings, practice assiduously on the side with a parent or older sib, improve gradually, gain the respect of his peers as they appreciate his determined efforts and improvement, until he finally becomes an accepted and modestly competent member of the ball team. Here again, the successful achievement enhances self-esteem and a confidence that successful direct struggle is possible even when the stress is substantial.

Where the dissonance is severe, however, and the stress correspondingly greater, direct mastery is not possible unless the level of demand and expectation is modified to bring it within the scope of the individual's capacities. If not modified, however, the excessive stress and impossibility of direct mastery make resort to one defensive strategy or another likely. This may happen for many reasons: dysphasia, dyslexia, temperament-environment dissonance, academic demands which are beyond an individual's intellectual abilities, overwhelming environmental stress, severe distortions of brain functioning. There are also many occasions in which an individual may have the capacity to cope directly and effectively with the new demand, yet fails to do so, and turns instead to some defensive strategy. This may happen for various reasons. Thus, certain past experiences may have created a conditioned response that any stress is dangerous. Or the demand may be presented by parent, teacher, or employer in an ambiguous or confusing form. As another example, the kind of effort required to master the demand may appear, rightly or wrongly, to alienate the individual from his peer group.

PSYCHOANALYTIC VIEW OF DEFENSE MECHANISMS

Our concept of the ontogenesis of defense mechanisms, as formulated in the preceding section, contrasts fundamentally with the psychoanalytic view. As stated, our position is that the basic positive adaptive interaction between individual and environment involves direct, appropriate, successful response to a new environmental demand or opportunity, without the need to resort to any defensive strategy. This is true whether it is the one-year-old who begins to feed himself, the two-year-old who brings his bowel movements under his conscious control, the three-year-old who begins to learn the rules of social interchange and play with his peer group, the six-year-old who begins to master reading, the adolescent who develops competence in sexual functioning, the young adult who experiences mature love, or the older adult who translates his moral, ethical, and career goals into reality. Defense mechanisms need not arise unless these and other sequential struggles for social competence and task mastery become frustrated, inhibited, the source of severe stress and anxiety, or unless the direct struggle appears too difficult or dangerous.

For Freud, on the contrary, all psychological development, whether healthy or pathological, necessarily involved the operation of defense mechanisms. The core of the psyche, in his view, consists of primitive instinctual id impulses (1949, p. 108). Freud described the id as "a chaos, a cauldron of seething excitement . . . the id knows no values, no good or evil, no morality. . . . The laws of logic—above all, the law of intradiction—do not hold for processes in the id" (1933, pp. 104-105). Socialization involves the constant struggle to control, neutralize and counteract this "seething cauldron." The process of development, therefore, inevitably involves defensive strategies to deal with id impulses, and these defenses are required for desirable positive psychological attributes to emerge. "The multifariously perverse sexual disposition of childhood can accordingly be regarded as the source of a number of our virtues, insofar as through reaction-formation it stimulates their development" (1964, pp. 238-239). Id impulses, for Freud, did not disappear, and therefore defensive strategies were essential throughout life. (In one of his last papers, "Analysis, Terminable and Interminable" [1937] Freud explained the problem of achieving a completely successful psychoanalytic treatment in terms of these ever-present id impulses.)

Thus, commitment to this psychoanalytical theoretical scheme denies the possibility that healthy psychological development with positive sequential growth in social competence and task mastery can be achieved by the direct utilization of capacities and abilities. Rather, from this viewpoint, positive adaptation requires the mediating influences of psychodynamic defense mechanisms. In healthy development, the use of more socially constructive defenses may be postulated than in maladaptive development, but *defensive* strategies remain all the same. The surgeon is a sublimated sadist; the gifts of the gentle philanthropist result from reaction formation against hostile, aggressive impulses; the passionate lover is displacing his oedipal fixation, and so on.

That we are not splitting hairs in making this issue, or setting up a straw man, can be seen by a consideration of George Vaillant's recent volume, *Adaptation to Life* (1977). In this volume, he summarizes the findings of the Harvard Grant Study, in which 95 Harvard graduates of the classes of 1942-1944 were studied intensively in their college years, and then followed for 30 years. He reports many findings of great interest: isolated traumas of childhood do not shape the future; life courses show many discontinuities; adaptive patterns change; linear predictability of adult development is not possible; retrospective explanations are filled with distortions; and development and change continue throughout adult life (p. 29). However, with his commitment to psychoanalytic theory, Vaillant conceptualizes the dynamics of development in terms of defense mechanisms. "Health is adaptation. . . . The terms *adaptation* and *defense* will be used interchangeably" (p. 13). Altruism becomes an "adaptive outgrowth of reaction formation, a defense mechanism that allows a user outwardly to steer a course exactly counter to some inner unconscious passion" (p. 110). "Sublimation . . . permits the counterfeit fantasies . . . to achieve real currency in everyday life. The artist is a man who can peddle his own most private dreams to others" (p. 101). "Con men, demagogues, and the great seducers of legend all deploy immature defenses to their short-term advantage" (p. 161).

DYNAMICS OF DEFENSE MECHANISMS

To challenge the thesis that all healthy adaptations are the product of defensive strategies does not mean we must adopt an opposite position, as some have done (Haan, 1963), that the use of defensive mechanisms is necessarily maladaptive and unhealthy.

An individual may at one time or another be faced with excessively stressful demands or conflicts which cannot be mastered directly. This may evoke the temporary utilization of a defensive strategy, which then gives the person the opportunity to resolve the stress positively. "In these situations it would appear that the use of the defense mechanism is necessary to organize the strengths and capacities needed for successful mastery" (Chess and Thomas, 1976). Thus, for example, an adolescent with the slow-to-warm-up temperament may experience his typically uncomfortable, shy response in joining a new peer group. He may rationalize his initial peripheral and outwardly detached involvement with the group by various excuses (he is worried about a friend who is ill, he has a sprained ankle, he has to get home early, etc.) and gain the time necessary to make his gradual positive adaptation. Or a woman in a new job may encounter blatant sexist attitudes in her co-workers and supervisors, suppress her anger, even perhaps displace it on to her family, wait until she has established her position securely, and then challenge these derogatory expressions and actions directly.

A defense mechanism may also serve an adaptive purpose over long periods of time, though usually at some cost. A man may allay the threat and anxiety of a serious chronic illness in himself or in a member of his family by denying the reality that no effective treatment for the illness exists. His continual search for a new remedy, for a new physician who promises a cure, will take its toll in time, energy, and repeated disappointments, but permit him to pursue his life activities without crippling anxiety. Or a man may be preoccupied with a fierce competitive drive, which makes his attitude to any competent co-worker potentially explosively jealous and hostile. He may attenuate or even eliminate these feelings by projecting them onto his co-workers, who are then seen as the jealous and competitive personalities. This paranoid defensive strategy will enable this individual to maintain his psychological equilibrium and work effectiveness, but at the cost of social and emotional alienation from many, if not all, people.

At times, the price paid for the achievement of psychological equilibrium through a defensive strategy is so high that it must be challenged at all costs. Thus, a child with a school phobia may avoid the anxiety of school attendance by the elaboration of various somatic symptoms. The child may be completely comfortable if not attending school, with no physical complaints and with active pursuit of friendships and other activities—but incapable of returning to school without severe acute anxiety. In such a case, this pattern of adaptation has so many serious consequences that it must be treated as a psychiatric emergency.

Finally, there are the instances in which a defense mechanism, no matter how strongly and decisively it is utilized, fails to achieve or sustain a state of psychological equilibrium. The disequilibrium which results may find expression in a panic state, acute dissociative state, severe depression, or behavioral disorganization.

Choice of Defense Mechanisms

Thus, defense mechanisms may play very different roles in different individuals and in the same individual at different times or different situations. As with all factors that influence psychological functioning, defense mechanisms always operate as one element in the sequential interactional process that determines the course of development.

This variability of defense mechanisms in importance, continuity, and consistency has been strikingly evident as we have reviewed the longitudinal data of our NYLS subjects from early infancy to early adult life. A substantial number have a consistent life history thus far of successful direct task mastery and growth in social competence at every age-period. At no time did symptoms of behavior disorder appear, and at no time did these youngsters resort to any defensive strategies. They were always characterized by parents, teachers and our staff interviewers and observers as functioning maturely and adapting positively, whether in infancy, preschool and school-age periods, at adolescence, or now as young adults. At the same time they are now distinctly individual personalities, with different goals and life-styles. In some of this group, family relationships were benign and without significant stress or conflict. In others, however, substantial, and in some cases serious, parental discord or excessive parental pressures were prominent. The youngsters were caught up in the resulting stress and conflict, but had the ability to face the issues directly and openly without defensive strategies. Resolution of these conflicts occurred either through change in parental functioning or the achievement of emotional independence by the youngster in adolescence, or both.

At the other extreme is the group with severe behavior disorders in which various defense mechanisms were actively utilized. One young man, who had been unable to meet rigid and excessive parental expectations since childhood, developed by adolescence a progressively negative self-image, hopelessness about attaining any worthwhile goal, and deterioration in social and school functioning. His openly expressed self-derogation and hopelessness were his prominent defensive strategies. In the past few years, however, this has changed. If anything, his functioning as a young adult is even more marginal, but his defense mechanism now is that of extreme denial. He asserts, in spite of all the evidence to the contrary, that he has no personal problems, his relationship with his parents is positive, a good job which will launch his career is in the offing.

A comment is in order on the personality characteristic of *hopelessness*—in this young man and in general. The hopelessness reflected the life experiences which have led to this adolescent's judgment and self-evaluation that he was incapable of successful mastery of any new environmental demand or expectation. Once formulated, it also became a defensive strategy, a rationalization to avoid engaging in the struggle to cope with any new life situation, a struggle which he anticipated could lead only to anxiety, pain, frustration, and the ignomy of a new failure. This defense mechanism, as is so often the case with defensive strategies, thus served as a self-fulfilling prophecy. With his hopelessness, he responded to any new demand either with complete avoidance or token effort, guaranteeing the failure which he had predicted ahead of time.

However, a derogatory self-image and a defensive posture of hopelessness are not the inevitable outcome of poorness of fit between capacity and demand, with severe stress and failure. Some of the youngsters in the NYLS group, and others we have seen in other settings, responded to such a dissonant interactive process by a realistic appraisal that their abilities were insufficient to achieve the goal, that "they had bitten off more than they could chew," gave up the effort without a sense of overall defeat, and redirected their energies and goals into directions where successful mastery was achieved. In such instances, the initial failure actually contributed to the growth of a positive self-image, through the realization that a failure was not disastrous, that they could "roll with the punches" and come back to other new challenges productively and effectively. In some cases, the youngster could master this difficult sequence on his own, in other instances he required help from parent, teacher, or therapist. Why one individual could respond with this positive adaptation to failure, and another sink into despair, even with help, is a most important issue for developmental theory for which there is as yet no simple answer.

As examples of this kind of variability in development: One young woman, who had functioned well in childhood without the need for defensive strategies, developed a severe problem of impulse control in adolescence, with projection and denial mechanisms very much in evidence. A young man with substantial perinatal brain damage, though with good intelligence, has had severe stress through life because of dyslexia, motor clumsiness, and lack of social competence. He never avoided issues, no matter how difficult or stressful, and now has elaborated a high level of sublimation. He is involved in a number of socially constructive activities, which serve as substitutes for his social difficulties, and which give him a sense of achievement and self-respect. By contrast, another young man of very superior intelligence, as early as three years exhibited an avoidance response to a difficult demand by verbal flippancy. At age 22 years, the same strategy is still evident.

An interesting sequence occurred in a girl with a bowel problem caused by a tight anal sphincter in infancy and intensified by
inconsistent maternal handling. Episodes of severe constipation,
painful evacuations, withholding, and soiling occurred through
childhood. Her defensive reaction was one of denial. As a young
child this took a motoric form, with the child attempting to hide
whenever she soiled herself. As she grew older, the denial took
an ideational form of insisting that no one noticed whenever an
accidental evacuation occurred. Finally, at age nine, at sleep-away
camp, she was confronted forcefully with the problem by her
counselor and bunkmates. She then came to one of us (S. C.) for
help, saying "I can't hide it so I better get over it." With this
determination, therapy was quickly and dramatically successful.
Now, at age 21, this young woman is functioning well socially
and academically and has no somatic or other symptoms. She has
no defensive strategies and no evidence of the personality characteristics which are presumed to derive from traumatic bowel training in childhood.

A most intriguing story is that of one of the NYLS youngsters
with a difficult temperamental pattern. The interactive pattern
with her parents began to be dissonant in middle childhood and
by the time she was 13 years old it had become sufficiently stressful for symptoms to appear. Conflict with an older sister was also
present. In the following three years her symptoms and disordered
behavior escalated progressively, with great turmoil, psychosomatic and phobic reactions, drug and alcohol abuse, unsatisfactory
sexual experiences, and severe conflict with her parents. At age
16 she suddenly experienced a dramatic religious conversion with
no apparent precipitating event. Following this, progressive improvement in symptoms and functioning developed, and at age
20 she is functioning well with a strongly positive self-image.
Residual circumscribed phobic reactions and mild psychosomatic
symptoms remain. There is no evidence of thought disorder or
anxiety in an interview situation.

Assuming that this young woman continues to do well psychologically, should we consider this religious conversion and its con-

sequences as the expression of a defense mechanism of sublimation? Or should we consider that her new religious faith gave her a basis for new goals and patterns of adaptive coping, which led to mastery of the life situations and expectations which previously were threatening and overwhelming? To call the sequence *sublimation* would imply, at least to us, that the basic dissonances and conflicts of her interactive patterns remain unresolved, and require the compensatory defense of sublimation. If there is evidence over the coming years for such a judgment, then she would be coping through this defense mechanism. If, on the other hand, she functions in the coming years with appropriately mature social competence and task mastery, retains her positive self-image, and symptoms are either absent or minimal, then a judgment of positive adaptation without the need for defensive strategies would be in order.

These abbreviated vignettes from the NYLS—and many others could be added—pose several challenging questions. Why did one youngster utilize one type of defense mechanism, and another a different type? Why did one individual show consistency in a defensive strategy from early childhood to adult life, another change from hopelessness to denial, and another from projection to hopelessness? It is clear to us that we do not have the answers. Our hypothesis is that the answers may be found at least partially in differences in temperamental attributes. However, our data do not as yet permit a definitive evaluation of this hypothesis.

CONCLUSION

To sum up, the analysis of the sequential organism-environment interactional process requires a consideration of the role of psychodynamic defenses, but always in their interplay with other influences. Such a consideration can rest on operational definitions and ratings of defensive strategies from empirical data, without assumptions as to the ontogenesis of these strategies or their relationship to presumed unconscious mental processes.

Defense mechanisms vary tremendously in their influence on

the developmental course of different individuals. These mechanisms may have little or no importance, they may be of transient significance at one or another time, they may be intermittent, or constitute a continuous and highly important factor. In this regard, they are similar to other influences on developmental course —temperament, intellectual level, specific abilities or defects, parental practices and attitudes, other family influences, special events, and the social environment—all of which also vary tremendously in their impact on different individuals.

Just as attempts to make one-to-one correlations between early life experience and later psychological functioning have proven simplistic and illusory, so any attempt to make such isomorphic linkages between specific defense mechanisms and later levels of maturity of functioning, personality characteristics, or occupational choice is bound to meet the same fate. Psychological functioning at any age, in any and all of its aspects, is always the outcome of the interaction of previous variables. No one variable can be expected to provide a direct causal relationship to later outcome.

Chapter XIII

The Self and Self-Concept

This above all: to thine own self be true,
And it must follow, as the night the day,
Thou canst not then be false to any man

Hamlet I:iii

The uniqueness of the human mind is perhaps most exquisitely manifested in the self and the self-concept or sense of

182

identity. It is true that a young chimpanzee can recognize and identify its reflection in a mirror, indicating at least a crude existence of "self" (Goodall and Hamburg, 1975, p. 38). However, there is no evidence that the development and differentiation of self in the chimpanzee or other nonhuman species proceed beyond this simple level. Humans, by contrast, have a conscious awareness of self—a sense of identity as separate unique persons. We change over time, as we cope with one sequence of life experience after another, yet always a central core of our psychological being appears to remain intact and to endure. The 60-year-old knows he is vastly different from the young adult he was at 20; at the same time, he feels deeply that he is the same as he was at 20. The adult experiences himself as a unique person who is at the same time similar to others. He has a sense of autonomy, yet only really knows himself through his social interactions with other human beings. The sense of self is the quintessence of the subjective, yet shows itself continuously to others in objective actions and communications. "Everyone knows what the self is," yet "despite the seeming clarity of the concept, people do not seem to agree by what they mean by it" (Becker, 1968, p. 194).

The self is the province of the poet, the philosopher, the social and behavioral scientist, and the clinician. It is a highly abstract and general concept, which makes its systematic study difficult. But, with its central place in the individual's psyche, it cannot be ignored either in developmental research, psychological theory or clinical practice.

DEFINITIONS

The terms *self, self-concept,* and *identity* are used loosely in the professional literature, not surprisingly for such general and abstract categories. "The self means one thing in a sociologist's theory and another in a psychologist's, one thing (even among sociological theories) in a structural-functional theory and another in a theory based on symbolic interaction" (Becker, 1968, p. 194). In this discussion, the term *self* will be used to denote the actual existing structure of the self, "abstracted from the indefinitely large number of 'identity' fragments concerning any of the person's characteristics, memberships, identifications, roles, values, beliefs, abilities, problems, goals, etc." (Gordon et al., 1975, p. 214) . Or, as another sociologist, Heine, put it, "Fundamentally, what all self theories have sought to locate and explain has been some unchanging identity of person that surpassed growth and maturity, that withstood time and circumstance, that remained despite manifest external transformations" (1963, p. 388).

The terms *self-concept* and *identity* are sometimes used synonymously, to denote the individual's consciousness of self, his evaluative self-assessment (Erikson, 1968, p. 23). Others use the terms self and identity interchangeably, to categorize the actual self, as in the quote from Heine above.

Self-evaluation may be accurate or distorted, may be inflated or denigrated. Two typical formulations illustrate this use of self-concept and identity categories as the reflection of the individual's self-evaluation. The anthropologist Spindler considers that identity "is composed in part of one's image of self, in part of one's perception of others' estimates, in part of the rationalization of discrepancies between the two. The form of, and emphasis upon, these estimates, images, and rationalizations are provided for the individual by his culture. The specific individual content is always idiosyncratic within the limits of the form" (1968, p. 336) . The psychoanalyst Erikson, whose formulations have been especially influential, states that "ego identity is more than the sum of the childhood identifications. It is the accrued experience of the ego's ability to integrate these identifications with the vicissitudes of the libido, with the aptitudes developed out of endowment, and with the opportunities offered in social roles. The sense of ego identity, then, is the accrued confidence that the inner sameness and continuity are matched by the sameness and continuity of one's meaning for others" (1950, p. 228) . In addition, Erikson speaks of "an optimal sense of identity," which encompasses" a feeling of being at home in one's body, a sense of 'knowing where one is going,' and an inner assuredness of anticipated recognition from those who count" (1968, p. 165) .

These formulations emphasize the general level at which the self is conceptualized, the enduring nature of the self-concept, and its intimate enmeshment in a social framework. An individual's sense of self, his feelings of competence and worth, derives from his experiences both in social relatedness and in task mastery.

DEVELOPMENT OF THE SELF

If the term *self* denotes the actual existing structure of the self, then what are the components that determine its structure? An endless list of items could be made as an inventory of the characteristics of any single individual—physical, psychological, demographic. Which should be considered part of his self, and which are irrelevant?

Empirically, we can include as significant components of the self those attributes which are both enduring and influential in determining the course of psychological development and functioning. Thus, a severe acute illness may have substantial psychological consequences, but being itself transient, it is not part of the self. A chronic physical illness or handicap which affects the individual behaviorally, because it is enduring, does become part of the self.

Societal values and demands clearly play a vital role in determining significant components of the self. In a society such as ours, in which hierarchical value judgments are made on the basis of sex, color, religion, national origin, and socioeconomic class, these aspects of an individual's identity become important attributes of the self. In a society where such value judgments were not made, these items might make useful demographic data for statistical purposes, but would not be significant aspects of the self. In a simple agricultural community, intellectual competence, except for extremes, might be of little importance, while physical strength, endurance and dexterity might be highly treasured assets and constitute very meaningful attributes of the self. In a technologically advanced society, these value judgments are reversed, and the cognitive capacities become significant aspects of the self.

The development of the self, therefore, will reflect the existence and influence of enduring and functionally important attributes. The meaning of any one attribute may change with time and lead to a corresponding change in the self. Thus, as an example, one of the young women in our NYLS group is intellectually superior and completing undergraduate studies with academic honors at a prestigious institution. Her expressed interest in a career as a social worker was sharply attacked by her friends as yielding to the stereotype of suitable careers for a woman. With her academic abilities, they insisted, she should make a more demanding career choice. The significance of her intellectual capacities for her self was now quite different than it would have been 50 or even 25 years ago.

DEVELOPMENT OF SELF-CONCEPT AND SELF-ESTEEM

The unique human capacity for sense of self or self-concept can be either a profoundly positive asset or a source of the greatest distress, unhappiness and disturbance in functioning. The former is true if the self-perception is accurate and evaluated favorably by the individual, i.e., with self-esteem. The latter is true if the self-perception is distorted and denigrated, or accurate but given no respect.

A number of studies suggest that definite evidence of self-differentiation can be identified in the infant, starting at or about nine months of age. Two studies of Lewis and Brooks are clear-cut. In a study of reactions to strangers (1974), they found that infants responded positively to strange children, as contrasted to negative reactions to strange female adults. They further observed an infant's response when, by the use of mirrors, it appeared that the baby was being approached by himself. The infant showed as much pleasure as he did to the approach of the mother. If the infant's negative reaction to a stranger reflects differentiation from the mother, as is usually assumed, then the response to the strange child and his own image in the mirror should be even more negative than to an adult female stranger. The positive response suggests that the infant compares faces not only to his mother's but also to his own. To do so requires at least the beginning of an organized self.

In their other study, Lewis and Brooks (1975) had mothers of children nine to 24 months unobtrusively rub a little rouge on the child's nose. The child was then brought in front of a mirror. If the child touched his rouged nose on viewing his image in the mirror, it indicated an ability to identify the image with his own self. Only a small percentage of the nine-month-olds did so, but the percentage increased linearly through the second year.

Does this mean that the development of the self begins only at nine months of age, or perhaps at most a few months earlier? This is basically the position advanced by Margaret Mahler, a most influential psychonalytic theorist on self-differentiation in infancy. Mahler has postulated two stages of early development following birth, in which the infant functions as a psychologically undifferentiated entity. The first month of life Mahler designates as "normal autism": "I have applied to the first weeks of life the term *normal* autism, for in it the infant seems to be in a state of primitive hallucinatory disorientation, in which need satisfaction belongs to his own omnipotent *autistic orbit.*" This is succeeded by a second stage of "normal symbiosis," starting in the second month of life. "The infant behaves and functions as though he and his mother were an omnipotent system—a dual entity within one common boundary. . . . The 'I' is not yet differentiated from the 'not-I,' and in which inside and outside are only gradually coming to be sensed as different" (Mahler, 1967, p. 710).

In Mahler's hypothetical scheme, the second symbiotic phase reaches its peak at four to five months of age, and only then does there begin the "first subphase of separation-individuation—called differentiation. It is synonymous in our metaphysical language with 'hatching from the mother-infant symbiotic common orbit' " (Mahler, 1972, p. 334)—in other words, the beginning of the development of a differentiated self.

Mahler's formulations have had wide acceptance in psychoanalytical circles. They have provided a theoretical basis for speculation as to the origin of various psychopathological syndromes of later life, such as the so-called "borderline syndrome," in distortions of healthy progression through the infantile stages of "symbiosis" and "separation-individuation" (Shapiro, 1978).

Anna Freud, like Mahler, feels that the development of self does not begin until the latter part of the first year (when so-called "object constancy" is achieved). She speaks of the egocentricity which governs the infant's relations with the object world. "Before the phase of object constancy has been reached, the object, i.e., the mothering person, is not perceived by the child as having an existence of her own; she is perceived only in terms of the role assigned to her within the framework of the child's needs and wishes" (1965, p. 58).

Erikson appears to place the beginning of self and identity in the first few months of life. His first developmental stage, which he designates as trust versus mistrust, includes "a rudimentary sense of ego identity." During this stage, the infant learns that "one may trust oneself . . . and that one is able to consider oneself trustworthy" (1950, p. 220).

Our own view is that individuation and self-differentiation begins at birth, and not at some later period, as Mahler and Anna Freud postulate. With this concept of individuation beginning at birth, the clear objective evidence of an organized self, beginning around nine months, as reported in the studies of Lewis and Brooks, reflects a new level of the development of self, rather than its beginning. (We do not impute to Lewis and Brooks any commitment to the position that the development of self begins only at nine months.) This would parallel the sequential evolution of language development, in which the first spoken words at nine or 12 or 18 months are not the beginning of language function, but a new stage which evolves from the preceding period of preverbal activity from birth onward.

This view flows from the concepts that link the development of self and identity to social activity. Thus, Lidz refers to G. H. Mead's thesis that "a self-concept arises through social transactions and recognition of how others evaluate the self" (1968, p. 267). And Erikson emphasizes that "the growing child must, at every step, derive a vitalizing sense of reality from the awareness that his individual way of mastering experience (his ego synthesis) is a successful variant of a group experience and is in accord with its space-time and life plan . . . ego identity gains real strength only from wholehearted and consistent recognition of real accomplishment—i.e. of achievement that has meaning in the culture" (1950, p. 208).

The young infant's social transactions and individual way of mastering experience can be assumed to lead to the beginnings of self-differentiation very soon after birth. This assumption is confirmed by observations of young infants. By the third month or even earlier, infants will spend many minutes at a time gazing at their hands, turning their hands at the wrists and looking intently as they do so. At the same age, or perhaps a few weeks later, many infants when alone in a crib will not only babble for long periods, but at times will keep repeating the same sound. As Dunn points out, "We know that by the third month of life babies are delighted by events that follow from their own acts (this is well shown by some of the research on smiling, for instance), and are upset if their own behavior with other people fails to produce the reaction they expect" (1977, p. 34).

In all these instances the young infant is initiating behavior that has consequences (movement of his hand, a sound, actions of other people). This is certainly the beginning of that basic constituent of positive self-concept, that "I" can produce changes in the external world. "I" must be a separate entity from the outside world if "I" can accomplish this.

Many a 10-month-old infant will already be insisting on trying to accomplish many tasks by herself, such as holding the bottle, using a spoon, putting on her shoes. These efforts must reflect a further development of self-concept, that "I" have the ability to attempt these actions which previously only the caretakers could accomplish. Failure often accompanies these first efforts, as it will for more complex tasks at later ages, like writing the alphabet and riding a bicycle. But persistence and eventual success are fundamental building blocks for a firm structure of self-esteem.

Growth of a positive self-concept in later infancy takes additional other forms as well. The 18-month-old who says "shoes" to a visitor and thrusts her foot forward with a beaming face to have her new shoes inspected is conveying a sense of self-pride. The two-year-old who makes scribbles on a paper and brings it to the parent with a smile is expressing some level of awareness of her worth to her parent.

SELF-CONCEPT AND SELF-ESTEEM IN LATER CHILDHOOD

Whatever the disagreements as to the beginnings of self-differentiation and individuation in infancy, there can be no question as to the rapid development of the self and self-concept through the preschool and middle childhood years. As the child's world expands in all areas, the elements for the formation and differentiation of the self come together in a mutually influential interactive process. If there is consonance between child and environment, the foundation for a healthy self-concept and stable self-esteem is laid down. If there is dissonance, a negative, denigrated self-evaluation begins to crystallize. The development of self-esteem is always a social process. There are no a priori built-in mechanisms by which the child can assess by himself the worthiness of his achievements, the appropriateness of his efforts at task mastery, and the competence of his social functioning. Communication and judgments from others provide the first standards and the basis for development of his own standards. The parent who approves uncritically of everything the child does is doing a great disservice to the youngster, as is the parent who criticizes every imperfection of performance.

SPECIAL STRESS AND SELF-ESTEEM

The physically handicapped child is frequently subject to special stress in the efforts to achieve task mastery and social competence. His best efforts may still leave him lagging significantly behind his non-handicapped peer at home, in school, in play or in social settings, or in all situations, depending upon the type and severity of the handicap. This may make it harder but by no means impossible, for such a child to develop a positive self-evaluation. Over and over again, we have been impressed, even awed, by the struggles of our handicapped congenital rubella children to reach a level of functioning which gains them the acceptance and respect of their parents, sibs, peers and teachers. Those who succeed gain enormously in self-esteem. Those who fail, because the handicap is too severe, the demands too excessive, or the defense mechanisms too self-defeating, are left with great injury to their self-assessments (Chess et al., 1980).

For the black child, a social system in which "white is right" presents special stresses and threats to the development of self-esteem. As Kenneth Clark has observed, "Human beings who are forced to live under ghetto conditions and whose daily experience tells them that almost nowhere in society are they respected and granted the ordinary dignity and courtesy accorded to others will, as a matter of course, begin to doubt their own worth" (1965, pp. 63-64). But the threat to self-esteem does not have uniform consequences. Some children may be overwhelmed. Others become aware of the sources of the threat, develop appropriate anger at the injustices they suffer, and reject the racist judgment of their inferiority. Robert Coles, in his classic study of the black children involved in the extraordinarily stressful school desegregation struggless in the 1960s, has described their resiliency, their dignity and their self-respect. "A thematic analysis of the hundreds of drawings and stories they have produced shows their kinship with all children. . . . With only one or two exceptions these children were in no sense 'sick.' They had no symptoms, gave no clinical evidence of serious trouble with eating and sleeping, with nursery school or regular school, with family and friends. They did not come to see me in a clinic, it was I who sought them out because of their role in a social struggle" (1967, pp. 64-65).

Findings on self-esteem may also depend on the historic period and social context of the study. In their historic investigations in the late 1930s, the Clarks found that black children tended to deprecate themselves when asked to choose between dark-skinned and white dolls in terms of "being bad" or "looking nice" (Clark and Clark, 1939). However, a study done by Spurlock in the late 1960s found that a group of black middle-class children, aged four to nine, all showed definite awareness of racial differences as related to color, and none manifested negative feelings about their own color. "This situation has shifted since black has become beautiful. . . . Coloring books for the young child are geared to black identity; black dolls are flooding the market" (1969, p. 506).

SELF AND IDENTITY IN ADOLESCENCE

The developmental significance of the middle childhood years may be underestimated by many. No such tendency exists when it comes to adolescence. The profound biological changes, the new level of social peer group functioning, the expanded academic and work demands, the change in relationships with parents, the beginning confrontation of the issue of independence—all make adolescence a period of significant change and development obvious to the observer and the adolescent himself.

For the adolescent period, the writings of Erikson, especially his concept of the "identity crisis," have been most influential in recent years. Erikson's thesis is that the development of the self in childhood (his term is "ego growth") occurs in early childhood through the mechanism of introjection, "the satisfactory mutuality between the mothering adult (s) and the mothered child," and in later childhood through the mechanisms of identification, that is, "the child's satisfactory interaction with trustworthy representatives of a meaningful hierarchy of roles as provided by the generations living together in some form of family." During these childhood periods "tentative crystallizations of identity take place," but identity formation finally arises in adolescence "from the selective repudiation and mutual assimilation of childhood identifications and their absorption in a new configuration, which, in turn, is dependent on the process by which a society (often through subsocieties) identifies the young individual" (1968, pp. 159-160).

For Erikson, the "identity crisis" of adolescence "is not an affliction but a normative crisis, i.e., a normal phase of increased conflict characterized by a seeming fluctuation in ego strength as well as by a high growth potential" (p. 163). He emphasizes that the term *crisis* does not connote "impending catastrophe," but designates "a necessary turning point, a crucial moment, when development must move one way or another" (p. 16). (One is reminded of the old saying that a crisis is both a danger and an opportunity.)

One can, however, question Erikson's thesis that the process of self and identity development in childhood can be mediated exclusively or even primarily through two psychodynamic mechanisms, introjection and identification, acting in sequence. The sense of self is a central psychological formation in scope, which brings together many separate elements of thought, emotion and behavior and all the complexities of interaction with environmental factors. To encompass all this within the framework of the operation of a single psychodynamic mechanism, followed by a second single one, can hardly do justice to the richness, complexity and variety of mechanisms, processes and factors which must be involved in the progressive differentiation and individuation of the self.

ADULT DEVELOPMENT

Erikson considers that the definitive crystallization of identity occurs in adolescence, defining "the final identity, then, as fixed at the end of adolescence" (1968, p. 161). He does, however, say that the process of identity development "is a process of increasing differentiation. . . . It does not 'end' until a man's power of affirmation wanes" (p. 23).

A commitment to an interactionist concept of the developmental process, in which sequential organism-environment interactions may produce significant psychological changes at any stage, implies that major changes in the self, the sense of identity, and self-concept can occur at any time in adult life, as well as in child-hood or adolescence. And in truth, there is no question but that this happens in individual people. The novelists and playwrights have always been keenly aware of the dramatic transformations that can occur. A qualitative change in role functioning (Levinson et al., 1974), a radical alteration in the social environment, an important success or failure in life, a crisis which is surmounted or not—all these can have important and even profound consequences for the self and self-concept. Intervention in the lives of individuals, through psychotherapy, women's consciousness-raising sessions, or intensive group dynamic experiences can also reshape the individual's central core of self and identity.

SOME CLINICAL CONSIDERATIONS

Shakespeare's injunction "to thine own self be true" actually provides a theme for some of the central goals of psychotherapy. Whatever the theoretical commitment of the therapist, the aims of treatment for the nonpsychotic patient are typically formulated in terms of self-discovery, self-awareness, self-realization, self-ful-fillment. The psychologically disturbed individual is considered to have a low self-esteem, which is inappropriate, downgraded as the result of unfavorable life experiences. "The person's personi-fication of himself is not very estimable by comparison with his personification of significant other people" (Sullivan, 1953, p. 350). This degraded self-concept, according to Sullivan, will then create anxiety and various defense mechanisms to avoid or contain the anxiety.

In our own professional experience, whether with older chil-dren, adolescents, or adults, we are impressed with the role of the individual's judgment of the consequences of his own behavior. A person who believes that his behavior can influence the attitudes and behavior of others so that he can thereby achieve his goals is likely to show a positive self-image, self-assurance, and effective-ness in coping with environmental demands. The individual who, by contrast, is defeatist about his ability to utilize his behavior to promote his goals, and who feels that his behavior typically results in unfavorable consequences for himself, will inevitably have a seriously downgraded estimate of his self. Therapy is then focused on delineating the positive constructive aspects of the patient's "true self," doing this in such a way that the patient achieves insight into his "true self" and embraces it, and then utilizes his capacities to change his interaction with the environment. This model of the key significance of the individual's sense of control versus lack of control of the outcomes of his behavior has received substantial verification in the experimental psychological literature in recent years (Perlmutter and Monty, 1977; Abramson and Seligman, 1978).

Ideologically, Shakespeare's "to thine own self be true" spells out the ethical value of individualistic self-fulfillment as a categorical imperative in modern bourgeois democratic industrial society. It is a value we take for granted and treasure, though other types of societies may not find this goal to have the same value or pertinence.

OVERVIEW

A major challenge to developmental theory and clinical psychiatry is the elaboration of suitable methodologies for the systematic study of the self, self-concept and identity. A beginning has been made by a few investigators, but as yet there is "very little solid research establishing sizable and dependable relationships between self-evaluation and important social-structural circumstances, attitudinal correlates, or consequences for subsequent conduct" (Gordon et al., 1975, p. 213).

In the interim, the researcher and clinician must be satisfied with general characterizations and impressionistic judgments. Even these can be extremely valuable in defining individual psychological patterns and in tracing the developmental dynamics of personality formation. At the same time, it is important to avoid using speculative hypothetical entities to fill in gaps in our knowledge, speculations which do not contribute to a fuller understanding of developmental processes and which give the illusion, but not the reality, of the explanation of empirical data.

Chapter XIV

Conscious and Unconscious Mental Processes

The previous chapter has considered the development of that special human characteristic, the self-concept. The awareness of self involves a consciousness of one's ideas, emotions, attitudes, and goals; this consciousness grows and expands at succeeding age-periods, as both the functioning of the mind and the capacity for self-knowledge mature. At the same time, psychological development also brings an increasing range of automatic mental activities of which the individual has little or no awareness.

The relationship between mental activity which is conscious and that which is unconscious, and the significance of each for psychological functioning, have long been a major focus of attention in psychiatric theory and practice. (In this discussion the terms *conscious* and *unconscious* will be used according to standard psychiatric practice. Conscious mental activity is that of which the individual is aware or of which he can become immediately aware; unconscious mental activity exists out of awareness. Freud also used the term *preconscious* to designate those ideas, emotions, and motives which, while unconscious at the moment, were capable of easily entering consciousness.)

FREUD'S "DYNAMIC UNCONSCIOUS"

Any discussion of the relationship of conscious and unconscious mental processes must start with a consideration of Freud's concept of the "dynamic unconscious." Of all his theoretical statements, this has been undoubtedly his most fundamental and influential formulation. As with all new broad generalizations in science, this idea was not unique, but developed against a background of increasing interest in unconscious mental processes among Western philosophers, psychologists, and essayists. Whyte, who has documented this intellectual trend in detail in his volume *The Unconscious Before Freud,* sumarizes this background. "The general conception of unconscious mental processes was *conceivable* (in post-Cartesian Europe) around 1700, *topical* around 1800, and *fashionable* around 1870-1880 . . . it cannot be disputed that by 1870-1880 the general conception of the unconscious mind was a European commonplace, and that many special applications of this general idea had been vigorously discussed for several decades" (1960, pp. 169-170). Whyte quotes a typical statement, made by Oliver Wendell Holmes in 1870: "The more we examine the mechanism of thought, the more we shall see that the automatic, unconscious action of the mind enters largely into all its processes. Our definite ideas are stepping-stones; how we get from one to the other, we do not know; something carries us, we do not take the step" (p. 171).

In the same period, the leading British psychiatrist Henry Maudsley stated that "it may now be affirmed that the most important part of mental action, the essential process on which thinking depends, is unconscious mental activity" (1867, p. 20). The philosopher Nietzsche in various writings asserted not only the existence, but the primacy, of unconscious thoughts, feelings and motives.

To show this linkage between Freud's ideas and the intellectual currents of his and preceding generations in no way detracts from the originality of Freud's systematic development of his own concept of the unconscious mind. Whyte puts it well:

> Freud's supreme achievement was to force the attention of the Western world to the fact that the unconscious mind is of importance in every one of us, by giving dramatic illustrations of the way in which it works, particularly when its spontaneous formative processes are deformed by inhibition. He was the first systematically to connect the general idea with a wide range of particular distortions of behavior in a way that is manifestly valid to unprejudiced minds. Freud changed, perhaps irrevocably, man's image of himself. Beside this it is of secondary importance that some of his valid ideas were not new, his special conceptions questionable, and his therapeutic methods uncertain (1960, p. 177).

Freud's great contribution in this area was to point the way to the systematic study of unconscious mental processes. As Lidz points out, "The explorations of the unconscious processes have been a major achievement of psychoanalysis. Freud did not discover unconscious thought, but he discovered the dynamic force of unconscious processes and their far-reaching consequences; and through the study of dreams, the neuroses, the associations of patients in psychoanalysis, and the meanings of slips of the tongue, etc., went far in unraveling one of the most difficult and diaphanous topics ever studied. However, it is essential to keep in mind that . . . many questions remain unanswered, if not, indeed, unasked" (1968, p. 245). It is also essential to keep in mind that, even if with the utilization of Freud's concept of "unconscious psychic determinism, a host of seemingly fortuitous and purpose-less psychological occurrences turned into potentially meaningful data" (Kohut and Seitz, 1963, p. 117), it still becomes a highly oversimplistic formula to interpret *all* slips of the tongue, for-tuitous events, feelings, attitudes, etc. as reflections of such "un-conscious psychic determinism" (Thomas, 1970).

Freud's Conscious-Unconscious Dichotomy

With regard to the characteristics of conscious versus uncon-scious, Freud had a clear-cut and categorical formulation. The un-conscious was the seat of the primary primitive instinctual drives, the id, and "the one and only endeavor . . . is toward satisfaction" (1949, p. 108). The id is "a chaos, a cauldron of seething excite-ment . . . the id knows no values, no good or evil, no morality. . . . The laws of logic—above all, the law of contradiction—do not hold for processes in the id" (1933, pp. 104-105). Conscious men-tal processes, on the other hand, occur "in the outermost cortex of the ego" (1949, p. 41) and regulate the individual's relation-ship with external reality. The ego controls the instinctual drives for satisfaction by coming "to a decision whether the attempt to obtain satisfaction is to be carried out or postponed or whether it may not be necessary for the demand of the instinct to be al-together suppressed as being dangerous. Just as the id is directed exclusively to obtaining pleasure, so the ego is governed by safety. The ego has set itself the task of self-preservation, which the id appears to neglect" (1949, pp. 110-111).

With these formulations, we have the categorical dichotomy between unconscious and conscious which has dominated psycho-analytic theory and practice. The unconscious mind is irrational, antisocial or at best asocial, and the basic source of psychopathol-ogy; the conscious mind is, or can be, rational, socially construc-tive, and the healthy counterweight to the unconscious mind's pathology. "We are justified in calling abnormal or unhealthy or neurotic any act in the determination of which unconscious processes are dominant" (Kubie, 1954, p. 184). The goal of psychotherapy is "the substitution of something conscious for something unconscious, the transformation of the unconscious thoughts into conscious thoughts. . . . We do nothing for our patients but enable this one mental change to take place in them; the extent to which it is achieved is the extent of the benefit we do them" (Freud, 1943, p. 377).

It is, of course, true that in recent years many psychoanalysts have introduced extensive modifications of Freud's categorical opposition of the conscious and unconscious mind (Lidz, 1968, Marmor, 1974). A rejection of Freud's libido theory and topographical id and ego model (with the superego added in middle childhood) requires more than a modification of the psychoanalytic conscious-unconscious dichotomy. It requires a different approach to the characteristics of conscious and unconscious mental processes and their relationship to each other.

An Alternative View

Freud's dichotomy of conscious-unconscious raises a number of basic questions. Are unconscious mental processes irrational, asocial, or antisocial, and characterized by so-called primitive "primary process thinking"? Is the unconscious dominated by a pleasure principle," while the preconscious and conscious ego is governed by a "reality principle"? Is the unconscious the source of potential or actual psychopathology because of the character of its drive states that continually press for satisfaction? Our own answers to these questions are in the negative. Rather, in our view, the unconscious can become conscious, and the conscious unconscious—sometimes easily, sometimes with difficulty—and both function to further the same goals of social competence and task mastery. Developmental and dynamic considerations determine when and how specific unconscious mental processes become conscious; this may occur spontaneously and with ease or may require planning and effort.

We have come to this position not only on theoretical grounds, but on the basis of our extensive clinical experience with children and adults over many years. This view is parsimonious, does not require the elaborate set of assumptions required by Freud's formulation, and, in our judgment, is in better accord with the empirical data.

Piaget has formulated a critique of Freud's theory of the unconscious from his own detailed study of children's dreams and fantasies, which takes the same approach as the view presented here. His data show that there is no separation between the child's conscious symbolism (as in make-believe play) and unconscious hidden symbolism. "Symbolic thought forms a single unit," states Piaget; he concludes that "the unconscious is not a separate region of the mind, since in every psychic process there is a continual and continuous coming and going from the unconscious to consciousness. . . . The unconscious is everywhere and there is an intellectual as well as an affective unconscious. This means that it does not exist as a 'region,' and that the difference between consciousness and the unconscious is only a matter of gradation or degree of reflection" (1962, pp. 170-172).

An alternative view also has to provide explanations for the actual phenomena of unconscious mentation. Why are some thoughts, emotions or motives unconscious and others conscious? Why are some that are unconscious easily accessible to consciousness and others not? Why does an individual resist, sometimes very strongly, accepting consciously certain of his unconscious thoughts or attitudes, but not others? What developmental mechanisms are responsible for the differences and even contradictions that can exist between some conscious and unconscious thoughts, emotions and motives? These questions we will also consider.

RATIONAL UNCONSCIOUS IDEATION

The conscious mind has no monopoly on rational thought and abstract problem-solving. It is a common experience to wrestle with a problem on a conscious level, to find the solution elusive, to put the problem out of one's conscious mind, and then have the answer suddenly and unexpectedly flash into consciousness. Or, again commonly, one can tackle some question in the evening, be unable to resolve it, go to bed and "sleep on it," and awaken in the morning with the solution clearly in mind. This sequence can only mean that rational thought processes proceed actively and successfully on an unconscious level, outside of conscious awareness. The terms "intuition" and "flash of inspiration" so frequently used to explain sudden unexpected conscious understanding and insight again attest to the frequency and effectiveness of rational unconscious ideation.

The capacity of the unconscious mind for logical thought extends even into the most creative and abstract levels of artistic and scientific activity. The creative artist traditionally has defined and elaborated his profound insights and mastered the extraordinarily complex task of translating these insights into words, sounds, or visual forms, through a combination of conscious and unconscious mental activity. The same is true of the creative scientist. A number have attested to the vital role played by the unconscious mind in rational, imaginative thought processes. Thus, the great French mathematician Poincaré (1958) has described how several basic ideas on Fuchsian functions came to him suddenly and unexpectedly, at times when consciously he had not been thinking of these problems. He called "this appearance of sudden illumination, a manifest sign of long, unconscious prior work." He also stated of this unconscious work that "it is possible, and of a certainty is it only fruitful, if it is on the one hand preceded and on the other hand followed by a period of conscious work (pp. 2044-2046). In other words, the character of the unconscious and conscious mental activity was not contradictory, but complementary.

A vivid description of creative problem-solving in sleep has been given by the chemist Kekule, whose concept of the ring structure of the benzene nucleus was one of the great intellectual achievements of nineteenth century organic chemistry. He had been baffled by this problem for years until the day when he fell asleep in a chair before his fireplace and began to dream of snakes and atoms whirling round and round. "All at once, I saw one of the snakes seize hold of its own tail, and the form whirled mockingly before my eyes. As if by a flash of lightning I awoke and spent the rest of the night in working out the consequences of the hypothesis" (cited in Jaffe, 1956, p. 533).

The Nobel laureate biochemist Szent-Gyorgi (1961) has also described his own pattern of working out problems in his sleep. And the supreme creative scientist Einstein always spoke of his "intuitions." "He seemed somehow to be able to sense the truth by some miraculous combination of penetrating clear thinking and an extraordinary instinct for the workings of the natural world" (Penrose, 1979, p. 7) —again the combination of the conscious and the unconscious.

The phenomenon of unconscious problem-solving has been demonstrated by Maier (1931) in an ingenious experiment. He gave each of a group of subjects a problem to work out, the solution of which depended on swinging a hanging rope as a pendulum. Some solved the problem, but many could not. Maier gave each unsuccessful subject a hint by casually swinging the cord on the window shade as he walked back and forth observing the subjects struggling with the task. With this cue 19 out of 37 subjects were suddenly able to solve the problem within one to three minutes. However, 13 of the 19 denied having noticed the cue and insisted that the solution had come entirely from their own conscious efforts.

DOES CONSCIOUS-UNCONSCIOUS CORRELATE WITH HEALTHY-UNHEALTHY?

Is the unconscious mind asocial and antisocial, dominated by the drive for pleasure and the source of psychopathology? Is it the conscious mind which provides the integration with social reality and the basis for mature psychological health? Again, as with the issue of rational thought, the conscious mind has no monopoly on psychological and social health. This becomes especially clear in the data obtained from patients in psychotherapy.

If the therapist has no a priori assumption that what is unconscious must be unhealthy, it is possible with great regularity to delineate healthy attitudes and behavior patterns which are operating unconsciously. And patients may show the same strong resistance to the conscious acceptance of such a healthy unconscious pattern as they may to the interpretation of an unhealthy one. The conscious acceptance of the healthy may be resisted because it will challenge certain neurotic defenses or because it may call for a difficult decision or sacrifice. For example, one individual's behavior clearly indicated a desire and an ability for warm personal relationships with people. Consciously, however, he denied this desire through a posture of cynicism and an expressed decision to avoid any intimate emotional relationships. The conscious attitude turned out to be a defense against an anxiety reaction to any closeness with another person; the acceptance of his unconscious desires and ability became anxiety-provoking and was strongly resisted.

As another example, a patient professed consciously a conviction that a serious work commitment was a surrender to "the Establishment" and "the rat race." He was even aware that this posture included the fear that his abilities would be inadequate to any work situation demanding a substantial level of performance. It became clear, however, as separate items of his behavior and comments formed a coherent pattern, that unconsciously he had strong interests and aptitudes for a specific field of professional work. When faced with this evidence, he became very anxious and insisted these interests were not "genuine," but a competitive reaction to his hardworking father. Eventually he accepted the validity of his unconscious interests, went into graduate training, and developed a successful and satisfying professional career.

From time immemorial, writers have recognized the existence of unconscious healthy motivations and attitudes in people which lead them to socially desirable behaviors. Typical is the perennial literature theme, as in *The Christmas Carol,* of the self-centered stingy cynic who finds himself functioning according to totally different unsuspected values within himself under the stimulus of some special situation.

Furthermore, consciousness and awareness of self, as vital as they are to humane and rational existence, do not ipso facto guarantee this humanity. The corrupt individual operates according to moral and ethical values which are socially undesirable, but these values may be fully conscious and in no way a reflection of unconscious drives or conflicts. The deceptive politician, the grafting official, the dishonest contractor, and the ruthless executive all wisely avoid public discussion of their activities, but there is no doubt that they are fully aware of their goals and behavior.

THE CREATIVE ARTIST

The creative artist has presented an exquisite dilemma for classical psychoanalytic theory. On the one hand, the writer and other artists express the highest aspirations and values of humanity, have the perceptiveness and judgment to be most cogent social critics, and have the sensitivity to understand the dynamics of behavior and emotional life in great depth. On the other hand, so much of this creativity clearly comes from unconscious sources within the artist that, according to psychoanalytic theory, it should be primitive, asocial, irrational, and pathological. Freud did recognize this dilemma in his comment that the psychoanalyst would have to lay down his arms before the problem of the artist and the creative process. This did not, however, inhibit psychoanalytic theorists from developing an elaborate ideology of the relationship between artistic creativity, especially in the writer, and potential psychopathology. Freud himself, in spite of his own caveat, initiated this trend with his thesis that the artist "has not far to go to become neurotic. He is one who is urged on by instinctual needs which are too clamorous; he longs to attain to honour, power, riches, fame and the love of women; but he lacks the means of achieving these gratifications. So, like any other with an unsatisfied longing, he turns away from reality and transfers all his interest, and all his libido too, onto the creation of his wishes in the life of phantasy" (1943, p. 327).

206 The Dynamics of Psychological Development

This formulation is reaffirmed by the leading psychoanalyst concerned with studies of art, Hanns Sachs. "We know what it means to the poet if he can elicit responsive emotions in his audience. It makes his guilt, caused by his forbidden, repressed, unconscious desires, bearable when he gets out of the isolation of the day-dreamer. Encouraged by their participation, he can shape in his mind and utter with impunity what without this help would remain shapeless and unutterable" (1942, p. 55).

This concept of the creative writer as urged on by instinctual needs which he expresses without guilt because he gratifies the unconscious pleasure needs of others has shaped a host of psychological and psychiatric writings. As Hatterer points out, "The tendency of such studies is to fit the artist to the theory. Each writer attempts, in a more or less schematic fashion, to prove that early sexual conflict and fixation (an unresolved oedipal complex) and traumas of one sort or another explain the creative process. A tedious repetition of any number of such one-noted theories is supported only by fragmentary, often apocryphal historical evidence, the weight of accumulated authority, and incantations of the original dogmas" (1965, p. 21). Beyond this, it seems an absurdity to look for the origins and motivations of artistic creativity, which constitutes a sublime level of the truly unique human capacity for *social* functioning, in a psychological force, namely the unconscious, which is considered to be "the part of the personality which is most remote from all social interests and considerations; since it obeys only the pleasure-principle, it is necessarily asocial, often anti-social" (Sachs, 1942, pp. 22-23).

Freud's belief that "the artist has not far to go to become neurotic" was consistent with a widespread nineteenth century view linking "madness" and "genius" (Andreasen, 1978). The stereotype of the artist as eccentric, unstable, unpredictable was (and still is) fashionable, and his difficult and deviant behavior was tolerated as "artistic temperament." (The present century has added a similar stereotype of the "mad scientist.") In evaluating this stereotype, it is first of all clear that mental illness does not promote the creative process. On the contrary, it interferes with and even destroys the artist's creative functioning, as witness the lives of Virginia Woolf, William Schumann, and Vincent Van Gogh, among others. Mental illness is a disruptive, disorganizing psychological process, which must of necessity interfere with any mental activity demanding a high level of complex, organized, and integrated mental functioning (Hatterer, 1965).

What is true is that the nature of creative activity and the relationship of the artist to society at large subject him to unusual and severe psychological stress. The emotional and intellectual effort required for original creation, for finding the right combination of words, sounds, and visual images that will express accurately and vividly his deepest feelings and ideas, taxes the artist's psychological capacities and resources to the utmost. As Hutchinson put it, the "demonic unrest and mental tension" of the artist "grow out of the fact that a balance cannot be effected between the intense and often over-ambitious creative drive and the rate of integration and accomplishment. It is the result of unfulfilled effort, not the cause of accomplishment" (1949, p. 415).

The artist requires long periods of lonely, single-minded devotion to work, isolated from other people, at the same time that his concerns are deeply social. He requires great self-confidence to pursue this dedicated course, yet has no source of external validation of his work in progress. Being creative, his ideas and representations must go beyond the conventional, yet he must find a bridge to effective communication with other people. He has to struggle not to be seduced by adulation if he achieves recognition, and not to yield to despair if his work is ignored or misunderstood. Subject as he is to such special stresses and conflicts, it is inevitable that the artist may have difficulty in consistently maintaining an optimal psychological adaptive level. Whether this results in eccentricities of behavior, exaggerated mood swings, neurotic symptomatology, or episodes of serious mental illness, it in no way merits an assumption of any intrinsic relationship between creativity and psychological deviance. If anything, the true link is between mental health and creativity, as demonstrated by the lives of some of the greatest artists—

Shakespeare, Bach, Rubens. For the others, where psychopathology of one kind or another is evident, the marvel is how much creative activity is sustained in *spite* of, and not *because* of, such interfering psychological disturbance.

DREAMS AND THE UNCONSCIOUS MIND

For Freud, dreams were "the royal road to the unconscious." In his view, the function of the waking ego in inhibiting unconscious id impulses is weakened during sleep, and these impulses press for expression. This is done in the dream, but in disguised form to elude the censorship of the repressive ego (1949, pp. 46-60). The dream, in this formulation, tells us the nature of underlying instinctual drives, once we can pierce its disguise. The dream also tells us the nature of "primary thought processes" in the unconscious (illogicality, condensation, displacement, etc.).

If one rejects Freud's instinct theory and the concept of "primary process thinking," this does not negate the linkage of dream mentation with the unconscious mind. Consciousness is absent or at most peripheral and hazy during sleep. The dreamer at most knows the dream passively, as an onlooker, without any active conscious influence on its content or direction. Typically, he experiences the dream as happening to him, and not something that he is making happen. The emotional and cognitive activity so evident in dreams does, therefore, reflect unconscious mental processes. What is not required for the clarification of the meaning of dreams are hypotheses regarding instinctual "wish-fulfillment," "censorship" of such hypothesized wishes, "manifest versus latent dream content," etc.

What are the special characteristics of dream mentation? Let us consider several typical dreams:

A woman of 40 came for psychotherapy because of painful anxiety symptoms. In her first session with the male therapist, she expressed unsureness about coming. She knew she needed help, but was doubtful regarding the usefulness of psychotherapy. That night she dreamed that she was being impaled on a fence of wooden stakes, and awakened with acute anxiety. After she reported the dream at her next session, the therapist suggested that perhaps she found coming for treatment threatening in some way. After a few minutes of silence, the patient poured out with great feeling memories of frightening sexual assaults by men in her early adolescence. It seemed clear that the male therapist appeared as a threatening figure to her, evoking unconscious fears of a repetition of the traumata of her earlier life. The sexual symbolism of the dream was obvious. She insisted that she had not had any awareness of this fear before going to sleep, but only the diffusely unfocused uneasiness regarding psychotherapy.

A man, active in a community organization, was debating with himself whether to accept a leadership role in this organization. That night he had an elaborate dream in which he was confronted with some obscure physical danger that he tried to escape from through various devices, but finally decided his only recourse was to remain and face whatever happened. He awoke with a clear decision to accept the leadership position. He also realized that he had been afraid of a certain political risk this decision entailed, but had been trying to deny such a fear.

A woman dreamed that a fire alarm was ringing, telling her that her house was on fire. She awakened to hear her alarm clock ringing.

In the first dream, a new situation (the psychotherapy setting) evoked by association a set of previous life experiences with intense emotional significance. A psychoanalytic interpretation would have speculated that the anxiety over being assaulted camouflaged an underlying sexual wish toward the therapist, representing a transference of an unresolved oedipal complex. (Such interpretations easily become self-fulfilling prophecies, by stimulating such feelings where they did not previously exist.) In the second dream, an unresolved problem which was not being faced in consciousness was decided during sleep. In the third dream, a simple external stimulus, the ringing of the alarm, was transformed into a more elaborate danger signal.

As illustrated in these three examples, thinking processes in dreams are those of cognition in general—the association of a new situation in meaningful ways with specific past life experiences, problem-solving, evaluation of a sensory stimulus, the spinning of fantasy, and symbolization. As Piaget (1962) has emphasized, unconscious thought, including dream thought, is not qualitatively different from conscious thought. What is characteristic of dream thought is rather the form it takes—the presentation of an idea or emotion through story telling, the intense and even extravagant display of emotion, the extensive use of symbols, the vividness of visual imagery, the discontinuities of time and space, the abrupt shift in action and characters.

It is intriguing to speculate on the striking similarity between these characteristics of the dream and those of poetry. Perhaps both the dream and poetry have this is common—a separation from the social environment and its demands for logic and order in our thoughts and emotions. The dreamer achieves this separation through sleep, the poet through the special license and privilege he assumes in his use of language. The daydreamer, who spins fantasies so frequently similar to that of the night-dreamer, has also achieved a partial transient separation from his immediate environment, a state of "abstraction" which may be the cause rather than the effect of the daydream.

This hypothesis as to the dynamics of dream thought is of course speculative. Hopefully, the extensive dream research programs in progress at various centers will produce the data required to validate or refute this formulation. Some suggestive supportive evidence does come from the experimental studies in sensory deprivation (Solomon et al., 1961). In these studies, various strategies are used to deprive subjects of several sensory inputs at the same time. Most often deprivation of vision and hearing are induced, and sometimes tactual-kinesthetic stimuli. In other words, significant interference of the subject's intimate relationship with the environment is produced. Disturbances have been found in perception, cognitive changes, and emotional reactions such as boredom, irritability, and anxiety. Of special interest are the reports of distortions in spatial and time orientation and vivid imagery production in some subjects—findings typical of normal dreams as well.

Bruner (1961), in reviewing these findings, emphasizes "not only the need for variable sensory stimulation as a condition for maintaining a functioning organism, but also the need for continuing social contact and stimulation" (p. 205) and concludes that "sensory deprivation in normal adults disrupts the vital evaluation process by which one constantly monitors and corrects the models and strategies one has learned to employ in dealing with the environment" (p. 207).

RELATIONSHIP OF CONSCIOUS TO UNCONSCIOUS

The empirical data, as reviewed above, challenge the validity and necessity for a categorical dichotomy between conscious and unconscious mental processes. To quote Piaget's judgment again, "symbolic thought forms a single unit" (1962, p. 170). And the psychologist Ernest Hilgard concludes from a review of data from hypnosis studies and the phenomena of dissociated or split personalities, that "the mind as a whole has unity, though one's acquaintance with it is always partial," and suggests "a division of consciousness into parallel parts instead of higher and lower levels" (1978, p. 42).

Conscious thought cannot be differentiated from unconscious thought in terms of a higher versus lower level, logical versus irrational, reality versus pleasure orientation, healthy versus pathological, or social versus asocial-antisocial. Neither does the resistance to conscious awareness or to change provide a reliable criterion for a special category of an unconscious mind. Some unconscious phenomena easily become conscious; others do not. Some resist change; others do not. Conscious ideas and attributes may be as subject to suppression and resistant to change as unconscious ones. To declare that those unconscious phenomena that come easily to consciousness are not truly unconscious, but "preconscious," as is done in psychoanalytic theory, is really begging the question. The "preconscious" is first defined as including those unconscious ideas that do not resist conscious awareness; the proof for a "preconscious," then, consists of pointing to unconscious ideas which can easily become conscious.

What, then, is the relationship between conscious and unconscious mentation? What different functions, if any, does each serve? A useful approach is to examine the characteristics of conscious mental processes—self-awareness being, like self and identity, a special human psychological attribute. The striking phenomenon of consciousness is its *focus* and *selectivity*. It is only possible to give conscious attention at any one time to one or at most a few situations, stimuli, goals, ideas, emotions. At the same time, conscious attention can typically be shifted quickly from one issue to another. The individual who focuses exclusively on one issue when a shift is indicated gets the label of a "one-track mind." The individual who shifts so quickly and often that he loses a selective focus gets the label "scatterbrained."

With this characteristic of selective focus, consciousness serves the mind as "active agent, planner and controller; for only through consciousness can we think ahead, have images of our goals, and formulate plans" (Hilgard, 1978, p. 48). As Hilgard emphasizes, the mental controls of behavior through consciousness are diverse, and "at any one time, they are arranged in a kind of preferential order, so that some dominant control system has access to behavior, while other available control systems are in abeyance. Then position in the order changes as demands upon the person change. For example, the control system that operates when a pianist sits down to play remains in abeyance when the pianist goes about other business. If it were not for some sort of preferential order, any triggered impulse might lead to a spasm of inchoate activity" (p. 49).

To spell out these generalizations, several illustrative examples can be given. An unskilled 26-year-old hospital worker is given the opportunity for job advancement through a special program of technical training. He accepts with delight, and decides on which of his recreational activities to eliminate to give him the necessary time. As the time approaches for his classes to begin, he finds himself anxious and worrying that he will fail academically. He then remembers his past school experiences, in which he was poorly motivated, always restless in school, and considered by his family inferior to his highly achieving older brother. His school performance at that time in the past deteriorated, he rationalized that school was unimportant, and he finally became a school dropout. But now, highly motivated by contrast, he determines to stick to it and study as hard as necessary, no matter how anxious, restless, or tempted by other recreational interests he becomes. This conscious decision and motivation sustain him through initial anxious and difficult weeks, and with the proof of academic competence and mastery, he gains self-confidence, relaxes and pursues his training successfully.

An adolescent girl of 16 had developed over the years an increasing interest and absorption in science and mathematics. Easily sociable as well, she had been a favored member of her peer group. Now she found her girl friends turning increasingly to parties and dating. The boys she knew began to look askance at her serious academic interests. Her family warned her that if she got a reputation as an intellectual, her chances for an active social life and marriage would suffer seriously. She felt convinced by these reactions of her family and peers, worried about her future social life, and decided to cut back on her academic commitments. As she did this, she became increasingly distressed and finally became aware that these academic commitments were deeply meaningful to her, more than she had realized. She changed her decision, firmly convinced that she had to follow her own direction and take her chances with her social life.

In both these cases, a new conscious decision and plan came into conflict unexpectedly with unconscious attitudes and reactions resulting from previous life experience. For the hospital worker, the conscious decision to pursue technical training was in his best interest and became, in Hilgard's phrase, his dominant control system. For the adolescent girl, the conscious decision to cut back on her academic commitment went contrary to her own value system, the depth of which she had not appreciated. Her change in her conscious plans resolved the conflict with her own previously largely unconscious attitudes and desires, with the inevitable cost of potential or actual conflict with her social environment. In both cases, the outcome could have been different, as it so often is. If the hospital worker's anxiety had been greater or his motivation weaker, or both, he might have given up the training opportunity with some defensive rationalization, or started, found himself unable to concentrate, and dropped out. If the adolescent girl had been less sure of the validity of her own interests and more intimidated by the threat of social isolation, she might have given up her academic ambitions and continued her favored social status in a conventional sexist role. The long range consequences of such failures of healthy self-fulfillment would be another matter.

As these examples indicate, consciousness shows its selective focus whenever quick change in ongoing behavior, thinking, or feeling is desired or demanded. The change may be a major one, as in the two examples above. Or it may be a minor transient shift, as in switching conscious focus from reading the newspaper to answering the ringing telephone. The routinized, ongoing activities not requiring conscious attention are the unconscious aspects of mentation and the reflection of the cumulative past experiences of the individual. When consciousness makes a demand for change, the unconscious routinized functions may respond in some cases to facilitate this change, in other cases to impede change, and in still other instances to block change altogether. Which it will be depends on the specific conditioned reflex pattern, memory trace, attitude, motivation, or psychodynamic defense that is stimulated and challenged by the demand for change.

Unconscious psychological processes can also lead to change, by the gradual cumulative effect of life experience. Attitudes, goals, and behavior patterns may change, often without the individual's awareness, until some event or experience brings the change into sharp conscious focus. Conscious mental activity, on the other hand, can at times serve to resist change. An individual's ideological system may promote continuity of behavior and, if rigid enough, create a barrier to desirable change in functioning. As an overall generalization, however, conscious and unconscious psychological processes can be said to complement each other in their adaptive functions. Conscious mentation facilitates change; unconscious mentation facilitates continuity. In healthy functioning the conscious-unconscious systems mesh in an interactive unity. Where this unity is disrupted, the consequence is some type of psychopathology.

Chapter XV

Personality and Its Development

The term *personality* has long been used in traditional psychiatry and psychology. Despite the difficulty in formulating objective criteria for its categorization, it has proven a useful concept, especially for practical clinical activities, and has withstood numerous challenges to its viability. As of now, any overall examination of the dynamics of psychological development cannot ignore an evaluation of its meaning and pertinence for developmental theory.

The use of the term personality in many ways overlaps that of the term self-concept. Both refer to an intuitive subjective sense of psychological identity which underlies the momentary vagaries and surface inconsistencies of day-to-day behavior. "The experience of subjective continuity in ourselves—of basic oneness and durability in the self—is perhaps the most compelling and fundamental feature of personality. This experience of continuity seems to be an intrinsic feature of the mind, and the loss of a sense of felt consistency may be a chief characteristic of personality disorganization" (Mischel, 1969, p. 1012).

As with the self-concept, innumerable definitions of personality have been offered. "There are nearly as many definitions as authors who have dealt with the problem" (Rioch, 1972, p. 576). Yet there is a basic difference in the approach of these two ambiguous, complex, yet profoundly meaningful concepts. Systematic detailed methods of categorizing and classifying the self and self-concept have not been developed and the researcher and clinician must be satisfied with general characterizations and impressionistic judgments. By contrast, a voluminous literature of personality studies exists and keeps growing with each passing year. Clinicians and academic psychologists contribute theories and methods and offer data to support their particular theoretical or methodological biases and to challenge opposing formulations. These efforts have not brought a consensus, to say the least. To some of the thoughtful researchers who have wrestled with personality issues it has brought pessimism. David Rioch, a clinical behavioral scientist, concluded from his review of concepts and data that "the term 'personality' with its rich, socially inclusive connotations, is germane to the clinic, but has no place in the laboratory" (1972, p. 785). And Gardner Murphy, an academic psychologist, after decades of highly respected work, gave the sad judgment that "the scientific effort to study personality has proved to be extraordinarily difficult. It is a labor fraught with conflict, frustration, the discovery of one's limitations and mistakes, the endless necessity for backtracking and doing over" (1968, p. 16).

Frustrating and difficult it may be, but any developmental theory must come to grips with a conceptualization of personality, unless one takes the mechanical behaviorist stance that personality is part of the unknowable "black box" of the mind.

DEFINITION OF PERSONALITY

With such a complex, ambiguous, and pervasive psychological entity as is subsumed under the term personality, a precise objective definition is impossible—at least up to the present time. As Rioch points out, "In many respects, the ambiguity of personality . . . is one of the characteristics of the term which maintain its popularity and keep it from becoming obsolete. Its use implies shared understanding or communication, with mutual agreement that an issue of precise definitions will not be embarrassingly raised" (p. 576). An imprecise definition, which will serve the purposes of this discussion, considers personality to be the composite of those enduring psychological attributes which constitute the unique individuality of the person, and which are expressed in diverse behaviors in different life situations, both concurrently and over time.

APPROACHES TO PERSONALITY STUDY

Emmerich (1968) has suggested a useful classification of the different approaches to personality study and the various concepts of personality development. His three groups include classic developmental theory, differential analysis, and the ipsative approach.

The classic developmental approach, according to Emmerich, posits invariant sequences of developmental stages out of which specific personality constellations crystallize. Thus, the Freudian sequence of instinctual development was presumed to lead to the so-called oral, anal, and genital personality types. Erikson's developmental stages were considered to lead to such characteristics as basic trust or mistrust, autonomy or fear and doubt, initiative or guilt, etc. Piaget's system of cognitive development conceptualized various developmental levels of cognitive functioning, which can be considered as one aspect of the personality. More recent variants of this developmental approach are found in Vaillant's classification of personality patterns in terms of a hierarchy of psychodynamic defenses, Kohlberg's theory of moral stages, and Loevinger's theory of ego stage development.

The second approach, that of differential analysis, in general leads to trait psychology, in which personality is characterized and defined in terms of some number of specific traits. These may be few, such as Jung's introversion-extroversion, or Adler's inferiority-superiority complexes. Or the number of traits may be multiple, such as the 16 proposed by Cattell (1970), the nine proposed by Beiser et al. (1972), and the five male and six female types derived by factor analysis by Block (1971) from the data of the Berkeley Longitudinal Study.

The third approach described by Emmerich is the ipsative one, in which intra-individual consistencies and change in specific psychological attributes over time are studied. Our own temperament studies fall within this approach, which has also characterized the work of others such as Lois Murphy, Kagan and Witkin.

THE SEARCH FOR TRAIT STABILITY

Traditionally, the field of personality study has been dominated by the search for traits which could be rated reliably, and which would show stability and consistency from one situation to another at the same time period, and also from one age-period to another. Clinicians approach this search primarily from data obtained from psychologically disturbed individuals. Academic psychologists concentrate on the statistical analyses of quantitative data obtained from standard observations, interviews, questionnaires, or experimental situations. .

Some 10 years ago, a trenchant challenge to the trait psychologists was formulated by several psychologists, notably Walter

Mischel (1968, 1969). "The initial assumptions of trait-state theory were logical, inherently plausible, and also consistent with common sense and intuitive impressions of personality. Their real limitation turned out to be empirical—they simply have not been supported adequately" (1968, p. 147). Mischel also asserted that extensive evidence supported the view that "noncognitive global personality dispositions are much less global than traditional psychodynamic and trait positions have assumed them to be" (1969, p. 1014). This traditional global position assumes that a durable trait will be operative and influential in the same direction, irrespective of the specific situation in which the overt behavior is manifested. Personality measurements, Mischel pointed out, usually took no serious account of the influence of the situation in which the behavior occurred. "Literally thousands of tests exist to measure dispositions, and virtually none is available to measure the psychological environment in which development and change occur" (1969, p. 1014).

Since the publication of Mischel's critiques, the academic psychologists concerned with personality studies have tended to generate a debate in terms of polarized oppositional positions of trait versus situation as the prime determinant of personality. A leading protagonist of the trait position has been Block with his analysis of data from the Berkeley Longitudinal Study (1971). Using sophisticated Q-sort techniques and multiple ratings, he has constructed a number of traits on the study subjects at the junior high school level, senior high school level, and the fourth decade of life. Statistically significant levels of correlation across situations and between the different age-periods for the specific traits were found. However, Block's study has been criticized by Cronbach (1972), among others, on the basis that his traits are little better than arbitrary. "Other groupings with an equal degree of coherence could have been clustered around almost any set of four to six well-spaced individuals" (p. 786). Cronbach further pointed out that Block's methodology left him no way to report divergences in later life for each of the early adolescent types.

THE INTERACTIONIST APPROACH

In the past few years, the trait versus situation controversy has been influenced by the increasing acceptance of the interactionist concept in developmental studies. This emphasis is evident in the symposium *Personality at the Crossroads,* edited by Magnussen and Endler. They state that "the dynamic model stresses an interactionist *process* in which persons and situations form an inexplicably interwoven structure" (1977, p. 18). In this same symposium, Mischel reviews this concept of the "interaction of person and situation" in what appears to us to be a highly thoughtful fashion. He makes it clear that no one "seriously doubts that lives have coherence and that we perceive ourselves and others as relatively stable individuals that have substantial identity and continuity over time, even when our specific actions change. However, this recognition of continuity exists side by side with the equally compelling evidence that complex human behavior is regulated by interactions that depend intimately on situational conditions (stimulus variables) as well as on dispositions. Humans are capable of great differentiation in their behavior, and they show extraordinary adaptiveness and discrimination as they cope with a continuously changing environment" (pp. 334-335). Mischel points out that traditional trait labels may serve as convenient summaries of our impressions of each other, but they do not illuminate the interactional dynamics between person and situation or the causes of behavior. Actually, traits require scientific explanation, but do not provide it.

Mischel suggests that the term "discriminative ability," with its positive connotations, be substituted for the category "behavioral inconsistency," with its usual negative implications. Behavioral consistency across different situations is not necessarily optimal. It may be adaptive or it may represent a rigidity and inflexibility of psychological functioning which can be highly maladaptive. As a general rule it may even be said that the behavior of psychologically disturbed individuals shows less variability and flexibility in different life situations than the behavior of healthy persons, unless the disturbance is so severe as to create a pattern of disorganization and behavioral disruption.

Mischel also warns against the attempt to find specific traits which show the same pattern of consistency in different individuals. Thus, one person may show relatively consistent friendliness, another consistent dependency, a third consistent honesty, and so on, but no one person is likely to be consistent with regard to all of these dimensions. "Consequently, when an investigator tries to compare many people on any given dimension, only some may be found consistent with regard to it but for most the dimension is one on which their behavior is highly discriminative. In many cases the dimension may even be entirely irrelevant" (1977a, p. 336).

In the same discussion Mischel raises a crucial issue with regard to the interactionist position. As he puts it, without an analysis of the psychological mechanisms and dynamics involved, "an emphasis on interaction is in danger of being little more than an announcement of the obvious" (1977a, p. 340). We ourselves are proposing an interactional model which utilizes the concept of goodness of fit between the individual's capacities and abilities and the demands and expectations of the environment. We have considered the characteristics of the individual or person variables, as Mischel labels them, under the categories of temperament, abilities, and motivations.

Mischel proposes a set of person variables which are of interest. He starts with the question, "When people respond to the environment they are confronted with a potential flood of stimuli; how are these stimuli selected, perceived, processed, interpreted, and used by the individual?" (pp. 340-341). The variables he proposes are in the areas of cognition and social learning; hence he calls them "cognitive social learning person variables" (p. 341). His variables include:

1) the competence to construct and generate diverse behaviors under appropriate conditions;
2) the encoding and categorization of situations—the process

by which individuals group information from stimulus inputs into categories and organize them actively into meaningful units;

3) the expectancies regarding outcomes: "We generate behavior in line with our expectancies even when they are not in line with the objective conditions in a situation" (p. 343);

4) the subjective values of behavioral outcomes. Such subjective values will depend on the individual's past experience. In any new situation, performance will depend on past experience outcome in similar situations. New information, however, may modify or change expectation as to outcome and influence behavior in that situation, even if the subjective variables are unchanged;

5) self-regulatory systems and plans: "Although behavior depends to a considerable extent on externally administered consequences for actions, everyone also regulates his own behavior by self-imposed goals (standards) and self-produced consequences. Even in the absence of external constraints and social monitors, we set performance goals for ourselves and react with self-criticism or self-satisfaction to our behavior depending on how well it matches our expectations and standards" (p. 345).

Mischel emphasizes that these person variables are overlapping and should be seen as suggestive and open to revision. He is emphatic in warning against any attempt to transform these variables into generalized traits. "If the above person variables are converted into global traitlike dispositions and removed from their close interaction with situational conditions, they are likely to have a limited usefulness" (p. 346).

We are impressed with the value of Mischel's approach in specifying dynamic social learning variables. This is in contrast to formulations in which broad generalizations regarding individual differences are made, and in which social learning is used in a global fashion, even within the framework of an interactionist approach. Mischel's variables fit very well within a goodness of fit-poorness of fit model. For each person, patterns of functioning on these cognitive social learning attributes, as derived from past life experiences and learning capacities, will influence significantly the degree to which any new specific environmental demand or expectation is consonant or dissonant with the individual's capacity for effective mastery.

MULTIPLE ROLE FUNCTIONS

A central thesis of traditional trait psychologies has been that diverse and even overtly contradictory behaviors in an individual at different times and in different situations can still reflect the same underlying trait. Thus, for example, a person may show aggressive self-serving behavior in one situation and generous altruistic tendencies in another setting. It will be assumed that he has the same self-centered trait in the second setting and that the altruistic behavior is a camouflaged or sublimated expression of the same self-serving goals. Or if a person shows passive dependent tendencies in one situation, but is assertive and takes initiative in another setting, the judgment may be that the assertive behavior, rather than being genuine, actually represents a defensive reaction formation to the underlying dependency pattern.

We have challenged this global approach with regard to emotions. The same challenge is necessary to the assumption that one fixed global personality trait must underlie diverse behavioral expressions. Most typically, this global approach tends to assume that the socially undesirable or psychopathological behavior is the one which gives the clue to the "real" basic personality, and that the healthy behavior is in one way or another a distorted reflection of such a pathological trait. Lawrence Kolb, a leading psychiatric clinician and teacher, has dealt with this issue concisely in a recent presentation (1978). He points out that psychiatric training always tends to emphasize the liabilities of individuals and their psychopathology, rather than their healthy assets. He suggests, in contrast to usual psychodynamic formulations, that the positive aspects of personality "undoubtedly derive from developmental processes quite different in origin and action from those productive of psychopathology. In the ill, those processes concerned with mastery of the environment are either inhibited or have failed in their evolution." Kolb emphasizes that reliance upon explanations of successful coping based on the concept of defense mechanisms are unsatisfactory. For example, "sublimation," which is so frequently invoked as a mechanism to explain the transformation of a socially undesirable personality trait into an acceptable one, "subsumes too much an explanation of effective and gratifying adult behavior and is assumed to have its origin as a means of escaping anxiety."

The data from our own longitudinal studies affirm the formulations of Mischel and Kolb. Individuals may genuinely play many roles in life depending on the specific situation and its meaning to them. Each role may be as real as any other in terms of its reflecting a significant and durable aspect of the personality. There is no justification for an a priori hierarchy, in which certain behaviors or traits are given greater importance than others in the conceptualization of overall personality structure. An individual's personality, as it evolves through his life experiences, will show many complexities, ramifications and even contradictions. The specific behavioral manifestations at any one time will reflect the interplay among different aspects of his personality, the meaning of that life situation to him, and the consequences of the coping mechanisms employed. It is, of course, true that, for any one individual in some specific situation, an overt behavioral expression may represent a façade or other defensive maneuver to conceal some underlying attitude, thought, or emotion. Thus, for example, an individual may have great hostility toward another person, be afraid to express it openly, and conceal his feeling with an elaborate overt expression of ingratiation. However, before assuming that the ingratiation really reflects on opposite underlying feeling, one must have other evidence indicating that this is indeed the case. It might actually be true that an individual who is easily hostile to most persons in most situations has a different positive reaction to other individuals in other situations. This can be seen even in psychotic paranoid individuals with elaborate delusions of persecution involving almost everyone in their environment, whether family, friends, or strangers. Yet even in such an individual, in whom this pathological trait thoroughly dominates his psychological functioning, there may be a few individuals who are not incorporated into this paranoid system. Expressions of trust and confidence in these special people may actually be genuine and not some special reflection of paranoid thinking.

Robert Coles has described vividly the phenomenon of contradictory role function in his study of migrant farmers. These families live and work in an environment in which they have no roots, in which they are usually mercilessly exploited, and in which they feel helpless. On the other hand, family ties are cohesive and strongly positive. Coles puts it:

> It is our impression that many migrants seem to have constructed a split in their personalities which results in two distinct personality styles. With their children and husbands or wives they will often be warm, open and smiling. At work, with strangers and often with one another while traveling or even walking the streets, they are guarded, suspicious, shrewdly silent or sullenly calculating in what they do have to say; and sometimes clearly apathetic, humorless or even bitter, resentful and touchy. Such alterations in mood and attitude appear to us as grim and striking examples of the capacity of the human mind to respond to its environment and keep itself intact by developing a high order of ability to divide itself severely and categorically. Nowhere in our years with these people did we hear this put better than by the mother of one of our 10 families: "We switches back and forth, from being in a good mood to a bad one because you learns how to travel and you just make your head travel with you, so you gives yourself and the kids a break from the field" (1965, pp. 282-283).

Much has been made of the lack of success that psychiatrists have in predicting levels of functioning in specific life situations, in spite of their presumed expertise in evaluating personality characteristics, psychodynamics, and coping mechanisms. Typical is the report by Fisher et al. in which psychiatrists interviewed and rated a group of Peace Corps volunteers entering that service. After one year of service the volunteers were rated by three field supervisors. "Intercorrelations among the interviewer's predictor ratings and the criterion raters were generally of the order of zero. In the few instances where the correlations departed from chance to about the 5% level, they were found to be in the opposite direction from what was predicted or expected. In general, the findings reveal no relationship between the psychiatrists' and field supervisors' ratings" (1967, p. 749). A possible explanation for this finding is that Peace Corps service represented an entirely new type of life experience and demand, while the psychiatrists' judgments were necessarily based on the evaluation of functioning in previous situations and the interview itself. It can be assumed that different personality attributes were dominant and influential in the volunteers' earlier life and in the psychiatric interview as contrasted to the Peace Corps work and life. Attempts at predicting this future Peace Corps functioning based on the previous psychiatric evaluations were therefore bound to be unreliable. Whether for the migrant farmers, the Peace Corps volunteers, or any group or individual having to adapt either simultaneously or sequentially with qualitative different environmental expectations and demands, it is fruitless and incorrect to debate which personality attributes are the "real" ones. Such a question has meaning only to those who conceive of personality structure as a static global hierarchical entity.

Judgments as to the meaning of different role functions for an individual can have practical importance in psychotherapy. A young woman, for example, had been dominated by her mother, older sister, and other relatives as she grew up. They assigned her the role of "cute" ineptitude and immaturity, which she accepted. In her mid-twenties, she married an older widower with two difficult children, and proceeded to take charge of the complex household in a highly competent and assertive manner. She took initiative as required, dealt effectively with the many domestic problems that occurred, and went back to finish her college education as well. At the same time, she was startled to find that when she was with her own family, she reverted to the role of an immature youngster with such giggling, foolish mannerisms, and expressions of helplessness with regard to family problems. To have tossed a coin to decide which personality was genuine to her and which was reactive and defensive would have missed the basic issue. Both roles were genuine; both reflected different aspects of her personality. As is typically the case, the different roles were expressed in different life situations and individuals, which had qualitatively specific and contradictory meaning for her. The issue then was one of clarifying this to her, so that she could make a decision as to which role she preferred and what measures to take to implement such a decision.

In intensive psychotherapy, a frequent phenomenon is the development of strong emotional reactions on the part of the patient toward the therapist, the so-called transference reaction. Here, the traditional interpretation has tended to be that these emotional reactions reveal the real basic personality of the patient, which must be operative in disguised or disturbed form in other situations as well. An alternative explanation, which makes for a very different approach, is that the psychotherapeutic situation is a very different and even unique one in the patient's experience and therefore may bring out special attitudes, feelings, and ideas, which may or may not be important in the patient's functioning in other life situations. The therapist's responsibility then is to decide from the other evidence which becomes available which possibility is indeed true and apply his therapeutic approach accordingly.

INTERACTION OF PERSON AND SITUATION VARIABLES

The interactionist view of psychological development, as presented throughout this volume, emphasizes the dialectical unity of simultaneously operative and mutually opposite dynamic forces —heredity and environment; biology and culture; continuity and change; emotion and thought. Nowhere is this enmeshment of opposing interacting factors more evident than in the person versus situation variables which influence personality development and structure. Person variables are highly influenced by past and present life situations; situation variables must be evaluated within the context of an individual's specific person attributes.

Thus, Magnusson and Endler suggest sex, socioeconomic background and educational level as significant person variables that can be studied "as independent main factors in personality research" (1977, p. 23). True, yet each of these factors is deeply influenced by social experience, and differently in different individuals. For any one person, the effect of sex role, social class position, or educational level may be quite different in different situations. For example, an individual's response to a competitive challenge may be related to being a man or a woman. Yet, at the same time, whether man or woman, the response may be very different if the challenge comes from a man versus a woman, or comes in a new, unfamiliar work setting versus a familiar, secure setting. Again, an individual's response to unfair criticism can be related to being white or black. Yet, at the same time, whether white or black, the response may be very different if the criticism comes from a white versus a black or from a friend versus a stranger. Mischel's cognitive social learning variables, as summarized above, emphasize the significance of an individual's durable patterns of response to environmental stimuli in determining the influence of the situation and situation variables. At the same time, as Mischel points out, these person variables are not global traits, but are themselves influenced by specific situations; "if the above person variables are . . . removed from their close interaction with situational conditions they are likely to have limited usefulness" (1977, p. 346). Even the relatively simple person variables of temperament and abilities can never be assessed globally or in the abstract, but only in the context of the specific life situations within which they are expressed.

With regard to situation variables, there has always been a

230 The Dynamics of Psychological Development

major emphasis on the influence of person variables. Whether these person variables were formulated as psychodynamic patterns or trait categories, their role in shaping the meaning and significance of specific situations to an individual has been documented. Further, it is clear that durable traits can also affect the types of situations a person experiences. An assertive, self-confident individual may be granted positions of initiative and leadership by others; a timid, self-deprecatory person may find that he is frequently the object of manipulation and exploitation; a paranoid, suspicious individual may find that he does encounter many situations of hostility and antagonism. The dramatic evidence of the influence of the person on the situation has tended in the past, as indicated above in this chapter, to a belittlement of the influence and significance of the situation on personality. .

Just as with the argument as to whether heredity or environment was more fundamental, so it is with the argument as to whether traits or situations are more basic determinants of personality. Both are fundamental, both influence each other, and personality always reflects the dynamic continuous process of interaction between traits and situations.

PERSONALITY DEVELOPMENT

The one generalization that can be made with regard to the course of personality development is that, as of now, no broad systematic generalization can be made that is applicable to all, or even most, individuals. In our own New York Longitudinal Study we have seen all variants in personality evolution from childhood to early adult life. One girl impressed her nursery school teacher at age four years as unusually competent, self-confident and responsible, and impressed our interviewer at age 21 as exactly the same kind of a person. Another girl who in early and middle childhood was a friendly, cooperative, and openly communicative member of her family, in adolescence and early adult life became self-centered, impulsive, secretive, and unreliable. A boy who in early childhood played the role of *enfant ter-*

rible, delighted in making embarrassing remarks about adults and peers, and was indifferent to serious activities, became at age 22 a serious, thoughtful and responsible young adult. In a similar vein, Vaillant (1977) has documented in his vivid vignettes both the continuities and wide range of changes in personality from the college years through the decades of middle age in the men of the Harvard Grant Study. .

As difficult as it is to predict the course of behavioral development in any individual because of the multiplicity of variables and the complexities of their interaction with each other, this problem is compounded by the subtle and subjective, yet pervasive and basic, psychological entity we identify as personality structure. So many person and situation variables are influential in its development, so many different outcomes are possible, so many different traits can be the significant ones for different individuals, so much differentiation and so many different roles can be evident, and differently from one person to another—that the search for simple formulas and categorizations would appear to be totally unrealistic. And yet it is just this kind of complexity, ambiguity, and unpredictability that makes the search for simple global answers so tempting to so many.

The study of personality is most fascinating and important. But from where we stand now in the behavioral sciences, this study appears to offer promise to the extent that it can be individualized. The broad conceptualizations will have to relate to the developmental process, and not to any catalogue of traits. Mischel (1977b) describes our present position very well. Personality research, he says, gives us a view of:

> . . . the person as so complex and multifaceted as to defy easy classification and comparisons on any single or simple complex dimension, as multiply influenced by a host of interacting determinants, as uniquely organized on the basis of prior experiences and future experiences, and yet as a rule-guided in systematic, potentially comprehensible ways that are open to study by the methods of science. It is an image that has

moved a long way from the instinctual drive-reduction models, the static global traits, and the automatic stimulus-response bonds of traditional personality theories. It is an image that highlights the shortcomings of all simplistic theories that view behavior as the exclusive result of any narrow set of determinants, whether these are habits, traits, drives, reinforcers, constructs, instincts, or genes and whether they are exclusively inside or outside the person. It will be exciting to watch this image change as new research and theorizing alter our understanding of what it is to be a human being (p. 253).

Chapter XVI

Poorness of Fit
and Psychopathology

Any general theory of development must be able to encompass the dynamics of both normal and pathological psychological phenomena within its conceptual scheme. In previous chapters we have focused primarily on general issues, with a main emphasis on normal development. In this chapter we will formulate the application of our interactionist and goodness of fit-poorness of fit theoretical model to the developmental dynamics of psychopathology and symptom formation and evolution.

233

In this discussion, we are not concerned with specific theories of the etiology of various mental illnesses. Rather, the issue here is the categorization of different *types* of pathological psychological functioning, whatever the cause or causes may be, the *consequences* of such disturbed functioning for behavior and maladaptation, and the evolution of specific symptom complexes out of the different types of maladaptive organism-environment interactional processes.

To restate briefly our basic concept of the dynamics of development, this involves a formulation of the interactionist model in terms of *goodness of fit* versus *poorness of fit*. Goodness of fit results when properties of the environment and its expectations and demands are in accord with the individual's own capacities. When this *consonance* between organism and environment is present, optimal development in a progressive direction is possible. Conversely, poorness of fit involves discrepancies and dissonances between the individual's capacities and environmental opportunities and demands, so that distorted development and maladaptive functioning occur. Goodness of fit is never an abstraction, but is always formulated in terms of the values, demands, and expectations of a given culture or socioeconomic group.

Poorness of fit and pathological development can occur if: 1) environmental demands and expectations are excessive even for an individual with normal capacities and characteristics; 2) defect or distortion in brain functioning make it excessively difficult or impossible to cope with environmental demands and expectations which other members of the same culture master quite adequately; or 3) a combination of the first two situations occur.

We will consider these three possibilities in turn, and then apply the formulations to the explication of the dynamics of specific psychopathological entities and symptom complexes.

DEMANDS AND EXPECTATIONS OF THE ENVIRONMENT

As discussed earlier, the primary goals of behavior can be conceptualized as social competence and task mastery. The development of social competence clearly derives from the standards, norms, and expectations of the individual's sociocultural group. This is no less true for task mastery. Society sets the tasks for the individual, whether child, adolescent, or adult, and provides the setting and resources for the achievement of task mastery. Our society demands that the young child achieve a regular feeding schedule, accomplish toilet training, and learn the rules of play with peers, and at the same time delegates the prime responsibility for the achievement of these goals to the parents or parent surrogates. A similar sequence is structured for language acquisition. When it comes to the mastery of reading and other learning skills, our society provides an elaborate structure of educational facilities and personnel, as adequate or inadequate as they may be, which has prime responsibility for the achievement of these goals. The adolescent's achievement of the goals of transition from dependency to independence, of the mastery of sexuality, of the enlargement of his capacity for intimate interpersonal relationships—all are delegated primarily to the peer group, and secondarily to the family and special community units. The adult's achievement of mature role functions is facilitated by academic and technical training institutes and a hierarchy of work and service institutions.

Society provides the structures and resources, and expects that the individual will utilize them to achieve sequential task mastery. Supporting ideologies assert that failure to achieve such mastery must be the fault of the individual and not the reflection of limitations and inadequacies in society's commitment and engagement. So we find pronouncements that the child who does not learn in a poor school is the victim of the "culture of poverty" or "minimal brain dysfunction"; that the handicapped adolescent who is bewildered by the complex rituals and conventions of teen-age society is imprisoned in an "unresolved oedipal complex"; that the adult worker who struggles desperately with a ruthless competitive society is reliving his "conflict with his father"; that the poverty-stricken mother who is overwhelmed by the inability to feed and clothe her family on a paltry welfare allowance is suffering from an "endogenous depression."

Beyond the overt demands and expectations—constructive and destructive—that society makes at sequential age-stage levels of development, there is an array of complex and subtle expectations that are demanded of the individual if he is to achieve a successful level of social competence. Thus, Goffman emphasizes the ubiquity of formalized rituals in social communication, rituals of which the actors themselves may be unaware. "Among adults in our society almost every kind of transaction, including every coming together into a moment of talk, is opened and closed by ritual" (1971, p. 139). And, Goffman emphasizes, this starts in childhood, at least for middle-class children, who "are taught a formal approach to social life; it is impressed upon them that all dealings, important or unimportant, extended or momentary, between the acquainted or unacquainted, mediated or face-to-face, in work or play, are to be treated as similar and isolable in that all are to be transmitted from within ritual brackets" (p. 138). And he documents this formalized structured approach, or ritual, with regard to the request for small favors, the response, the appreciation of the response; to the tripping over someone, with an apology, and an acceptance of the apology and the parting; to the unexpected meeting or passing in the streets, with the ritual of greeting and passing; etc.

Duncan and Fiske have detailed the complexities of the social environment in communication.

> Dozens of times each day we interact with others. To an observer even the most simple or routine interactions may seem fascinatingly complex. There are facial expressions and gesticulations, heads may nod or shake; eyebrows may rise. . . . Participants may touch themselves and each other. Postures, distances, and angles are taken by participants and sometimes changed . . . the voices may be loud or soft, harsh or warm, slow or fast. Also audible may be sniffs, clicks, coughs, laughs, hesitation sounds such as "uh," inhalations and sighs (1979, p. 90).

Humphrey emphasizes the inherent instability of a social situation: "A social transaction is by its nature a developing process, and neither party can be sure of the future of the other. . . . The first rule of any transaction is that the problem alters as a consequence of attempts to solve it. . . . In a social transaction there are definite constraints on what is allowed and definite conventions as to how specific actions by one agent should be answered by another" (1978, p. 46). (The resemblance of Humphrey's conventions" to Goffman's "rituals" is clear.)

For the individual relegated to an inferior social or class position by virtue of religion, race, sex, color, or type of work, an additional structure of social demands comes into play (Thomas and Sillen, 1972). The victims may even conform without being aware of the roles they are playing. Jean Baker Miller has described this socioeconomic phenomenon vividly.

> Once a group is defined as inferior, the superiors tend to label it as defective or substandard in various ways. These labels accrete rapidly. Thus, blacks are described as less intelligent than whites, women are supposed to be ruled by emotion, and so on. . . . Dominant groups usually define one or more acceptable roles for the subordinate. . . . Out of the total range of human possibilities, the activities most highly valued in any particular culture will tend to be enclosed within the domain of the dominant group; less valued functions are relegated to the subordinates. . . . The dominant group, thus, legitimizes the unequal relationship and incorporates it into society's guiding concepts. . . . Tragic confusion arises because subordinates absorb a large part of the untruths created by the dominants; there are a great many blacks who feel inferior to whites, and women who still believe they are less important than men" (1976, pp. 6-11).

As a consequence, "within each subordinate group, there are tendencies for some members to imitate the dominants." If, on the contrary, "subordinates move toward freer expression and action, they will expose the inequality and throw into question the basis for its existence. And they will make the inherent conflict an open conflict. They will then have to bear the burden and take the risks that go into being defined as 'troublemakers' " (Miller, 1976, p. 12).

Thus, the demands that society makes on the developing individual are extraordinarily diverse and complex. Mastery of a whole host of tasks of increasing complexity at sequential age levels of development are expected; the nuances and subtleties of social communication have to be comprehended and incorporated; and the dilemmas and conflicts of the innumerable victims who are ascribed to an inferior status because of religion, race, sex, color, or type of work have to be resolved in one fashion or another. As complex and even contradictory as these social demands or expectations are, most normal youngsters show successful patterns of mastery from birth onward. The dynamics of evolutionary natural selection has seen to that. Thus, most individuals are endowed biologically with the capacity to receive stimuli, information, and messages from the environment, to process these environmental inputs accurately and in orderly, organized sequences, and then to communicate effectively back to the environment.

PATHOGENIC PATTERNS OF BRAIN FUNCTIONING

For the individual with one or another deviation in cerebral capacity for adaptation, the story may be entirely different. What are the types of deviation and impairment in brain function which militate against successful adaptation to social demands and expectations, and what are the maladaptive phenomena and consequences which ensue?

It must first be emphasized that not all "deviations" represent pathology. Normal, healthy human behavioral functioning is characterized by wide diversity and individuality. However, society at large, or a specific sociocultural group or family, may, and often does, identify one behavioral pattern as normal and all deviations from that pattern as undesirable and pathological. The excessive stress imposed on such deviant individuals to either change their functioning or be labeled inferior or "sick," whether it be their sexual, temperamental, or ideological characteristics that are at issue, may put them at high risk for the development of psychopathology. For the propagators of the stereotype of what is normal and healthy, a self-fulfilling prophecy is achieved. The deviant individual, even though he starts out psychologically healthy, ends up with psychopathological manifestations which reflect stress and conflict imposed upon them.

To turn to the deviant patterns of brain functioning which are truly pathogenic, we suggest the following classification, based on an interactionist theoretical model:

1) Environmental inputs are received and processed accurately, but there is a diminished ability; quantitatively and qualitatively, to organize and integrate these inputs, i.e., an impairment in learning capacity.
2) Learning capacity is normal, but the ability to process multiple competing stimuli simultaneously is impaired.
3) The processing of incoming stimuli is distorted, so that accuracy of perception, ideation, and symbolization of reality is impaired.
4) Biochemically induced distortions of the brain's reactions to environmental inputs occur, so that the affective component of the brain's response is exaggerated and modified to produce symptoms of heightened or depressed mood.
5) Normal intrinsic brain functioning is present, but there is the development of a constellation of rigid, automatic coping responses to certain specific environmental demands or expectations, a constellation which is maladaptive, self-defeating and self-perpetuating.
6) Normal brain functioning exists, but highly excessive and inappropriate environmental demands and expectations result in symptoms such as anxiety and depression, which are painful and interfere with effective functioning.

For each of the above pathogenic patterns of brain functioning, the development of actual psychopathology requires the input of environmental stimuli, expectations, and demands which the brain cannot master effectively. Where the impairment of brain functioning is extreme, this may occur even with environmental inputs which are modest and limited. Where the impairment is mild, psychopathology may develop only with environmental expectations which are highly demanding.

BRAIN-ENVIRONMENT INTERACTION

Symptom development must always be analyzed in terms of the poorness of fit between the demands of the environment and the capacities and functional behavioral patterns of the individual. Symptoms also express not only the person's reactions to excessive stress and organism-environment dissonance, but also the attempts to repair this excessive stress. Thus, the demand on a temperamentally slow-to-warm-up child for immediate positive adaptation to a new group may result in anxiety, as the expression of excessive demand. In this regard, psychological symptoms are similar to physical symptoms. Cardiac impairment may produce precordial pain as the expression of the excessive stress on the heart imposed by physical exertion, as well as rapid breathing and tachycardia to cope with this stressful physical demand.

The nature of the organism-environment interaction may result in the production of different symptoms by the same etiology, or the same symptom by different etiologies. The same level of severity of mental retardation may lead one child to quiet withdrawal behavior and defensive rationalizations in school, and another to clowning or aggressive behavior, depending on the academic expectations and attitudes of teacher and classmates. Anxiety or depression, with similar defensive responses, may result from a number of different reasons for inadequate capacity for mastery—mental retardation, organic brain impairment, schizoid personality patterns, perceptual impairment by toxic substances.

No single formula can help to explain the origin and significance of any specific symptom as it manifests itself in different cases. In other words, when symptoms arise at the same age and presumed level of psychological functioning, they may reflect many different antecedent pathways of development. The form taken by the symptom in any individual case appears to be the result of a continuously evolving process of interaction between temperament and other organismic characteristics with specific environmental influences, at all times reflecting the child's level of behavioral organization and ideational capacities (Thomas, Chess, and Birch, 1968, p. 170).

Finally, the type of environmental demand which is excessively stressful is not necessarily the same for all individuals, but varies depending on the specific deficit or distortion of brain functioning. The individual who processes environmental inputs accurately, but has an impairment in learning ability, may show the greatest poorness of fit with cognitive demands and lesser dissonance with social expectations. The individual whose processing of incoming stimuli is subtly distorted may have the greatest difficulty with social situations, with their complexity, variability, and frequent rapid changes, and less with cognitive academic learning. The individual with a fixed automatic learned maladaptive pattern may be unable to cope effectively with one type of situation, such as interpersonal intimacy, and yet function effectively in other settings.

The above discussion has examined various types of environmental demands and expectations on the one hand, and different patterns of deviant or pathogenic brain functioning on the other. We will now consider some of the major clinical psychopathological syndromes to suggest a model of poorness of fit which may be appropriate for each and which may clarify the dynamics of symptom formation and evolution in each case. The scheme of clinical classification suggested by the new DSM-III system of the American Psychiatric Association will be utilized for syndrome categorization.

MENTAL RETARDATION

The mentally retarded individual suffers essentially from a limitation in learning capacity, though what he can learn he does without significant perceptual or integrative distortion. The determination of this limited cognitive ability has been preempted by the standard IQ tests, though the usual assumptions as to their validity and reliability have been increasingly questioned in recent years (McClelland, 1973; Mercer, 1974, Zigler and Trickett, 1978). For the mildly and even moderately retarded individual, social and vocational adaptation without excessive stress is possible if education, training, and family and community support systems are neither under- nor overdemanding. Environmental expectations which are excessive or which write off the youngster with a low IQ score as uneducable and untrainable will lead to poorness of fit and psychopathological symptoms that reflect excessive stress and defensive attempts at compensation.

Organic Mental Disorders

Disturbances of brain functioning due to cerebral damage can arise from many causes—infections, toxins, metabolic dysfunction, tumors, head injury, insufficiency of blood supply, etc. These can produce many specific effects, depending on the area and extent of the damage, acuteness of the damage, and premorbid personality; these effects include motor or sensory impairment, memory loss, perceptual and cognitive distortions, and confusion in spatial and temporal orientation. A more subtle but pervasive disturbance that is typical of the organic disorder is a difficulty in processing multiple competing environmental stimuli simultaneously, and an impairment in the ability to shift the focus of attention demanded by an environmental change. With these difficulties, the brain-damaged individual characteristically shows a narrow and perseverative focus of mental activity, repetitiveness in communication, and anxiety and resistance to the need for quick change in schedule and plans. If the competing and shifting environmental demands are excessive and cannot be easily avoided, the disorganization of brain functioning that occurs typically takes the form of the *catastrophic reaction* first described by Goldstein (1942), with acute anxiety, agitation, confusion, irritability, and autonomic disturbances. This reaction develops simultaneously with the attempt to respond to the overwhelming demand, and therefore does not represent a psychological reaction to failure at the task. The stress and anxiety produced by the difficulty in coping with multiple and shifting stimuli (which are most likely to occur in social interactions) can lead to various defensive patterns, such as social isolation, restriction of the environment, avoidance of new tasks, continuous repetitive activity, denial reactions, and excessive orderliness (Kolb, 1973, p. 269).

SCHIZOPHRENIA

Individuals with this serious, complex, poorly understood, and variable clinical syndrome present many frustrating questions and problems to researchers, clinicians, public health authorities, and families. It is no surprise that theories which deny the existence of this syndrome or take the position that schizophrenia is really a positive creative pattern of adaptation should find favor. Such ideologies offer a seductively easy and simple alternative answer to the heavy responsibility of providing treatment and support for huge numbers of afflicted individuals and their families whose lives are so seriously and tragically affected by this mysterious illness.

A very recent authoritative review by Cancro (in press) characterizes schizophrenia as "a syndrome which is heterogeneous in its etiology, pathogenesis, presenting picture, course, response to treatment, and outcome. . . . The clinical picture is seen as a modestly homogeneous state which derives from different initial conditions through different biosocially influenced pathways." The evidence for a genetic factor is impressive (Cancro, in press) and plausible hypotheses regarding biochemical mechanisms have emerged from recent research data (Wynne et al., 1978, pp. 85-158). Environmental factors, such as chronic family stress, undoubtedly are influential in interaction with biological factors (Rutter, 1978), though the previously influential concept of a parentally-induced psychogenic etiology for schizophrenia is now widely questioned, even by some who were previously strong advocates of this position (Arieti, 1977).

Theoretical formulations and research studies of the etiology and pathogenesis of the enigma we call schizophrenia are as varied and heterogeneous as the manifestations of the illness itself. Of special interest is "a dramatic new development in schizophrenia research during recent years: wide conviction that the concepts of attention and information processing are especially valuable because they bridge the gap between the biologic and psychologic realms" (Wynne et al., 1978, p. 13). If subtle but functionally significant distortions of attention and information processing, whatever their etiology, are characteristic of schizophrenia, then our interactionist poorness of fit model could be applicable. We suggest that such difficulties in attention and information processing could produce distorted intrapsychic representations of external reality. Such distortions in schizophrenia would not be on the gross perceptual and cognitive levels characteristic of organic mental disorders, but on subtle symbolic and ideational levels of cerebral integrative functioning. The formal signs of thought disorder, the most useful criterion variable for schizophrenia (Cancro, in press), can be considered to reflect both the impairment in symbolic and ideational functioning and the defensive attempts to compensate for the effects of the distorted intrapsychic representations of external reality. The severity of the illness will and does vary tremendously, depending on the degree of attentional and information processing disturbance, the nature of environmental demands and expectations, other characteristics of the individual which may intensify or ameliorate the maladaptive outcome of the primary impairment, and the feedback from the environment of the consequences of compensatory defensive strategies. At one extreme is the individual who is at no time psychotic but shows the characteristic thinking disorder and defensive strategies found in schizophrenia, the so-called "schizoid personality" or "latent schizophrenic." At the other extreme is the individual whose illness is so severe that his coping and defensive mechanisms are unable to maintain any level of adaptive functioning, with either an acute or even chronic period of behavioral disorganization.

AFFECTIVE DISORDERS

The major affective disorders—manic disorder, major depressive disorder, and bipolar affective disorder—appear to have significant genetic (Allen et al., 1974; Gershon, 1979), biochemical (Schildkraut et al., 1978) and environmental (Allen et al., 1974; Akiskal and McKinney, 1975) etiological components. These etiological factors, in one combination or another, can be assumed to alter the affective component of the brain's response to environmental stimuli so that either a manic or depressed mood is produced. This altered mood, in turn, distorts the individual's judgment and behavioral responses, so that maladaptive sequences of interaction with the environment develop and escalate. The manic person pursues unrealistic expansive ideas and projects, meets with strongly negative responses from others, becomes convinced that this interference arises from jealousy and incompetence, becomes more insistent that he is right and others must acknowledge it, gets an even greater negative response, and so on. The depressed individual interprets accidental events or behavior of others as confirmation of his pessimistic judgments and his self-condemnation and behaves accordingly; others then do begin to blame and criticize him; this increases or at least perpetuates his depression, and so on. The altered mood thus produces a poorness of fit between individual and environment which easily reinforces and even intensifies the manic or depressed affective state.

LEARNED MALADAPTIVE COPING PATTERNS

In the main, these conditions include those diagnosed as neuroses or personality disorders. In these conditions, brain functioning is basically normal, but there is poorness of fit between an individual's abilities and temperament and environmental demands and expectations, whether from the family, peer group, school, or work environment. A rigid, automatic coping mechanism develops to deal with these environmental demands, as with the child who develops passive dependent and avoidance responses to excessive and inflexible parental expectations. The consequences of such a pattern become highly maladaptive, self-defeating, but self-perpetuating at later age-periods (Thomas, 1970), with the development of anxiety, somatoform or dissociative symptoms and the manifestations of a personality disorder. A simpler mechanism may operate to produce phobic disorder; accidental contiguity of a specific stimulus with an anxiety situation may lead to a chronic phobic response to that stimulus.

ADJUSTMENT DISORDER

In these conditions, brain functioning is normal and preexisting maladaptive coping patterns are either absent or relatively insignificant. Healthy psychological functioning is disrupted, however, by environmental stress which is so severe as to overwhelm the individual's previously successful adaptive patterns. Dramatic instances of such overwhelming stress are seen in soldiers subjected to extensive unrelieved combat (Grinker and Spiegel, 1945) and communities disrupted by some natural disaster (Erikson, 1976). The sociologist Kai Erikson's careful, detailed study of the psychological consequences of a terrible flood that tore through the coal mining villages in a narrow mountain hollow in Appalachia called Buffalo Creek in 1972 is especially instructive. The flood was a sudden, unexpected disaster which killed over one hundred people and destroyed the homes and possessions of most of the survivors. Symptoms typical of traumatic neurosis occurred in almost all the survivors and were still actively present two years later. Erikson emphasizes "the remarkable uniformity of the complaints. . . . I knew that other students of disaster had noted the same thing. It was as if every man, woman, and child in the place —everyone—was suffering from some combination of anxiety, depression, insomnia, apathy or simple 'bad nerves,' and to make matters worse, those complaints were expressed in such similar ways that they almost sounded rehearsed . . . no matter how ruthlessly one probes, there is no getting around the conclusion that the survivors have responded to the disaster and have suffered from it in much the same way" (p. 136). Recovery from the initial shock, anxiety and demoralization at the destruction of their closely-knit community did not occur because the relief measures undertaken by governmental and other agencies, however well-intentioned, were by outsiders, impersonal and insensitive to the primary need to restore a sense of community and community support to the survivors. "When one's communal surround disappears, and with it a feeling of belonging and identity, one tends to feel less intact personally; and one also tends to turn to illness as a way of explaining one's own discontents" (Erikson, 1976, p. 233).

Erikson makes a highly significant challenge to conventional psychiatric theory. "It is a standard article of psychiatric wisdom that the symptoms of trauma ought to disappear over a period of time, and when they do not, as was generally the case on Buffalo Creek, a peculiar strain of logic is likely to follow. If one has not recovered from the effects of trauma within a reasonable span of time, or so the theory goes, then it follows that the symptoms themselves must have been the result of a mental disorder predating the event itself" (p. 184). But to follow this kind of logic, as Erikson points out, requires the assumption that virtually all the people on Buffalo Creek suffered from significant degrees of psychological disorder before the flood struck. Rather, the perpetuation of the disturbances resulted from the prolongation of the environmental stress that was so crucial to the initial development of symptoms—the loss of a sense of community and community support.

Erikson suggests that the dynamics of chronic symptom production in the survivors of the Buffalo Creek disaster may apply to many groups and individuals living under conditions of "chronic disaster." "It has long been recognized, for example, that living in conditions of chronic poverty is often traumatizing . . . one can scarcely avoid seeing the familiar symptoms of trauma—a numbness of spirit, a susceptibility to anxiety and rage and depression, a sense of helplessness . . . and a general loss of ego functions" (pp. 255-256) . As he says, it is "a standard article of psychiatric wisdom" to blame such symptoms on presumed mental disorders of intrapsychic origin. This is the "peculiar strain of logic" so aptly labeled by Ryan (1971) as "blaming the victim," in which "a social process is analyzed in such a way that the causation is found to be in the qualities and characteristics of the victim rather than in any deficiencies or structural defects in the environment."

Thus, although the interactionist model emphasized the continuous, evolving, reciprocal influence of organism and environment on each other, these studies of the impact of acute and chronic disaster indicate that in certain extreme circumstances the effect of environment alone may be decisive. Similarly, at the other extreme, in some cases, such as very severe organic brain impairment, schizophrenia or affective disorders, intraorganismic characteristics alone may be decisive.

OVERVIEW

The above discussion of the pathogenesis and symptom formation in various types of psychopathological states has been necessarily sketchy, schematic and oversimplified. A number of conditions, such as psychophysiological and psychosexual disorders, and drug and alcohol abuse, have also not been considered. A full discussion of this subject would require an entire volume. Our intent, rather, has been to indicate the possibility of applying the interactionist goodness of fit-poorness of fit theoretical model to the developmental dynamics of psychopathology as well as to normal development. This model does not require the kinds of speculations and assumptions that have been favored by traditional psychodynamic and behaviorist theories. Hopefully, this alternative interactionist model, as elaborated here and by other workers, will avoid what Mischel describes as "the shortcomings of all simplistic theories that view behavior as the exclusive result of any narrow set of determinants, whether these are habits, traits, drives, reinforcers, constructs, instincts, or genes, and whether they are exclusively inside or outside the person" (1977, p. 253) .

Chapter XVII

Overview:
The Development
of Human Individuality

Three passions, simple but overwhelmingly strong, have governed my life: the longing for love, the search for knowledge, and unbearable pity for the suffering of mankind. . . . Love and knowledge, so far as they were possible, led upwards toward the heavens. But always pity brought me back to earth.

BERTRAND RUSSELL,
The Autobiography of Bertrand Russell

The previous chapters of this volume have examined a number of key issues relevant to normal and deviant psychological development. These issues have been considered in the light of both the explosion of knowledge and new ideas in the past three decades and the previously existing body of knowledge. We have been most impressed by the growing consensus among research workers with regard to certain basic concepts: the inadequacy of simple linear models of development; the necessity for an interactionist model, in which the infant plays an active role from birth onward; the dynamics of development as a continuous dialectical unity of opposites—heredity and environment, biological and cultural, continuity and change.

The Homeodynamic View

All psychological processes show both continuity and change over time and at all stages of the life cycle. This concept flows from the formulation of development as a dynamic process which may reinforce, modify, or change specific psychological patterns at all age-periods. We have called this a *homeodynamic* view, a combination of sameness and change. This view is in contrast to those formulations which conceptualize the interplay of organism and environment as achieving one or another form of *homeostatic* equilibrium.

Psychological theories have always been strongly shaped by the currently influential models of the physical sciences, especially biology. It is therefore no surprise that the homeostatic formulation is explicit or implicit in the traditional psychological concepts of instinctual drive reduction, automatic stimulus-response bonds and static global personality traits. The French physiologist Claude Bernard put forward a view of the stability and constancy of the internal environment as necessary for the maintenance of life. This was one of the great generalizations of nineteenth century biology, further elaborated and documented in the early part of this century by the American physiologist Walter Cannon, who introduced the term homeostasis and called it "the wisdom of the body." The physicist Norbert Wiener gave the homeostatic view further emphasis and influence with the description of cybernetic feedback mechanisms.

Even for physiological functions, homeostatic mechanisms are not always optimally adaptive. As Dubos points out, in many situations "homeostatic mechanisms have indirect and delayed consequences that are responsible for chronic disorders. . . . All too often the wisdom of the body is a short-sighted wisdom" (1978, p. 79). And the unique adaptive capacity of the mind to master new and changing environmental demands would be stifled if it were bound within a homeostatic functional model. "Human health transcends purely biological health because it depends primarily on those conscious and deliberate choices by which we select our mode of life and adapt, creatively, to its experiences" (p. 80).

Optimal adaptation and mastery of the environment do, however, require the capacity for continuity and stability of behavioral functioning, as well as for change and flexibility. A coping mechanism learned in the past may be effective in dealing with a recurrent situation or even with certain new ones, and has the great advantage of being applied swiftly and even automatically. On the other hand, a habituated or automatic response to a new or even familiar situation may be unfavorable and maladaptive. Indeed, healthy human behavioral functioning is characterized by a flexible discriminative interplay of both the old and the new, with both equilibrium and change in evidence. Hence, neither a primarily *homeostatic* or primarily *dynamic* model, but only a *homeodynamic* approach can encompass this combination of continuity and change.

THE GOODNESS OF FIT MODEL

As indicated throughout this volume and in our previous writings (Thomas, Chess, and Birch, 1968; Thomas and Chess, 1977), we have found the goodness of fit model very useful in analyzing the mechanisms of the organism-environment interactional process. With this concept, optimal development occurs when the properties of the environment and its expectations and demands are in accord with the organism's own capacities, motivations, and styles of behaving. Conversely, distorted development and maladaptive functioning occurs when there is poorness of fit between environmental opportunities and demands and the capacities and characteristics of the organism. Both goodness or poorness of fit can influence continuity or change in the environment or in the individual's behavioral functioning, depending on the dynamics of the organism-environment interactional process. The various possibilities are indicated in Figures I and II.

As can be seen from these figures, the goodness of fit-poorness of fit model is not compatible with concepts of linear unidirectional continuity or change or with simple general rules of prediction from earlier to later age-periods that can be applied to all individuals. Rather, all kinds of permutations and combinations

Figure I
Goodness of Fit

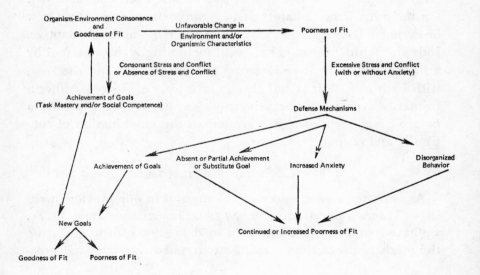

Figure II
Poorness of Fit

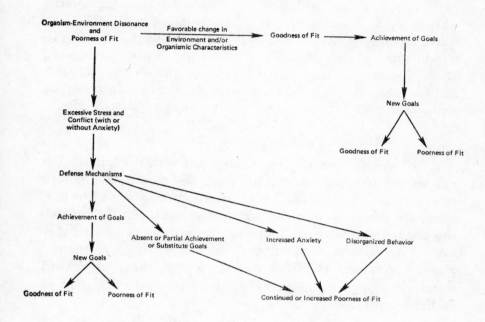

are possible. It should also be emphasized that goodness or poorness of fit are rarely global. At any age-period for any individual, certain environmental demands and expectations may be consonant with his capacities and coping mechanisms, while others may be dissonant. These consonances or dissonances may even shift at succeeding age-periods. Thus, it is not unusual in the treatment of someone with relatively mild psychopathology to find that he is functioning well with a good adaptive level in some or even most areas, and that his disturbed maladaptive behavior is present in only one or several areas.

If the goodness of fit model is to be useful, it must avoid the danger of circular reasoning that has bedevilled so many psychological theories. In other words, it would be very easy to explain adaptive versus maladaptive functioning as due to goodness versus poorness of fit and then "prove" the type of fit by the type of functioning. Independent criteria by which goodness or poorness of fit can be determined must be established for temperament (Thomas, Chess, and Birch, 1968; Thomas and Chess, 1977), cognitive capacity (Chess, 1980), racial, socioeconomic, and sex discrimination (Thomas and Sillen, 1972; Miller, 1976; Rutter et al., 1976), health, nutrition, and socioeconomic disadvantage (Birch and Gussow, 1970), physical handicap (Chess et al., in press), as well as for other organismic and environmental characteristics.

Specific Psychological Mechanisms

In this volume, we have been concerned with the formulation of a set of interrelated general principles and theories that govern the developmental process. These concepts are advocated by ourselves and others because they are in agreement with the expanding body of empirical research data, are so formulated that they can be tested, and eliminate the necessity for the hypothetical abstract constructs of earlier theories which cannot be defined operationally or tested. Kagan describes well the inadequacies of earlier formulations:

> Young sciences suffer the combined disadvantages of ambiguous propositions and weak methodology—a combination that makes it likely that original suppositions, usually loose metaphors taken from the philosophy of the larger culture, will be difficult to disconfirm. As a result these suppositions live longer than they should. It is useful to remain critically skeptical of the unexamined premises of an emergent discipline. We should expect that many of psychology's early advances will be disconfirmations of old prejudices (1976, pp. 195-196).

The acceptance of the general concepts of development presented in this volume still leaves, however, the formidable question of the specific mechanisms by which these principles are implemented. What kinds of neurochemical structures are formed as the result of the growing child's interaction with the environment? What are the neurophysiological properties of these structures, how are they activated, how are they modified by new life experiences? Are there qualitative differences in the structures linked with different psychological functions and different types of life experience? What is the nature of the interaction among the various structures, and how is this interaction expressed? As behavior, emotion, and cognition become more elaborated and their interactions more complex as development proceeds, how is this reflected in the characteristics and functioning of neurochemical processes?

To pose these questions does not imply an attempt to reduce psychological functions to physiological and biochemical phenomena. Just as sociology and anthropology cannot be reduced to psychology and biology (the sociobiologists notwithstanding), so psychology cannot be reduced to biochemistry and electrophysiology. But the human mind cannot be separated from the functioning of the brain, and the discovery of the laws of brain functioning is essential to an understanding of the processes of psychological development.

For example, we can present a general concept of conscious mental functioning and argue for its superiority to the psychoanalytic formulations in terms of objectivity, its correspondence with empirical data, its avoidance of "loose metaphors" and ambiguity, and its usefulness in understanding normal and pathological psychological phenomena. But, as Worden points out, the scientific study of consciousness demands much more:

> A science of conscious experience can begin by describing precisely what kinds of systems have the property of awareness, what conditions within these systems are necessary and sufficient for the emergence of this property, what aspects of brain systems are influenced by the conscious property, and what lawful relationships exist between the quality of consciousness and the nature of the effects it has on the brain. In this light, conscious experience is an enigma only insofar

as science cannot yet define either the systems having this property or those influenced by it (1975, p. 203).

One such brain system for psychological functions has been identified in one type of learning, the conditioned reflex, the structure formed as the result of the temporal contiguity of an unconditioned reflex and an environmental stimulus. Many of the laws of conditioned reflex formation, modification, extinction, and interrelationship between different conditioned reflexes have been identified and proven very useful in developmental psychology, learning theory, and certain psychopathological formulations. Beginnings in a similar direction have been made by Piaget (1952) with his concept of "the operation" and Kagan (1971) with his concept of "the schema." Biochemical studies of the properties and functions of the synaptic junction represent another approach.

PRACTICAL IMPLICATIONS

Theory always affects practice, and vice versa. Psychoanalytic and behaviorist theories have deeply influenced the approach to child-rearing, parent guidance, education, and the treatment of behavior disorders and the serious mental illnesses. The alternative to these theories presented in this volume necessarily involves a different approach to these practical issues. A number of these practical implications have been discussed in the preceding chapters. Worthy of reemphasis here is the inadequacy of any approach which applies the same unidimensional formula to all children and adults, to all students, to all patients. Beyond this, the constellation of characteristics of one psychologically healthy person may vary significantly from another's, and the important interactional determinants of goodness of fit may also vary from one to the other.

Does this mean that our ability to influence a person's developmental course is bound to be frustrated because so many interacting variables are involved? Not at all. The situation is no different in physical medicine. The symptom the patient brings to the physician may have many causes; the same cause may produce different symptoms. It is the physician's task, in each case, to identity the reasons for the poorness of fit between the individual and the environment in his physical functioning and adaptation.

In the prescientific era of medicine, when the available knowledge and methods of data collection were rudimentary, simple unidimensional formulae that were applied indiscriminately to all patients with the same symptom also flourished. In developmental psychology and psychopathology we are emerging from such a prescientific era. We now have enough knowledge and information gathering techniques that we can apply the same discriminative analysis of psychological problems as we do in physical medicine.

THE DIVERSITY OF HUMAN INDIVIDUALITY

In our last volume (Thomas and Chess, 1977), we reviewed some of the data from the New York Longitudinal Study from infancy through adolescence. We concluded by emphasizing how we had been

> . . . impressed by the range and variety of the behavioral repertoire of the young infant. We have seen how this behavior makes it possible for the child to play an active role in his development from birth onward. Any global concept of "personality" becomes untenable as one identifies the many different behaviors in different interactions that each child and adolescent exhibits. All of us play many roles as we go back and forth from one life situation to another. All our roles are interrelated, all are parts of our individuality, and no one can be entitled "the real self" at the expense of the others, and endowed with some mystique of personality. Above all, we have been deeply impressed at the breadth and scope of individual differences in behavior of even the youngest infants (pp. 208-209).

As we have reviewed in this volume the data and concepts flowing from the developmental studies of the past few decades, the profound significance of this phenomenon of human diversity has been dramatically evident. The dynamic interplay of the many factors that influence the course of psychological development ensures that the flowering of true individuality can take many forms. The poets, playwrights, artists, and philosophers have always marvelled at the many different ways there are to be a human being. Simplistic developmental theories, whether they relied on instinctual drive-reduction, conditioned reflex or global trait models, could not illuminate the significance of human diversity. But our present knowledge can do so. The neonate's capacity to learn, the plasticity of developmental pathways, the individual differences in temperament, the active role played by the infant in interaction with environment from the moment of birth onward, the enormous variability in the cultural influences brought to bear on the developmental process, the subtleties and complexities of the relationships among language, thought, and emotion—all promote a diversity of healthy psychological functioning from one individual to another.

The process of evolution has resulted in an almost infinite variety of living species, each with its own special patterns for survival and adaptation. The dynamics of psychological development in the human being fosters just such a variety of individual patterns of task mastery and social competence, of positive self-concept, of flexibility combined with stability in optimal active adaptation to environmental demands and expectations.

Societies can be judged on the basis of the kind of opportunities they give to how many of their members for the full development of this diversity of individuality. We can hope—and to be human means to hope—that social organizations will some day evolve so that human beings can realistically aspire to the "longing for love, the search for knowledge, and unbearable pity for the suffering of mankind" that now is possible for only a tiny number of fortunate and gifted individuals. Or, their passions may be more modest and limited, and still represent the full expression of their constructive aspirations. In the pursuit of these passions, which distill out the essence of true humanity, human beings would show the widest range of diversity in the patterns and qualities of their behavior and in the variability of their functioning from one situation to another. Yet, their functioning would be shaped by the same general laws of psychological development—laws which we now know not only permit but encourage the maximum exploitation of individual organismic differences, environmental influences and cultural influences, all operating in a dialectical interpenetration of opposites.

References

Abrams, S., and Neubauer, P. B. 1975. Object orientedness and transitional phenomena. In S. A. Grolnick, L. Barkin, and W. Muensterberger, eds., *Transitional Objects.*. New York: Jason Aronson.

Abramson, L. Y., and Seligman, M. E. P. 1978. Learned helplessness in humans, critique and formulations. *Journal of Abnormal Psychology,* 87:49-74.

Ackerman, N. 1958. *The Psychodynamics of Family Life.* New York: Basic Books.

Adelson, E., and Fraiberg, S. 1974. Gross motor development in infants blind from birth. *Child Development,* 45:114-126.

Ainsworth, M. D. S., and Bell, S. M. 1974. Mother-infant interaction and the development of competence. In K. J. Connolly and J. Bruner, eds., *The Growth of Competence.* New York: Academic Press.

261

Akiskal, H. S., and McKinney, W. T. 1975. Overview of recent research in depression. *Archives of General Psychiatry,* 32:285-305.

Allen, M. G., Cohen, S., Pollin, W., and Greenspan, S. I. 1974. Affective illness in veteran twins: A diagnostic review. *American Journal of Psychiatry,* 131:1234-1239.

Allport, G. W. 1961. *Pattern and Growth in Personality.* New York: Holt, Rinehart, and Winston.

Andreasen, N. C. 1978. Creativity and psychiatric illness. *Psychiatric Annals,* 8:23-45.

Arieti, S., 1975. Creativity and its cultivation: Relation to psychopathology and mental health. In S. Arieti, ed., *American Handbook of Psychiatry,* Vol. 3. 2nd ed. New York: Basic Books.

———. 1977. Parents of the schizophrenic patient: A reconsideration. *Journal of the American Academy of Psychoanalysis,* 5:347-358.

Bandura, A. 1974. Behavior theory and the models of man. *American Psychologist,* 29:859-869.

———. 1978. The self system in reciprocal determinism. *American Psychologist,* 33:344-358.

———, and Harris, M. B. 1966. Modification of syntactic style. *Journal of Experimental Child Psychology,* 4:341-352.

Barash, D. P. 1977. *Sociology and Behavior.* New York: Elsevier.

Baratz, S. S., and Baratz, J. C. 1970. Early childhood intervention: The social science basis of institutional racism. *Harvard Educational Review,* 40:29-50.

Barchas, J. D., Akil, H., Elliott, G. R., Holman, R. B., and Watson, S. J. 1978. Behavioral neurochemistry: Neuroregulators and behavioral states. *Science,* 200:964-973.

Becker, H. H. 1968. The self and adult socialization. In E. Norbeck, D. Price Williams, and W. M. McCord, eds., *The Study of Personality.* New York: Rinehart and Winston.

Becker, W. C., and Krug, R. S. 1965. The parent attitude research instrument—A research review. *Child Development,* 36:329-365.

Beiser, M., Feldman, J. F., and Egelhoff, C. J. 1972. Assets and affects. *Archives of General Psychiatry,* 27:545-549.

Bell, R. Q. 1968. A reinterpretation of the direction of effects in studies of socialization. *Psychological Review,* 75:81-95.

Belmont, I. In press. Perceptual organizations and minimal brain dysfunctions. In H. E. Rie and E. D. Rie, eds., *Handbook of Minimal Brain Dysfunction.* New York: John Wiley and Sons.

Bennett, E. L., Diamond, M. C., Krech, D., and Rosensweig, M. H. 1964. Clinical and anatomical plasticity of brain. *Science,* 146:610-619.

Bereiter, C., and Engleman, S. 1966. *Teaching Disadvantaged Children in the Preschool.* Englewood Cliffs, N. J.: Prentice-Hall.

Bernstein, B. 1961. Social structure, language and learning. *Educational Research,* 3:163-176.

Birch, H. G. 1954. Comparative psychology. In F. L. Marcuse, ed., *Areas of Psychology.* New York: Harper and Bros.

———. 1954. The relation of previous experience to insightful problem-solving. *Journal of Comparative Psychology,* 38:367-383.

———, and Gussow, J. D. 1970. *Disadvantaged Children: Health, Nutrition, and School Failure.* New York: Harcourt, Brace and World.

Birns, B. 1976. The emergence and socialization of sex differences in the earliest years. *Merrill Palmer Quarterly,* 22:3.

Block, J. 1971. *Lives Through Time.* Berkeley: Bancroft Books.

Bloom, B. S. 1964. *Stability and Change in Human Characteristics*. New York: John Wiley and Sons.

Bloom, L. 1978. Language development, language disorders, and learning disabilities. Paper read at New York Association for the Learning Disabled Conference, December 1978.

Borchas, J. D., Akil, H., Elliot, G. R., Holman, R. B., and Watson, S. J. 1978. Behavioral neurochemistry: Neuroregulations and behavioral states. *Science*, 200:964-973.

Boulding, K. 1956. General systems theory: The skeleton of science. *General Systems*, 1:11-28.

Bower, T. G. R. 1977. *A Primer of Infant Development*. San Francisco: W. H. Freeman.

Bowlby, J. 1969. *Attachment* Vol. 1. *Attachment and Loss*. New York: Basic Books.
———. 1951. *Maternal Care and Mental Health*. Geneva: World Health Organization.

Brazelton, T. B. 1973. Neonatal behavioral assessment scale. *Clinics in Developmental Medicine*, No. 50.
———. 1978. Introduction. In A. J. Sameroff, ed., *Organization and Stability of Newborn Behavior*. Monographs for Social Research in Child Development, Vol. 43, Nos. 5-6, pp. 1-13.

Bretherton, I. 1978. Making friends with one-year-olds: An experimental study of infant-stranger interaction. *Merrill-Palmer Quarterly*, 24:29-51.

Bridger, W. H., and Reiser, M. F. 1959. Psychophysiologic studies of the neonate. *Psychosomatic Medicine*, 21:265-276.

Bronowski, J. 1973. *The Ascent of Man*. Boston: Little, Brown.

Bronson, W. C. 1974. Mother-toddler interaction: A perspective on studying the development of competence. *Merrill-Palmer Quarterly*, 20:275-301.

Bruch, H. 1954. Parent education, or the illusion of omnipotence. *American Journal of Orthopsychiatry*, 24:723-732.

Bruner, J. S. 1961. The cognitive consequences of early sensory deprivation. In P. Soloman, P. E. Kubzansky, P. H. Lederman, J. H. Mendelson, R. Trumbull, and D. Wexler, eds., *Sensory Deprivation*. Cambridge: Harvard University Press.
———. 1978. Learning the mother tongue. *Human Nature*, 1:32-39.
———. 1973. Organization of early skilled action. *Child Development*. 44:1-11.

Buss, A. H., and Plomin, R. 1975. *A Temperament Theory of Personality Development*. New York: John Wiley and Sons.

Campbell, D. T. 1975. On the conflicts between biological and social evolution and between psychology and moral tradition. *American Psychologist*, 30:1103-1126.

Cancro, R. In press. Overview of schizophrenia. In H. Kaplan, A. Freedman, and B. Sadock, eds., *Comprehensive Textbook of Psychiatry*. 3rd ed. Baltimore: Williams and Wilkins.

Carey, W. B. 1972. Clinical application of infant temperament measures. *Journal of Pediatrics*, 81:823-828.
———, and McDevitt, S. C. 1978. Stability and change in individual temperament: Diagnoses from infancy to early childhood. *Journal of the American Academy of Child Psychiatry*, 17:331-337.

Carpenter, G. 1975. Mother face and the newborn. In R. Lewin, ed., *Child Alive*. London: Temple Smith.

Cattell, R. B. 1970. The integration of functional and psychometric requirements in a computerized diagnostic system. In M. S. Maher, ed., *New Approaches to Personality Classification*. New York: Columbia University Press.

――――. 1950. *Personality: A Systematic and Factual Study*. New York: McGraw-Hill.

Chess, S. 1971. Autism in children with congenital rubella. *Journal of Autism and Childhood Schizophrenia*, 1:33-47.

――――. 1944. Developmental language disability as a factor in personality distortion in childhood. *American Journal of Orthopsychiatry*, 14:483-490.

――――. 1979. Developmental theory revisited: Findings of longitudinal study. *Canadian Journal of Psychiatry*, 24:101-112.

――――. 1977. Follow-up report on autism in congenital rubella. *Journal of Autism and Childhood Schizophrenia*, 7:69-81.

――――. 1964. Mal de mère. *American Journal of Orthopsychiatry*, 34:613-614.

――――. In press. The mildly mentally retarded child in the community: Success versus failure. In S. B. Sells, R. Crandall, M. Roff, J. S. Strauss, and W. Pollin, eds., *Human Functioning in Longitudinal Perspective*. Baltimore: Williams and Wilkins.

――――. 1978. The plasticity of human development. *Journal of the American Academy of Child Psychiatry*, 17:80-91.

――――. 1953. The social factors in delinquency. *American Journal of Orthopsychiatry*, 23:1-5.

――――, Clark, K. B., and Thomas, A. 1953. The importance of cultural evaluation in psychiatric diagnosis and treatment. *Psychiatric Quarterly*, 27:102-114.

――――, Fernandez, P., and Korn, S. 1980. The handicapped child and his family: Consonance and dissonance. *Journal of the American Academy of Child Psychiatry*, 19:56-57.

――――, and Hassibi, M. 1978. *Principles and Practices of Child Psychiatry*. New York: Plenum.

――――, Korn, S., and Fernandez, P. 1971. *Psychiatric Disorders of Children with Congenital Rubella*. New York: Brunner/Mazel.

――――, and Thomas, A. 1976. Defense mechanisms in middle childhood. *Canadian Psychiatric Association Journal*, 21:519-525.

――――, and Thomas, A. 1959. The importance of nonmotivational behavior patterns in psychiatric diagnosis and treatment. *Psychiatric Quarterly*, 33:326-334.

――――, Thomas, A., and Birch, H. G. 1965. *Your Child is a Person*. New York: Viking Press.

――――, Thomas, A., and Cameron, M. 1976. Sexual attitudes and behavior patterns in a middle-class adolescent population. *American Journal of Orthopsychiatry*, 46:689-701.

――――, Thomas, A., and Cameron, M. 1976. Temperament: Its significance for school adjustment and academic achievement. *New York University Educational Review*, 7:24-29.

Chodoff, P., Friedman, S. B., and Hamburg, D. 1964. Stress, defenses and coping behavior: Observations in parents of children with malignant disease. *American Journal of Psychiatry*, 120:743-749.

Chomsky, N. 1957. *Syntactic Structure*. The Hague: Mouton.

Cichetti, D., and Sroufe, L. A. 1978. An organizational view of affect: Illustration from the study of Down's Syndrome infants. In M. Lewis and L. A. Rosenblum, eds., *The Development of Affect*. New York: Plenum Press.

Clark, K. B. 1965. *Dark Ghetto*. New York: Harper and Row.

――――, and Clark, M. P. 1939. The development of consciousness of self and emergence of racial identification in Negro preschool children. *Journal of Social Psychology*, 10:591-599.

Clarke, A. D. B. 1978. Predicting human development: Problems, evidence, implications. *Bulletin of the British Psychological Society*, 31:249-258.

Clarke, A. M., and Clarke, A. D. B. 1976. *Early Experience: Myth and Evidence.* London: Open Books.

Clarke, B. 1975. The causes of biological diversity. *Scientific American,* 233:50-60.

Cohen, J. D., Caparulo, B., and Shaywitz, B. 1976. Primary childhood aphasia and childhood autism. *Journal of the American Academy of Child Psychiatry,* 15:604-645.

Coleman, J. C. 1978. Current contradictions in adolescent theory. *Journal of Youth and Adolescence,* 7:1-11.

Coles, R. 1967. *Children of Crisis.* Boston: Little Brown.

———. 1965. The lives of migrant farmers. *American Journal of Psychiatry,* 122:271-285.

Condon, W. S., and Sander, L. W. 1974. Neonate movement is synchronized with adult speech: Interactional participation and language requisition. *Science,* 183:99-101.

Connolly, K. 1972. Learning and the concept of critical periods in infancy. *Developmental Medicine and Child Neurology,* 14:705-714.

———, and Stratton, P. 1969. An exploration of some parameters affecting classical conditioning in the neonate. *Child Development,* 40:431-441.

Cronbach, L. J. 1972. Book Review of *Lives Through Time* by J. Block. *Science,* 176: 785-786.

Davis, H. V., Sears, R., Miller, H. C., and Brodbeck, A. J. 1948. Effect of cup, bottle, and breast feeding on oral activities of newborn infants. *Pediatrics,* 2:549-558.

deVilliers, J. G., and deVilliers, P. A. 1978. *Language Acquisition.* Cambridge: Harvard University Press.

Dobzhansky, T. 1966. A geneticist's view of human equality. *The Pharos,* 29:12-16.

———. 1962 *Mankind Evolving.* New Haven: Yale University Press.

Dorfman, D. D. 1978. The Cyril Burt question: New findings. *Science,* 201:1177-1186.

Dubos, R. 1965. *Man Adapting.* New Haven: Yale University Press.

———. 1978. Health and creative adaptation. *Human Nature,* 1:74-82.

Duncan Jr., S., and Fiske, D. W. 1979. Dynamic patterning in conversations. *American Scientist,* 67:90-98.

Dunn, J. 1977. *Distress and Comfort.* Cambridge: Harvard University Press.

Eibl-Eibesfeldt, I. 1975. *Ethology, the Biology of Behavior.* New York: Holt, Rinehart and Winston.

Eisenberg, L. 1972. The *human* nature of human nature. *Science,* 176:123-128.

———. 1977. Development as a unifying concept in psychiatry. *British Journal of Psychiatry,* 131:225-237.

Emde, R. N. 1978. Commentary. In A. J. Sameroff, ed., Organization and Stability of Newborn Behavior. *Monographs for Social Research in Child Development,* Vol. 43, Nos. 5-6.

———, Gaensbauer, T. J., and Harmon, R. J. 1976. *Emotional Expression in Infancy. A Biobehavioral Study.* Psychological Issues, Vol. 10, Monograph 37. New York: International Universities Press.

———, and Harmon, R. J. 1972. Endogenous and exogenous smiling systems in early infancy. *Journal of Child Psychology and Psychiatry,* 11:177-200.

Emmerich, W. 1968. Personality development and the concept of structure. *Child Development,* 39:671-690.

Engel, G. L. 1967. Ego development following severe trauma in infancy: A 14 year study of a girl with gastric fistula and depression in infancy. *Bulletin of the Association of Psychoanalytic Medicine,* 6:57.

Erikson, E. H. 1950. *Childhood and Society*. New York: Norton.
———. 1963. *Childhood and Society*. 2nd ed. New York: Norton.
———. 1968. *Identity, Youth and Crisis*. New York: Norton.
Erikson, K. 1976. *Everything in Its Path*. New York: Simon and Schuster.
Fantz, R. L., and Nevis, S. 1967. Pattern preferences and perceptual-cognitive development in early infancy. *Merrill-Palmer Quarterly*, 13:77-108.
Fisher, J., Epstein, L. J., and Harris, M. R. 1967. Validity of the psychiatric interview. *Archives of General Psychiatry*, 17:744-750.
Flavell, J. H. 1972. An analysis of cognitive-developmental sequences. *Genetic Psychology Monographs*, 86:279-350.
———. 1963. *The Developmental Psychology of Jean Piaget*. Princeton: D. van Nostrand.
Fraiberg, S. 1977. *Every Child's Birthright: In Defense of Mothering*. New York: Basic Books.
———. 1977. *Insights from the Blind*. New York: Basic Books.
Freud, A. 1965. *Normality and Pathology in Childhood*. New York: International Universities Press.
Freud, S. 1962. *Analysis, Terminable and Interminable* (1937). In J. Strachey, ed., *Standard Edition of the Complete Psychological Works of Sigmund Freud*, Vol. 23. London: Hogarth Press.
———. 1950. *Collected Papers*, Vol. 2. London: Hogarth Press.
———. 1924. *Collected Papers*, Vol. 4. London: Hogarth Press.
———. 1950. *Collected Papers*. Vol. 5. London: Hogarth Press.
———. 1943. *A General Introduction to Psychoanalysis*. New York: Garden City Publishing Company.
———. 1900. *The Interpretation of Dreams*. In J. Strachey, ed., 1953. *Standard Edition of the Complete Psychological Works of Sigmund Freud*, Vols. 4 and 5. London: Hogarth Press.
———. 1933. *New Introductory Lectures in Psychoanalysis*. New York: Norton.
———. 1949. *An Outline of Psychoanalysis*. New York: Norton.
———. 1964. *Three Essays on the Theory of Sexuality* (1905). In J. Strachey, ed., *Standard Edition of the Complete Psychological Works of Sigmund Freud*, Vol. 7. London: Hogarth Press.
Furth, H. G. 1971. Linguistic deficiency and thinking. *Psychological Bulletin*, 76:58-72.
Gardner, R. A., and Gardner, B. T. 1969. Teaching sign language to a chimpanzee. *Science*, 165:664-672.
Gazzaniga, M. S. 1977. Consistency and diversity in brain organization. In *Proceedings Conference on Evolution and Lateralization of the Brain*. New York: New York Academy of Science.
Gershon, E. S. 1979. Genetics of the affective disorders. *Hospital Practice*, 14:117-122.
Goffman, E. 1961. *Asylums*. New York: Doubleday.
———. 1971. *Relations in Public*. New York: Basic Books.
Goldfarb, W. 1945. Effects of psychological deprivation in infancy and subsequent stimulation. *American Journal of Psychiatry*, 102:18-33.
Goldstein, K. 1942. *After-effects of Brain Injuries in War*. New York: Greene and Stratton.
Goodall, J., and Hamburg, D. A. 1975. Chimpanzee behaviors as a model for the behavior of early man: New evidence on possible origins of human behavior. S. Arieti, ed., *American Handbook of Psychiatry*, Vol. 6. 2nd ed. New York: Basic Books.

References

Gordon, C., Gaitz, C. M., and Scott, J. 1975. Self evaluations of competence and worth in adulthood. In S. Arieti, ed., *American Handbook of Psychiatry*, Vol. 6. 2nd Ed. New York: Basic Books.

Gordon, E. W. 1973. Affective response tendencies and self-understanding. In *Proceedings of 1973 Invitational Conference on Testing Problems*. Princeton: Educational Testing Service.

———. 1975. New perspectives on old issues in education for the minority poor. *IRCD Bulletin*, 10:5-17. New York: Columbia University Teachers College.

———, and Green, D. 1974. An affluent society's excesses for inequality: Developmental, economic and educational. *American Journal of Orthopsychiatry*, 44:4-18.

Gould, R. L. 1972. The phases of adult life: A study of developmental psychology. *American Journal of Psychiatry*, 129:521-531.

Graham, P., Rutter, M., and George, S. 1973. Temperamental characteristics as predictors of behavior disorders in children. *American Journal of Orthopsychiatry*, 43:328-339.

Grinker Sr., R. R. 1975. The relevance of general systems theory to psychiatry. In S. Arieti, ed., *American Handbook of Psychiatry*, Vol. 6. 2nd ed. New York: Basic Books.

———, and Spiegel, J. P. 1945. *Men Under Stress*. New York: Blakiston.

Grossman, H. J., and Greenberg, N. Y. 1957. Psychosomatic differentiation in infancy. *Psychosomatic Medicine*, 19:293-306.

Guilford, J. P. 1959. *Personality*. New York: McGraw-Hill.

Guillemin, R. 1978. Peptides in the brain: The new endocrinology of the neuron. *Science*, 202:390-401.

Haan, N. 1963. Proposed model of ego functioning: Coping and defense mechanisms in relation to IQ change. *Psychological Monographs*, Vol. 77, No. 8. American Psychological Association.

Hamilton, W. D. 1964. The genetical theory of social behavior: I and II. *Journal of Theoretical Biology*, 7:1-52.

Hartman, H. 1950. Comments on the psychoanalytical theory of the ego. *Psychoanalytical Study of the Child*, 5:74-95.

———. 1958. *Ego Psychology and the Problem of Adaptation*. New York: International Universities Press.

Hatterer, L. 1965. *The Artist in Society*. New York: Grove Press.

Hauser, S. T. 1976. Loevinger's model and measure of ego development: A critical review. *Psychological Bulletin*, 83: 928-955.

Hearnshaw, L. S. 1979. *Cyril Burt, Psychologist*. London: Hodder and Stoughton and Ithaca, N. Y.: Cornell University Press.

Heine, P. J. 1963. The problem of personality in sociological theory. In J. P. Wegman and R. W. Heine, eds., *Concepts of Personality*. Chicago: Aldine.

Henry, J. 1967. Discussion of Erikson's *Eight Ages of Man*. In *Current Issues in Psychiatry*, Vol. 2. New York: Science House.

Hertzig, M. E., Birch, H. G., Thomas, A., and Mendez, O. A. 1968. *Class and Ethnic Differences in the Responsiveness of Preschool Children to Cognitive Demands*. Monographs of the Society for Research in Child Development, Vol. 33, No. 1.

Hess, E. H. 1972. Imprinting in a natural laboratory. *Scientific American*, 227:24-31.

Hess, R. D. 1970. Social class and ethnic influences on socialization. In P. M. Mussen, ed., *Carmichael's Manual of Child Psychology*. New York: John Wiley and Son.

Hilgard, E. R. 1978. Hypnosis and consciousness. *Human Nature*, 1:42-49.

Hinde, R. 1966. *Animal Behavior: A Synthesis of Ethology and Comparative Psychology.* New York: McGraw-Hill.

Hindley, C. B., and Owen, C. F. 1978. The extent of individual changes in IQ for ages between 6 months and 17 years in a British longitudinal sample. *Journal of Child Psychology and Psychiatry,* 19:329-350.

Houston, S. H. 1970. A reexamination of some assumptions about the language of the disadvantaged child. *Child Development,* 41:947-963.

Humphrey, N. K. 1978. The origins of human intelligence. *Human Nature,* 2:42-47.

Hutchinson, E. D. 1949. Period of frustration in creative endeavor. In P. Mullahy, ed., *A Study of Interpersonal Relations.* New York: Hermitage Press.

Izard, C. E. 1977. *Human Emotions.* New York: Plenum Press.

Jaffe, B. 1956. *New World of Chemistry.* New York: Silver Burdett.

Jan, J. E., Freeman, R. D., and Scott, E. P. 1977. *Visual Impairment in Children and Adolescents.* New York: Grune and Stratton, pp. 97-111.

Jensen, A. R. 1969. How much can we boost IQ and scholastic achievement? *Harvard Educational Review,* 39:274-277.

Kagan, J. 1978. The baby's elastic mind. *Human Nature,* 1:66-73.

———. 1971. *Change and Continuity in Infancy.* New York: John Wiley and Sons.

———. 1972. Do infants think? *Scientific American,* 226:74-82.

———. 1976. Emergent themes in human development. *American Scientist,* 64:186-196.

———. In press. Heart rate and heart rate variability as signs of a temperamental dimension in infants. In C. Izard, ed., *Measurement of Emotion in Children.*

———. 1969. Inadequate evidence and illogical conclusions. *Harvard Educational Review,* 39:274-277..

———. 1978. On emotion and its development: A working paper. In M. Lewis and L. A. Rosenblum, eds., *The Development of Affect.* New York: Plenum Press.

———. 1976. Resilience and continuity in psychological development. In A. M. Clarke and A. D. B. Clarke, eds., *Early Experience: Myth and Evidence.* London: Open Books.

———, Kearsley, R. B., and Zelazo, P. R. 1978. *Infancy, Its Place in Human Development.* Cambridge: Harvard University Press.

———, and Klein, R. E. 1973. Cross-cultural perspectives on early development. *American Psychologist,* 28:947-961.

———, Rosman, B. L., Day, D., Albert, J., and Phillips, W. 1964. Information processing in the child: Significance of reflective attitudes. *Psychological Monographs,* Vol. 78. No. 1. American Psychological Association.

Kanner, L. 1943. Autistic disturbances of affective contact. *Nervous Child,* 2:217-250.

Kaye, K., and Brazelton, T. B. Mother-infant interaction in the organization of sucking. Paper presented at the Society for Research in Child Development, Minneapolis, 1971.

Kearsley, R. B. 1973. The newborn's response to auditory stimulation. *Child Development,* 44:582-590.

Kessen, A. 1978. Review of *Infancy, Its Place in Human Development* by J. Kagan, R. B. Kearsley, and P. R. Zelazo. *New York Times Book Review,* December 10, 1978.

Kogan, N. 1971. Educational implications of cognitive style. In G. S. Lesser, ed., *Psychological and Educational Practice.* Glenview, Ill.: Scott, Foreman.

Kohut, H., and Seitz, P. F. D. 1963. Psychoanalytic theory of personality. In J. M. Wepman and R. W. Heine, eds., *Concepts of Personality.* Chicago: Aldine.

Kolb, L. C. 1978. Ego assets: An overlooked aspect of personality organization. Paper presented at Menas S. Gregory Lecture, New York University Medical Center, April 20, 1978.

———. 1973. *Modern Clinical Psychiatry.* Philadelphia: W. B. Saunders.

Kohlberg, L. 1978. The cognitive developmental approach to behavior disorders: A study of the development of moral reasoning in delinquents. In G. Serban, ed., *Cognitive Defects in the Development of Mental Illness.* New York: Brunner/Mazel.

———. 1964. Development of moral character and moral ideology. In M. L. Hoffman and L. W. Hoffman, eds., *Review of Child Development,* Vol. 1. New York: Russell Sage Foundation.

Kubie, L. 1954. The fundamental nature of the distinction between normality and neurosis. *Psychoanalytic Quarterly,* 23:167-204.

Labov, W. 1970. The logic of nonstandard English. In W. Labov and Associates, eds., *Language and Poverty: Perspectives on a Theme.* Chicago: Markham.

Lamb, M. E. 1978. Influence of the child on mental quality and family interaction during the prenatal, perinatal and infancy periods. In R. M. Lerner and G. B. Spanier, eds., *Child Influences on Marital and Family Interaction.* New York: Academic Press.

Lehrman, D. 1953. A critique of Konrad Lorenz's "Theory of Distinctive Behavior." *Quarterly Review of Biology,* 28:337-363.

———. 1970. Semantic and conceptual issues in the nature-nurture problem. In L. R. Aronson and E. Tobach, eds., *Development and Evolution of Behavior, Essays in Memory of T. C. Schneirla.* San Francisco: W. H. Freeman.

Lerner, R. M. and Spanier, G. B., eds. 1978. *Child Influences on Marital and Family Interaction.* New York: Academic Press.

Levinson, D. J. 1978. *The Seasons of a Man's Life.* New York: Knopf.

———, Darrow, C. M., Klein, E. B., Levinson, M. H., and McKee, B. 1974. The psychological development of men in early adulthood and the mid-life transition. In D. Ricks, A. Thomas, and M. Roff, eds., *Life History Research in Psychopathology,* Vol. 3. Minneapolis: University of Minnesota Press.

Levy, D. 1957. Capacity and motivation. *American Journal of Orthopsychiatry,* 27:1-8.

Lewin, K. 1935. *A Dynamic Theory of Personality.* New York: McGraw-Hill.

Lewin, R., ed. 1975. *Child Alive.* London: Temple Smith.

Lewis, M., and Brooks, J. 1975. Infants' social perception: A constructive view. In L. B. Cohen and P. Salapatek, eds., *Infant Perception from Sensation to Cognition,* Vol. 2. New York: Academic Press.

———, and Brooks, J. 1974. Self, other and fear: Infants' reactions to people. In M. Lewis and L. A. Rosenblum, eds., *The Origins of Fear.* New York: John Wiley and Sons.

———, and Feiring, C. 1978. The child's social world. In R. M. Lerner and G. B. Spanier, eds., *Child Influences on Marital and Family Interaction.* New York: Academic Press.

———, and McGurk, H. 1972. Infant intelligence scores—true or false. *Science,* 178:1174-1177.

———, and Rosenblum, L. A., eds. 1978. *The Development of Affect.* New York: Plenum Press.

Lewis, O. 1966. The culture of poverty. *Scientific American,* 215:19-25.

Lidz, T. 1968. *The Person.* New York: Basic Books.

———, Fleck S., and Cornelison, A. R. 1965. *Schizophrenia and the Family.* New York: International Universities Press.

Lipsitt, L. 1969. Learning capacities of the human infant. In R. J. Robinson, ed., *Brain and Early Behavior.* London: Academic Press.

———, and Kaye, H. 1964. Conditioned sucking in the newborn. *Psychonomic Science,* 1:29-30.

Loevinger, J. 1969. Theories of ego development. In Augusto Biasi, ed., *Clinical-Cognitive Psychology: Models and Integrations*. Englewood Cliffs, N. J.: Prentice-Hall.

Lorenz, K. 1952. *King Solomon's Ring: New Light on Animal Ways*. New York: Thomas Y. Crowell.

———. 1966. *On Aggression*. New York: Harcourt, Brace and World.

MacFarlane, A. 1975. The first hours, and the smile. In R. Lewin, ed., *Child Alive*. London: Temple Smith.

MacFarlane, J. W. 1964. Perspectives on personality consistency and change from the guidance study. *Vita Humana*, 7:115-126.

Magnusson, D., and Endler, N. S. 1977. Interactional psychology: present status and future prospects. In D. Magnusson and N. S. Endler, eds., *Personality at the Crossroads*. New York: John Wiley and Sons.

Mahler, M. S. 1967. On human symbiosis and the vicissitudes of individuation. *Journal American Psychoanalytic Association*, 15:710-762.

———. 1972. On the first three subphases of the separation-individuation process. *International Journal of Psychoanalysis*, 53:333-338.

Maier, N. R. F. 1931. The solution of a problem and its appearance in consciousness. *Journal of Comparative Psychology*, 12:181.

Marks, M., and Gelder, M. G. 1966. Common ground between behavior therapy and psychodynamic methods. *British Journal of Medical Psychology*, 39:11-23.

Marmor, J. 1974. *Psychiatry in Transition*. New York: Brunner/Mazel.

———. 1966. Psychoanalysis at the crossroads. In J. Masserman, ed., *Science and Psychoanalysis*, Vol. 10. New York: Grune and Stratton.

———. 1942. The role of instincts in human behavior. *Psychiatry*, 5:509-516.

Matas, L., Arend, R. A., and Sroufe, L. A. 1978. Continuity of adaptation in the second year: The relationship between quality of attachment and later competence. *Child Development*, 49:547-556.

Maudsley, H. 1867. *The Physiology and Pathology of the Mind*. London: Mac-Millan and Company.

Mayr, E. 1961. Cause and effect in biology. *Science*, 134:1501-1506.

McCall, R. B. 1977. Challenges to a science of developmental psychology. *Child Development*, 48:333-334.

———, Eichorn, D. H., and Hogarty, P. S. 1977. *Transitions in Early Mental Development*. Monographs of the Society for Research in Child Development, Vol. 42, No. 3.

———, Hogarty, P. S., and Hurlburt, N. 1972. Transitions in infant sensory motor development and the prediction of childhood IQ. *American Psychologist*, 27:728-748.

McClelland, D. C. 1973. Testing for competence rather than for intelligence. *American Psychologist*, 28:1-14.

Mendelson, M. J., and Haith, M. M. 1976. *The Relation Between Audition and Vision in the Human Newborn*. Monographs of the Society for Research in Child Development, Vol. 41, No. 4.

Mercer, J. R. 1974. A policy statement on assessment procedures and the rights of children. *Harvard Educational Review*, 44:125-141.

Messick, S. 1976. Personality consistencies in cognition and creativity. In S. Messick and Associates eds., *Individuality in Learning*. San Francisco: Jossey-Bass.

Miller, J. B. 1976. *Toward a New Psychology of Women*. Boston: Beacon Press.

Mischel, W. 1969. Continuity and change in personality. *American Psychologist*, 24:1012-1018.

———. 1977a. The interaction of person and situation. In D. Magnusson and N. S. Endler, eds., *Personality at the Crossroads*. New York: John Wiley and Sons.

———. 1977b. On the future of personality measurement. *American Psychologist,* 32:246-254.

———. 1968. *Personality and Assessment.* New York: John Wiley and Sons.

Modgil, S. 1974. *Piagetian Research: A Handbook of Recent Studies.* New York: Humanities Press.

Moskowitz, B. A. 1978. The acquisition of language. *Scientific American,* 23, Nov., 92-108.

Murphy, G. 1947. *Personality: A Biosocial Approach to Origins and Structure.* New York: Harper.

———. 1968. Psychological views of personality and contributions to its study. In E. Norbeck, D. Price-Williams, and W. M. McCord, eds., *The Study of Personality.* New York: Holt, Rinehart and Winston.

Murphy, L. B. and Moriarity, A. E. 1976. *Vulnerability, Coping and Growth.* New Haven: Yale University Press.

Mussen, P. H., Conger, J. P., and Kagan, J. 1979. *Child Development and Personality.* 4th ed. New York: Harper and Row.

Nelson, K. E. 1975. Facilitating syntax acquisition. Paper presented at the April meeting of Eastern Psychological Association in New York.

———. 1973. Structure and strategy in learning to talk. *Monographs for Social Research in Child Development,* Vol. 38, No. 149.

Neugarten, B. L. 1979. Time, age, and the life cycle. *American Journal of Psychiatry,* 136:887-894.

New York Daily News, 2 April, 1978. Interview with Dr. Lee Salk.

Norris, M., Spaulding, P., and Brodie, F. 1957. *Blindness in Children.* Chicago: University of Chicago Press.

Osgood, C. E. 1952. Nature and measurement of meaning. *Psychological Bulletin,* 49:197-237.

Owens, H., and Maxmen, J. S. 1979. Mood and affect: A semantic confusion. *American Journal of Psychiatry,* 136:97-99.

Panier, G. B., Lerner, R. M., and Aquiino, W. 1978. The study of child-family interactions—a perspective for the future. In R. M. Lerner and G. B. Spanier, eds., *Child Influence on Marital and Family Interaction.* New York: Academic Press.

Papousek, H. and Papousek, M. 1975. Cognitive aspects of preverbal social interaction between human infants and adults. In Ciba Foundation Symposium No. 33, *Parent-Infant Interaction.* Amsterdam: ASP.

Pasamanick, B., and Knobloch, H. 1966. Retrospective studies on the epidemiology of reproductive casualty: Old and new. *Merrill-Palmer Quarterly,* 12:7-26.

Pavlov, I. P. 1928. *Lectures on Conditional Reflexes,* Vol. 1 New York: International Publishers.

———. 1941. *Lectures on Conditional Reflexes,* Vol. 2. New York: International Publishers.

Peiper, A. 1963. *Cerebral Function in Infancy and Childhood.* New York: Consultants Bureau

Penrose, R. 1979. Einstein's vision and the mathematics of the natural world. *The Sciences,* 19:6-9.

Perlmutter, L. C., and Monty, R. A. 1977. The importance of perceived control: Fact or fancy? *American Scientist,* 65:759-765.

Piaget, J. 1954. *The Construction of Reality in the Child.* New York: Basic Books.

————. 1962. *Play, Dreams and Imitation in Childhood.* New York: W. W. Norton.

————. 1932. *Language and Thought of the Child.* London: Rutledge and Kegan Paul.

————. 1963. *The Origins of Intellience in Children.* New York: International Universities Press.

Pinneau, S. R. 1961. *Changes in Intelligence Quotient from Infancy to Maturity.* Boston: Houghton Mifflin.

Plomin, R., and Rowe, D. C. 1977. A twin study of temperament in young children. *Journal of Psychology,* 97:107-113.

Poincaré, H. 1958. Mathematical creation. In J. R. Newman, ed., *The World of Mathematics,* Vol. 4. New York: Simon and Schuster.

Rheingold, H., and Eckerman, C. 1973. Fear of the stranger: A critical examination. In H. Rees, ed., *Advances in Child Development and Behavior.* New York: Academic Press.

Richardson, S. 1976. The influence of severe malnutrition in infancy on the intelligence of children at school-age: An ecological perspective. In R. N. Walsh and W. T. Greenough, eds., *Environments as Therapy for Brain Dysfunction.* New York: Plenum, pp. 256-275.

Richmond, J. B., and Lipton, E. L. 1959. Some aspects of the neurophysiology of the newborn and their implications for child development. In L. Jessner and E. Pavenstadt, eds., *Dynamic Psychopathology in Childhood.* New York: Grune and Stratton.

————, and Lustman, S. L. 1955. Automatic function in the neonate. *Psychosomatic Medicine,* 17:269-275.

Riesen, A. H. 1960. Effects of stimulus deprivation on the development and atrophy of the visual sensory system. *American Journal of Orthopsychiatry,* 30:23-36.

Rioch, D. M. 1972. Personality. *Archives of General Psychiatry,* 27:575-580.

Russell, B. 1967. *The Autobiography of Bertrand Russell.* Vol. I. Boston: Little, Brown.

Rutter, M. 1978. Communication deviance and diagnostic differences. In L. C. Wynne, R. L. Cromwell, and S. Matthysse, eds., *The Nature of Schizophrenia.* New York: John Wiley and Sons.

————. 1978b. Diagnosis and definition of childhood autism. In M. Rutter and E. Schapler, eds., *Autism: A Reappraisal of Concepts and Treatment.* New York: Plenum Press.

————. 1975. *Helping Troubled Children.* Middlesex: Penguin Books.

————. 1972. *Maternal Deprivation Reassessed.* Middlesex: Penguin Books.

————. 1970. Psychological development: Predictions from infancy. *Journal of Child Psychiatry and Psychology,* 11:49-62.

————. 1978c. Separation experiences. A new look at an old topic. Paper read at the Bakwin Memorial Lecture, New York University Medical Center, 17 October, 1978.

————, Tizard, J., Yule, W., Graham, P., and Whitmore, K. 1976. Isle of Wight studies, 1964-1974. *Psychological Medicine,* 6:313-332.

Ryan, W. 1971. *Blaming the Victim.* New York: Pantheon.

Rycroft, C. 1976. Action louder than words. *New York Review,* 23:12-14.

Sachs, H. 1942. *The Creative Unconscious.* Cambridge: Sci-Art Publishers.

Sagan, C. 1977. *The Dragons of Eden.* New York: Random House.

Sahlins, M. 1976. *The Use and Abuse of Biology.* Ann Arbor: University of Michigan Press.

References

273

Sameroff, J. J. 1975. Early influences on Development; Fact or fancy? *Merrill-Palmer Quarterly*, 20:275-301.

———, and Chandler, M. J. 1975. Reproductive risk and the continuum of caretaking casualty. In S. Scarr-Salapatek and G. Siegel, eds., *Review of Child Development Research*, Vol. 4. Chicago: University of Chicago Press.

Schafer, R. 1976. *A New Language for Psychoanalysis*. New Haven: Yale University Press.

Schaffer, R. 1977. *Mothering*. Cambridge: Harvard University Press.

Scheerer, M. 1963. Problem-solving. *Scientific American*, 208:118-128.

Schildkraut, J. J., Orsulak, P. J., Schatzberg, A. F., Gudeman, J. E., Cole, J. O., Rohde, W. A., and La Brie, R. A. 1978. Toward a biochemical classification of depressive disorders. *Archives of General Psychiatry*, 35:1427-1439.

Schlesinger, H., and Meadows, K. 1972. *Sound and Sign: Childhood Deafness and Mental Health*. Berkeley: University of California Press.

Schneirla, T. C. 1972. An evolutionary and developmental theory of biphasic process underlying approach and withdrawal. In L. R. Aronson, E. Tobach, J. S. Rosenblatt and D. S. Lehrman, eds. *Selected Writings of T. C. Schneirla*. San Francisco: W. H. Freeman.

———. 1957. The concept of development in comparative psychology. In D. B. Harris, ed., *The Concept of Development*. Minneapolis: University of Minnesota Press.

———, and Rosenblatt, J. S. 1961. Behavioral organization and genesis of the social bond in insects and mammals. *American Journal of Orthopsychiatry*, 31:223-253.

Sears, R. R. 1951. A theoretical framework for personality and social behavior. *American Psychologist*, 6:476-483.

———, Macoby, E. E., and Levin, H. 1957. *Patterns of Child Rearing*. Evanston, Ill.: Row, Peterson.

Senn, M. F. E., and Solnit, A. J. 1968. *Problems in Child Behavior and Development*. Philadelphia: Lea and Febiger.

Shapiro, E. R. 1978. The psychodynamics and developmental psychology of the borderline patient: A review of the literature. *American Journal of Psychiatry*, 135:1305-1315.

Shapiro, T., and Perry, R. 1976. Latency revisited, the age 7 plus or minus 1. *Psychoanalytic Study of the Child*, 31:79-105.

Simpson, G. G. 1963. Biology and the nature of science. *Science*, 139:81-88.

Skinner, B. F. 1957. *Verbal Behavior*. New York: Appleton-Century-Crofts.

Solomon, P., Kubzansky, P. E., Leiderman, P. H., Mendelson, J. H., Trumbull, R., and Wexler, D., eds. 1961. *Sensory Deprivation*. Cambridge: Harvard University Press.

Spindler, G. D. 1968. Psychocultural adaptation. In E. Norbeck, D. Price-Williams, and W. M. McCord, eds., *The Study of Personality*. New York: Holt, Rinehart and Winston.

Spitz, R. A. 1965. *The First Year of Life*. New York: International Universities Press.

———. 1950. Relevancy of direct infant observation. *Psychoanalytic Study of the Child*, 5:66-73.

———, and Wolf, K. M. 1946. The smiling response: A contribution to the ontogenesis of social relations. *Genetic Psychology Monographs*, 34:57-125.

Spurlock, J. 1969. Problems of identification in young black children—static or changing. *Journal of National Medical Association*, 61:504-507.

Sroufe, L. A. 1978. Affective constructs and continuity in adaptation. Paper presented at the NIMH Advisory Workshop on Emotional Development in Infancy, Rockville, Md., 14 February, 1978.

———. 1977. Wariness of strangers and the study of infant development. *Child Development*, 48:731-746.

Stein, M., Schiavi, R. C., and Camerino, M. 1976. Influence of brain and behavior on the immune system. *Science*, 191:435-440.

Stein, S. P., Holzman, S., Karasu, T. B., and Charles, E. S. 1978. Mid-adult development and psychopathology. *American Journal of Psychiatry*, 135:676-681.

Stern, W. 1927. *Psychologic der Fruhen Kindheit, bis zun Sechsten Lebensjahre.* 4th ed. Leipzig: Quelle and Meyer.

Stewart, W. 1969. *Historical and Structural Bases for the Recognition of Negro Dialect.* School of Languages and Linguistic Monograph Series, No. 22. Washington, D.C.: Georgetown University.

Stoch, M. B. and Smythe, P. M. 1963. Does undernutrition during infancy inhibit brain growth and subsequent intellectual development? *Archives of Diseases of Children*, 38:546-552.

Stoller, R. J. 1973. Overview: The impact of new advances in sex research on psychoanalytic theory. *American Journal of Psychiatry.* 130:241-251.

Sullivan, H. S. 1953. *The Interpersonal Theory of Psychiatry.* New York: W. W. Norton.

Suomi, S. J., and Harlow, H. F. 1972. Social rehabilitation of isolate-reared monkeys. *Developmental Psychology*, 6:487-496.

Szent-Gyorgi, A. 1961. Discussion of scientific creativity. Paper presented at Third World Congress of Psychiatry, Montreal, Canada, 7 June, 1961.

Tavolga, W. N. 1970. Levels of interaction in animal communication. In L. R. Aronson, E. Tobach, D. S. Lehrman, and J. S. Rosenblatt, eds., *Development and Evaluation of Behavior, Essays in Memory of T. C. Schneirla.* San Francisco: W. H. Freeman..

Thomas, A. 1962. Pseudo-transference reactions due to cultural stereotyping. *American Journal of Orthopsychiatry*, 5:894-900.

———. 1970. Purpose vs. consequence in the analysis of behavior. *American Journal of Psychotherapy*, 24:49-64.

———, Birch, H. G., Chess, S., and Hertzig, M. E. 1961. The developmental dynamics of primary reaction characteristics in children. *Proceedings Third World Congress of Psychiatry*, Vol. 1. Toronto: University of Toronto Press.

———, Birch, H. G., Chess, S., and Robbins, L. C. 1961. Individuality in responses of children to similar environmental situations. *American Journal of Psychiatry*, 117:798-803.

———, and Chess, S. 1957. An approach to the study of sources of individual differences in child behavior. *Journal of Clinical Experimental Psychopathology and Quarterly Review of Psychiatry and Neurology*, 18:347-356.

———, and Chess, S. 1972. Development in middle childhood. *Seminars in Psychiatry*, 4:331-341.

———, and Chess, S. 1976. Evolution of behavior disorders into adolescence. *American Journal of Psychiatry*, 133:539-542.

———, and Chess, S. 1975. A longitudinal study of three brain damaged children. *Archives of General Psychiatry*, 32:457-465.

———, and Chess, S. 1977. *Temperament and Development.* New York: Brunner/Mazel.

———, Chess, S., and Birch, H. G. 1968. *Temperament and Behavior Disorders in Children.* New York: New York University Press.

————, Chess, S., Birch, H. G., Hertzig, M. E., and Korn, S. 1963. *Behavioral Individuality in Early Childhood.* New York: New York University Press.

————, Chess, S., Sillen, J., and Mendez, O. 1974. Cross-cultural study of behavior in children with special vulnerabilities to stress. In D. Ricks, A. Thomas, and M. Roff, eds., *Life History Research in Psychopathology*, Vol. 3, pp. 53-67. Minnesota: University of Minnesota Press.

————, Hertzig, M. E., Dryman, I., and Fernandez, P. 1971. Examiner effect in IQ testing of Puerto Rican working-class children. *American Journal of Orthopsychiatry*, 41:809-821.

————, and Sillen, S. 1972. *Racism and Psychiatry.* New York: Brunner/Mazel.

Thomas, L. 1979. *The Medusa and the Snail.* New York: Viking.

Tinbergen, N. 1968. On war and peace in animals and man. *Science*, 160:1411-1418.

Tizard, B., and Rees, J. 1974. A comparison of the effects of adoption, restoration to the natural mother, and continued institutionalization on the cognitive development of four-year-old children. *Child Development*, 45:92-99.

Tobach, E., and Schneirla, T. C. 1968. The biopsychology of social behavior of animals. In R. E. Cooke and S. Levin, eds., *Biologic Basis of Pediatric Practice*. New York: McGraw-Hill.

Turkewitz, G., and Birch, H. G. 1971. Neurobehavioral organization of the human newborn. In J. Hellmuth, ed., *Exceptional Infant: Studies in Abnormalities*, Vol. 2: 24-40. New York: Brunner/Mazel.

Trivers, R. L. 1971. The evolution of reciprocal altruism. *Quarterly Review of Biology*, 46:35-57.

Vaillant, G. E. 1977. *Adaptation to Life.* Boston: Little, Brown.

Viedemar, M. 1979. Panel Reports, Monica: A 25-year longitudinal study of the consequences of trauma in infancy. *Journal of the American Psychoanalytic Association*, 27:107-126.

von Bertalanffy, L. 1962. General system theory: A critical review. *Yearbook of the Society of General Systems Theory*, 7:1-21.

von Frisch, K. 1950. *Bees, Their Vision, Chemical Senses and Language.* New York: Ithica.

Vygotsky, L. S. 1978. *Mind in Society.* Cambridge: Harvard University Press.

————. 1962. *Thought and Language.* Cambridge: Massachussetts Institute of Technology Press.

Walter, G. 1953. Electroencephalographic development of children. In J. M. Tanner and B. Inhelder, eds., *Discussion of Child Development*, Vol. 1. New York: International Universities Press.

Waters, E. 1978. The reliability and stability of individual differences in infant-mother attachment. *Child Development*, 49:483-494.

Watson, J. 1928. *Psychological Care of Infant and Child.* New York: W. W. Norton.

Wender, P. 1971. *Minimal Brain Dysfunction in Children.* New York: John Wiley and Sons.

Wertheimer, M. 1961. Psycho-motor coordination of auditory-visual space at birth. *Science*, 134:1692.

White, B. L. 1975. *The First Three Years of Life.* Englewood Cliffs, N. J.: Prentice-Hall.

White, R. W. 1959. Motivation reconsidered: The concept of competence. *Psychological Review*, 66:297-333.

Whyte, L. L. 1960. *The Unconscious Before Freud.* New York: Basic Books.

Williams, R. J. 1956. *Biochemical Individuality.* New York: John Wiley and Sons.

————, 1978. Nutritional individuality. *Human Nature*, 1:46-53.

Wilson, E. O. 1975. *Sociobiology, The New Synthesis.* Cambridge: Harvard University Press.

Wilson, R. S. 1978. Synchronies in mental development: An epigenetic perspective. *Science,* 202:939-948.

Winick, M., Meyer, K. K., and Harris, R. C. 1975. Malnutrition and environmental enrichment by early adaptation. *Science,* 190:1173-1175.

Witkin, H. A. 1973. A cognitive style perspective on evaluation and guidance. In *Measurement for Self-Understanding and Personal Development.* Princeton: Educational Testing Service.

———, Dyk, R. B., Faterson, H. F., Goodenough, D. R., and Karp, S. A. 1962. *Psychological Differentiation: Studies of Development.* New York: John Wiley and Sons.

Wohlwill, J. F. 1973. *The Study of Behavioral Development.* New York: Academic Press.

Wolff, P. H. 1966. *The Causes, Controls and Organization of Behavior in the Neonate.* Monograph No. 17. Psychological Issues, Vol. 5, No. 1. New York: International Universities Press.

———. 1970. Critical periods in human cognitive development. *Hospital Practice,* 11:77-87.

———. 1978. Critical remarks. In G. Serban, ed., *Cognitive Defects in the Development of Mental Illness.* New York: Brunner/Mazel.

———. 1960. *The Developmental Psychologies of Jean Piaget and Psychoanalysis.* New York: International Universities Press.

———. 1963. Observations on the early development of smiling. In B. M. Foss, ed., *Determinants of Infant Behavior,* Vol. 2. London: Methuen and Company.

Wolff, S., and Chess, S. 1965. An analysis of the language of fourteen schizophrenic children. *Journal of Child Psychology and Psychiatry,* 6:29-41.

———, and Chess, S. 1964. A behavioral study of schizophrenic children. *Acta Psychiatrica Scandinavica,* 40:433-466.

Wood, D., Bruner, J. S., and Ross, G. 1976. The role of tutoring in problem solving. *Journal of Child Psychology and Psychiatry,* 17:89-100.

Worden, F. G. 1975. Scientific concepts and the nature of conscious experience. In D. A. Hamburg and K. H. Brodie, eds., *American Handbook of Psychiatry,* Vol. 6. 2nd ed. New York: Basic Books.

Wynne, L. C., Cromwell, R. L., Matthysse, S., eds. 1978. *The Nature of Schizophrenia.* New York: John Wiley and Sons.

———, and Singer, M. T. 1963. Thought disorder and family relations of schizophrenia. *Archives of General Psychiatry,* 9:191-206.

Zigler, E. Letter to the Editor. *New York Times Magazine,* 18 January, 1975.

———. 1973. Project Head Start: Success or failure? *Children Today,* 36:2-7.

———, and Trickett, P. K. 1978. Social competence and evaluation of early childhood intervention programs. *American Psychologist,* 33:789-798.

Index

277